The Romance of Democracy

The Romance of Democracy

Compliant Defiance in
Contemporary Mexico

Matthew C. Gutmann

UNIVERSITY OF CALIFORNIA PRESS
Berkeley · Los Angeles · London

University of California Press
Berkeley and Los Angeles, California

University of California Press, Ltd.
London, England

© 2002 by the Regents of the University of California

Library of Congress Cataloging-in-Publication Data

Gutmann, Matthew C., 1953-.
  The romance of democracy : compliant defiance in
contemporary Mexico / Matthew C. Gutmann.
      p.   cm.
  Includes bibliographical references and index.
  ISBN 0-520-22099-4 (alk. paper).—ISBN 0-520-
23528-2 (pbk. : alk. paper)
      1. Democracy—Mexico—Coyoacân—Public
opinion.   2. Working class—Mexico—Coyoacân—
Political activity.   3. Working class—Mexico—
Coyoacân—Attitudes.   4. Public opinion—Mexico—
Coyoacân.   5. Mexico—Politics and government—
1988-   6. Santo Domingo de los Reyes (Coyoacân,
Mexico).   I. Title.

JL1281 .J885   2002
320.972—dc21   2001058501

Manufactured in the United States of America
10 09 08 07 06 05 04 03 02
10 9 8 7 6 5 4 3 2 1

The paper used in this publication meets the minimum
requirements of ANSI/NISO Z39.48–1992(R 1997)
(*Permanence of Paper*). ⊗

To my father
Carl Mack Gutmann
and to my grandparents
James Gutmann and Helen Rosenthal

History will not absolve us.

Roger Bartra

Contents

Acknowledgments

My cultural trajectory from Gringo to *güero* in Colonia Santo Domingo, Mexico City, has been made possible because of several unique people there like Gabriel Saavedra, Angela Jiménez, Marcos Ruvalcaba, Fili Fernández, and Marcelo Nolasco. Since I first landed in their midst in summer 1991 as an ethnographic *paracaidista*, Norma López, Miguel Armenta, Héctor Jiménez, Valfre Jiménez, Bernardino Ramos, Juan López, María Elena López, and Noé López have also been especially gracious and generous in response to my stubborn ways. Like family, we are together for life. Of this, I am sure and grateful.

Tom Skidmore and David Kertzer have made the first years at Brown University infinitely more stimulating and pleasant. My thanks to colleagues at Brown in anthropology, Latin American studies, and ethnic studies, and to those who have improved my understanding of political cultures in Latin America, especially Liza Bakewell, Roger Bartra, Stanley Brandes, Daniel Cazés, Miguel Centeno, Sylvia Chant, Teresita de Barbieri, Miguel Díaz Barriga, Gudrun Dohrmann, Agustín Escobar, Mary Goldsmith, Meche González de la Rocha, Estela Guzmán, Donna Guy, Michael Herzfeld, Michael Higgins, Gil Joseph, Michael Kearney, Jeff Lesser, Larissa Lomnitz, Nelson Minello, Carlos Monsiváis, Eduardo Nivón, Nancy O'Connor, Orlandina de Oliveira, Lynn Stephen, Verena Stolcke, Eric Van Young, and Mara Viveros.

In her role as editor, Naomi Schneider once again had the foresight to choose two superb reviewers. John Gledhill provided comments that allowed me to reframe several chapters and Judith Adler Hellman helped make the study of interest to those outside anthropology. In the throes of final revisions on this book I was ever more appreciative of their detailed and insightful suggestions. Tom Skidmore, the *ur*-guru of so many Latin Americanists, was also generous with his reading of an early draft of this book. I am also grateful to Francisco Lomeli for his suggestions and to Andy Sieverman for his production craftsmanship.

Research assistance for this book was provided by several people. In Mexico, Elia Aguilar labored valiantly to produce dozens of magnificently accurate transcriptions of taped interviews, while Pedro Lewin helped in innumerable ways throughout several years of research. In Providence, I was able to count on the support of Miguel Calderón and María Elena García, and secretarial assistance at Brown from Kathy Grimaldi, Matilde Andrade, and Shirley Gordon. I have been very lucky to work with such good people.

Portions of this study have been presented at meetings of the American Anthropological Association; the Latin American Studies Association; the International Oral History Conference; and the Society for Latin American Studies; and in lectures at Brown University; California State University–Long Beach; Colby College; Cornell University; Harvard University; Princeton University; Syracuse University; the University of Arizona; the University of California at San Diego; the University of Connecticut; and Yale University. Thanks to the audiences on each of those occasions for their questions and criticisms.

Funding for various parts of this book project was provided by two Salomon Faculty Research Awards, two University Funded Small Grants, and a small research stipend that accompanies the Stanley J. Bernstein endowed assistant professorship at Brown University (1999–2001). I am sincerely grateful to Brown for financial support on this and other projects. My thanks also and again to the following institutions for financial support that enabled me to conduct research leading to the present book and an earlier one: National Institutes of Health Postdoctoral Training Grant (1996–97), National Institute of Mental Health National Research Service Award (1993–95), Fulbright–Hays Dissertation Research Abroad Training Grant, National Science Foundation Doctoral Dissertation Improvement Grant, Wenner–Gren Foundation Predissertation Grant, Institute for Intercultural Studies Grant, UCMEXUS Dissertation Research Grant (1992–93), and various small University of California at Berkeley grants for graduate students (1991–94).

A few technical words of clarification. First, my thanks to the art editors at the University of California Press for agreeing to reprint several leaflets and posters that were not up to their usual aesthetic standards. I take full responsibility for their poor reproduction quality—friends in Mexico City secured them for me and preserved them as best they could. Second, most of the names I use in this study for my friends and neighbors in Mexico City are their real names. When I have chosen other names to protect the identities of the people mentioned or information that I think needs to be concealed in some way, I do not indicate this in the text. Finally, unless otherwise indicated, translations from other languages to English are mine, as are photos unless otherwise indicated.

I dedicate this study to my father, Carl Gutmann, who many years ago when I was not quite six years old, provided me with a first precious lesson in politics: he led a movement to integrate a swimming pool in the North Avondale neighborhood of Cincinnati. His principled stand and actions—his politics—inspired me at the time and they still do. Thanks also for a treasured walk from Montmartre to the Musée de l'Armée.

This volume is also dedicated to my grandmother, Helen Rosenthal, and my grandfather, James Gutmann, both of whom helped me to find a political ethics in which I could flourish, even when on more than one occasion they disapproved of the ways I sought to practically apply these values. Were they still alive, we would have had some fun arguing about this book.

My appreciation to Audrey Gutmann and Ann Oliver for kindnesses small and large over the years. I am also fortunate to have gracious and loving in-laws; to Sarah Joyce Ham and Lonnie and Judy McKenzie, thanks especially for letting us leave the grandkids with you so I could go off to Mexico.

To Michelle, in our fourteenth year together, for sharing life, and Mexico, and for not killing me when I landed in San Diego in 1995 with Liliana having contracted *Shigella flexneri,* or when I returned in 2000 to Providence with Maya in a hip-to-toe cast (Maya chased a dog which chased a car which then hit Maya . . .). I will try to do better, I really will. To Liliana and Maya, for their endless curiosity, I promised you that we could spend another year in Mexico when this book was done. Well, it is. Just make sure you remember (in the words of Philip Pullman): "Be prepared for strangeness and for new ways, my bears."

M. C. G.
Oaxaca de Juárez, México
January 2002

Preface: Provoking Ten Burros and a Genius

For the first time in the history of humanity, the earth is truly round.

Marc Augé

In May 1994 I returned to Colonia Santo Domingo, in Mexico City, and quickly found myself part of a raucous street scene. Loud and disorderly streets are nothing new for residents of the neighborhood; indeed, public debates have been common here ever since thousands of *paracaidista* (parachutist) land squatters first invaded these volcanic rocks on the south side of the Mexican capital in September 1971. Still, this time there was something new to the excitement: rather than voicing concerns relating to the construction and protection of their particular *colonia,* residents were expressing anxiety about Mexico's political outlook in general and how elections might fit into this future. And they were arguing about these issues as if their words, actions, and opinions actually might make a difference in national political outcomes.

This kind of engagement with official politics and this kind of enthusiasm for electoral politics, albeit a wary enthusiasm, is not normal in the *colonias populares* of Mexico City.

I had been gone from Mexico City for several months, and now Gabriel, Marcos, Felipe, and Toño were bringing me up to date in their running argument with one another. As we shared various *caguamas* of Corona beer, Toño was once again expressing his staunch support for the government PRI party. "They're the only ones with the *infraestructura* to run the country. Things would quickly deteriorate, everything would be *un desmadre* [a total mess] if another party won," he chided the others.[1] Marcos, although an active member of a janitors' union and a sup-

xv

Figure 1. After the January 1994 uprising in Chiapas, Gabriel liked to put EZLN (Zapatista) stickers
on cars he was repairing.

porter of the PRD center-left opposition party, was explaining to Toño
that he too had problems with the PRD presidential candidate Cuauhtémoc Cárdenas. This was why, Marcos declared, he was a *PRDista sin
Cárdenas,* a supporter of the PRD but without Cárdenas.

Both Toño and Marcos then began chastising Gabriel, a celebrated
mechanic on Huehuetzin Street in Colonia Santo Domingo, for his notorious *abstencionista* politics—Gabi frequently berated customers and
passersby for getting too agitated about elections. After the January 1,
1994, Zapatista uprising, and for the remainder of 1994, Gabi would
plaster EZLN (Zapatista National Liberation Army) stickers on many
of the cars and jitneys he repaired, and would proselytize from his *taller*

(workshop) on the sidewalk about the virtues of effecting political change from outside the electoral party system.

As the lone *ecologista* in the group, Felipe limited his discussion to periodic reminders that his party was the only one with representatives that anyone on Huehuetzin Street had actually met.

Given the serious nature of the debate and the disagreements, there was an exhilarating sense that the political conflicts among these men concerned important issues and that opposing sides and positions had real consequences for the political fortunes of millions of other Mexicans.

For men and women in Colonia Santo Domingo, 1994 was an eventful year. As did their compatriots throughout the Republic, they witnessed and disputed the Zapatistas' uprising in January, the assassination of PRI presidential candidate Luis Donaldo Colosio in March, the presidential election in August, and a second major political assassination of José Francisco "Pepe" Ruiz Massieu in September. In addition, at the end of that year they suffered yet another major peso devaluation. All these events presented challenges to the political agnosticism of *chilango abstencionistas* and the *defeño* disaffected. For a while, for a few months, popular political culture was not the same in Mexico City.

DEMOCRACY AND ITS MALCONTENTS

In the United States I have never participated in a street debate among old friends such as the one I witnessed in Santo Domingo in May 1994. This is not a minor issue. My own curiosity about a periodic passion for politics in many parts of Mexico in the 1990s was sparked by the knowledge that this kind of interest had been largely lacking elsewhere in North America for several decades. In contemporary Mexico, however, I noted that popular politics involves a tumultuous history of new social movements and electoral politics, political activism and passivity, and, at least among many of my friends and neighbors in one neighborhood of Mexico City in the 1990s, a profound and personal engagement with concepts like democracy, agency, and resistance in the subjective lives of men and women.

How can we explain the periodic passion for politics among working-class people in Mexico City? And why did this fervor often die out as suddenly as it flared up?

In 2000, in Mexico as elsewhere across the globe, many people say that they believe in democracy, that they support democratic efforts and politics, and that to say and do otherwise would be, well, simply undemocratic. So if nearly everyone is enthusiastic about democracy, it seems good and appropriate to ask what everyone means by that term. The elusiveness of the term *democracy* is symptomatic both of the range of aspirations wrapped within its multiple meanings and, ultimately, of its imprecision. For these reasons, in these pages I will not be able to offer a sound-bite definition of democracy; rather, I will seek to show how democracy's very multivalence is a key reason for the zeal with which so many people have employed the term to dramatically different ends in recent world history. Passionate partisanship can disguise a multitude of semantic sins.[2]

Until quite recently, around 1988 to be precise, people from all walks of life in Mexico casually made fun of official politics in their country. There were jokes about the *sexenio* (the six-year presidential period) and how it resembled a rotating dictatorship; about the use of the *dedazo* (finger-tap) and *destape* (unveiling) to choose each presidential successor[3]; about *urnas embarazadas* (pregnant ballot boxes); about the old-guard political *dinosaurios* and the young-Turk *tecnócratas;* about *llevando a acarreados,* rented-and-transported crowds being trucked to campaign rallies; and about the ridiculously lopsided coverage of electoral politics by government-owned and -affiliated television stations.[4]

The presidential election of 2000, in which the government-PRI party (Partido Revolucionario Institucional) that had ruled Mexico virtually unopposed for decades went down in defeat, was internationally hailed as a historic watershed for democratization in poor nations everywhere. "A peaceful transition to multiparty democracy," the analysts applauded. In the wake of this transition, it would be a shame not to take advantage of the opportunity to learn from women and men of the capital city about democracy, resistance, and agency; to consider their experiences and hopes for building democratic communities; and to examine what common citizens in Mexico City think about exercising political sovereignty over their own lives.

In the 1980s and 1990s many leftist observers of Mexico came to place great hope in organized social movements as holding greater promise for democratization than political parties. These expectations were linked to romantic notions of popular resistance, as many searched for social forces to replace the class-struggle framework of orthodox Marxism. Political cultures and the cultures of politics (see Alvarez, Dagnino, and Escobar 1998) became key concepts for the study of politics in Latin America at the end of the twentieth century. The meanings and significance of public and private distinctions in political life, writ large and small, became vital to an understanding of the particular regional dilemmas that faced many Latin American societies seeking to make the transition from military dictatorships to more participatory forms of government. Although this specific situation did not apply literally to Mexico, many of the issues explored there during this period were relevant for emerging cultural politics in countries like Argentina, Chile, Ecuador, Brazil, and Guatemala. Similarly, grappling with the relationship between democracy, poverty, and inequality was of paramount importance in grounding broader discussions of the relationship between economic growth and development, on the one hand, and redistribution of resources—"poverty alleviation," in the words of the World Bank—on the other.

Throughout Latin America in the early 2000s, commentators used the term *redemocratization* to describe the political goals sought and the transformations underway in the region. Yet, once again, the ambiguity of the term *democracy* became readily apparent upon a more than cursory examination, because to talk of "redemocratization" begged the question: When was Latin America ever democratic? What parts of the region had ever enjoyed this democracy that was so cherished in these societies? What did this democracy look like and feel like, or was this preexisting democracy so indeterminate that this entire line of questioning seemed unfair? As Gills, Rocamora, and Wilson (1993, 3) wrote in the introduction to their volume on "low intensity democracy," "Whereas some regard formal democracy as sufficient in itself, if the content of this new democracy is critically examined it may be found to be seriously flawed on many counts."

Given the regularity with which the slogans of democracy and resistance were summoned, one would have expected more critical discussion and less ingenuous invocation of the terms. It was not hard to trace the trajectory of similar academic debate on other intricate conceptual and practical questions—for example, on "the indigenous problem" in Mexico. Since the second decade of the twentieth century, in alternating waves of assimilationism and demands for cultural autonomy, scholars, policy makers, and leaders of indigenous groups themselves have tried to find ways to do more than simply make the indigenous peoples of Mexico—numbering greater than ten million in the year 2000, some 10 percent of the population—emblems of chronic discrimination in the country. There needed to be similar debate about the conceptual and practical meanings of democracy and resistance.

For many observers of Mexico, a central concern in the past two decades has been to account for the emergence of popular social movements as expressions of "the central theme of poverty" (see Nivón 1998, 33). Yet, by themselves, these have not been sufficient to effect fundamental, lasting political change. Judith Adler Hellman has been exceptionally astute with respect to this last point, as when she noted, "It could be argued that it is not the role of a mass popular movement to formulate and promote an alternative vision of society—that this is the role of a political party" (1994a, 138; see also Hellman 1992). And it is precisely here that we can see certain problems inherent in earlier utopian visions of social movements as providing a panacea to deep-seated political inequalities in Mexico and elsewhere. Alternatives to both party politics as usual and stock resistance models need to be developed to more fully explore popular politics in contemporary Mexico.

Perplexingly enough, after decades of full-throttled participation by left intellectuals and activists in deliberations on questions of Mexican national identity, and clashes around the relationship of class to such nationalist concerns, in the past twenty years activists have largely confined themselves to organizing and leading social movements devoted far more to the issues of day-to-day survival than to questions of national sovereignty. Meanwhile, the intellectuals have delved ever deeper into questions of globalization, identity, and ethnohistory, seeking to expand the horizons of space and time, and in the process often abandoning these very issues of contemporary politics and power in a regrettably similar fashion.

U.S. EMPIRE: POINTS OF REFERENCE AND DEFERENCE

By the year 2000 opposition candidates in Mexico had been elected President of the Republic and mayor of the capital city, and therefore, one might assume, they could serve as political examples of democracy internal to Mexico. Nevertheless, comparisons with the United States continued to be a point of democratic reference in Mexico, especially with respect to various civil rights such as freedom of the press and freedom of assembly, and to a two-party system versus Mexico's single government-party system. Still, it is unclear whether it was actual political freedoms in the United States or, on the contrary, its superpower status that made claims to democratic standard-bearer status valid in the eyes of many people in Mexico.

One reason for questioning the aptness of comparisons between Mexico and the United States is the superficial quality of invidious analysis of the content of democracy in each country. Another reason is surely that, with Mexico and the United States, we are not discussing two hermetically sealed nation-states but rather two countries sharing a long border and a history of utterly unequal relations. And, as Steve Stern (1998a, 51) noted in an essay on the paradoxes of foreign presence in Latin America: "Perhaps we must begin all over again to conceptualize a foreign presence that is integral yet not totalizing in its power to mold, or a foreign-local relationship that constantly draws cultural boundaries of 'we' and 'they' yet fails to preclude dynamics that confound division into 'we' and 'they.'" Although some commentators seem even more tempted following the fall of the Berlin Wall in 1989 and the ensuing collapse of the Soviet Union, comparing democracy in the two countries must be done with great care.

Although many friends and colleagues in Mexico find comparisons to the United States odious on general principle, others there use the United States as a model of where Mexico should be headed. Thus, more than a few might wish to admit, the juxtapositions between these two countries divided by a two-thousand-mile border are, to one extent or another, the transnational currency in which we are dealing in the twenty-first century.[5] More importantly for readers of this book, perhaps, because people in the United States are unaccustomed to learning from the lives and experiences of people in other countries, especially regarding democracy, I would emphasize early on how much we have to *learn* from political events and ideas in Mexico. It is hardly a simple matter of what we in the United States have to teach the rest of the world.[6]

Regardless of comparisons, though, a persistent issue for many in Colonia Santo Domingo, and for intellectual and political leaders in the Mexican capital as well, concerns the ability of any society to develop democratically when severe political, economic, and cultural inequalities are obvious to all.[7] If the wealthiest 20 percent of the population made off with 50 percent of Mexico's income in the early 1990s, and the lowest 20 percent earned only 5 percent of the GNP (see Oppenheimer 1998, 89), by what standards are we to judge such mundane matters as popular participation in political decision making? Is survival to be the only salient issue for the poor, whereas the elites will have the liberty to dally in issues of statecraft?

Perhaps we should be less exclusively interested in gauging how well Mexicans are achieving so-called democratic values and institutions, how they are coping with the issue of campaign-financing limits, or how effectively election monitors that have been chosen from the international community have worked. There is a place and a real need for such research and speculation, and certainly the forms and substance of compliant defiance in contemporary Mexico can be comprehensively charted only by comparing studies utilizing mixed methodologies. But we need to ask other questions about political defiance and compliance as well.

AGENCY AND VICTIMIZATION

To what extent do people exaggerate their political influence? Whom should we regard as the ultimate arbiters of such influence—social actors or outside political observers? Without delving into the peculiar realm of the political unconscious, what people in my neighborhood of Mexico City claim to know and not know is often directly linked by them to their activity or inactivity. Further, these same friends in Santo Domingo often directly associate knowledge and actions, on the one hand, and culpability, on the other.

One way to approach the matter of the compliant defiance of working-class women and men in Mexico City is to (re)examine the concept of agency. The term *agency,* as it has been used in the past two decades or so, has been popular because it has the great merit of challenging determinist thinking in the social sciences. With agency, the dispossessed are seen to have a fuller voice in deciding their own fates and even have a hand in human tragedies, an example being the voluntarist fervor with which German citizens slaughtered Jews in Nazi Germany.[8] More often than not, however, "agency" has referred rather exclusively to politically progressive efforts of the poor and dispossessed only when they are able to break free of structural and systemic constraints. How one understands failures or situations when the poor and dispossessed dare not even attempt to break out are subjects that many of us have been reluctant to address.

Michael Herzfeld (1997) closely examines questions of agency in his development of the theory of "cultural intimacy." In discussing intra-cultural diversity and people who are more and less gifted practitioners in the arts of politics, for example, he writes that "skilled actors use the appearance of rigidity to get what they want. Unskilled (or simply unsuccessful) actors blame the system; this is the worldview whereby they also blame the state and so confirm its power" (Herzfeld 1997, 20). Skilled actors are not only compared to their unskilled (or unsuccessful)

counterparts, but are also utilized to adjudicate the anthropological or-
thodoxy wherein "social actors seemed to be locked into an ideational
predestination, the possibility of independent agency all but precluded"
(Herzfeld 1997, 29).

This propensity to romance the politically successful actors among
the dispossessed, as evidenced in many a barren homage to resistance
theory (see chapter 6), has unfortunately resulted in less than adequate
analyses with respect to the politically weak—those who are not successful, not interested, or not aware. Even to mention the possibility that
poor people may not be "aware," of course, conjures up charges of false
consciousness and other censured concepts today. Yet, paradoxically,
political passivity, and not simply agency, remains uncharted territory.
In her study of transvestites, queens, and machos in Mexico City, Annick Prieur (1998, 129) makes a similar point. Although her informants
are the victims of symbolic (and not so symbolic) violence, they are also
actors who *choose* certain elements of their lives. They are not simply
the passive subjects of history.

Most men and women in Colonia Santo Domingo are in the periphery of the mainstream politics of electoral parties, and are also marginal
actors in organized social movements, either barrio-based or citywide.
The study of popular political interests and activities is certainly more
easily accomplished by focusing on organized, public manifestations
of incumbent and oppositional institutions, movements, and leaders.
But by concentrating as much on abstentionism as on participation, as
much on individual political outrage and individual displays of nationalism as on organized forms of protest and rebellion, additional facets
of the picture come into focus. It is not that politics and power are ultimately more capillary (à la Foucault) than collective. Rather, it is that
there is much to be learned from a stratum of the population that is
not made up primarily of political activists, nor truly representative of
the inertia and disinterest often considered typical of the impoverished
masses.

Another topic related to democratization that has attracted widespread attention in diverse locales is the question of how to conceptualize citizenship as both a general category and with specific reference to
marginalized and oppressed groups. In the United States, for example,
scholars pose questions about the issue of pluralism. Should citizenship
be considered an ideal of inclusion rather than exclusion, and is this a
very realistic goal (see, e.g., Ong 1996; Rosaldo 1997). In other words,

to what extent can the values and demands of "full citizenship" be understood as a claim for recognition of multiple forms of civil participation from a diverse array of cultural groups within the larger society? Or, is the concept of equal citizenship really an illusion whose realization is utopian and unrealistic precisely because the larger society is, at its base, founded on and maintained by inequalities that are inherent in its very constitution?

That the right of the socially dispossessed to vote, along with other civil rights, has been a long sought and hard-won accomplishment in Mexico as elsewhere is beyond question. The fact of achieving suffrage and other civil rights, however, is not the same as recognizing how and when to use them effectively to change the world. Wendy Brown has written provocatively about "the emancipatory force of rights" (which would certainly include the right to participate in free elections):

> While rights may operate as an indisputable force of emancipation at one moment in history—the American Civil Rights movement, or the struggle for rights by subjects of colonial domination such as black South Africans or Palestinians—they may become at another time a regulatory discourse, a means of obstructing or co-opting more radical political demands, or simply the most hollow of empty promises. . . . The point is that rights converge with powers of social stratification and lines of social demarcation in ways that extend as often as attenuate these powers and lines. (Brown 1995, 98)

Commenting on this passage, John Gledhill argues for the inclusion of capitalist social relations in any discussion of rights, not because class determines all other modes of domination, but "because it remains a constitutive part of the positioning of social subjects in the arena of struggles over rights" (1997, 72). In chapter 8, I examine more closely the relationship between the right to vote and gender identities and relations. Among other things, recent work in gender studies in Latin America that has focused on questions of public and private spaces of power has substantially refined our overall understanding of civic rights, modes, and methods of political change at societal and more familiar levels.

Journalists and academics are constantly inventing terms to describe democracy's blemishes and blemished democracies: "rogue democracies," "shallow democracies," and "imperfect democracies" are a few of recent coinage (see Crossette 2000; Rosenberg 2000). The election of Hugo Chávez as Venezuela's president and the reelection of Alberto Fujimori in Peru in 2000 are widely deemed as exemplary of "shortcomings" in the realization of democratic ideals in Latin America; they are less often discussed in the press or in scholarly forums as illustrative of politics that really had very little to do with democracy in any meaningful sense.

The romance of democracy exists, to be sure, in the possibility of popular participation in politics, and, more irreverently, in the wooing of the populace to believe in utopian promises when their only political future is more of the same. The right to decide upon channels for political participation is on the agenda in Mexico, and the balance between compliance and defiance is, as always, at the center of the debate over the meanings and activities to be associated with citizenship. Yet, what do women and men in Santo Domingo who wish to participate as active citizens in a democratic Mexico actually do when they roll out of bed in the morning? Are their actual options limited to saying to themselves, "Well, only six more years until I can vote again in the presidential election"?

RESISTANCE AND THE PEOPLE

"A lot of people talk these days about democracy as the goal of all kinds of social struggle," I commented one day in 1997 to Gabriel, my mechanic friend.

"But ask those wise guys if they go to the marches, if they go to the meetings. 'Do you go out and raise hell?' Everyone talks about democracy . . ." Gabi complained.

"The Zapatistas, too?" I asked him.

"The Zapatistas practice democracy more because the groups who are prepared are the ones who are marginalized. Why? Because they are the groups who actually can see to it that democracy functions. But that's when people get together and analyze things so democracy doesn't become, as I was saying, ten burros and a genius."

Which, of course, raised for me the obvious question: "And who's to say who are the burros and who are the geniuses?"

"The burros are the ones who talk about democracy and don't practice it," Gabriel responded, just barely managing to keep a straight face.

"Are you a genius or a burro?" I needled him.

"Burro," he replied, laughing. Then, recovering his composure, he added in a half-serious, half-playful tone: "But I'm not a mountain burro, because even burros have hierarchies. There are burros who are more burros than I am, and there are burros less burros than I am. What

I do think is that there's a lack of *educación* and that the level of *educación* in our country is very low." [9]

"But even in countries where the level of formal education is very high there are assholes all over," I commented.

To which Gabi retorted, "And in the end, who's to blame?"

"I don't know," I lied, because I knew where this line of argument was leading. "Tell me," I requested, so I would not have to put words into his mouth.

"The people," Gabriel told me, just as he had on so many other occasions in the years we had been talking about politics and change in Mexico. "The people" bore some responsibility for their own misery, because only the people could, if they became "educated" in the broadest sense of being conscious of their situation, do something to rectify their lives.

And so, before proceeding further, this issue of "the people," sometimes also referred to as "the popular classes," must be briefly addressed. It is as unsettled a subject as any in the anthropology of Mexico today. Earlier taken-for-granted agreements about what constitutes a class are presently undergoing rigorous scrutiny. Skepticism abounds among many anthropologists in Mexico regarding the very utility of "class" as an analytic category (see, e.g., Nieto 1998). As one way of conceding the blurry boundaries of the social group that has been variously called the working class, the proletariat, the poor, the dispossessed, and the underdogs, while at the same time acknowledging the obvious fact that disparities of wealth are horrendously glaring and significant in all aspects of social life in Mexico, newer terms like *clases populares* have come into vogue since the 1980s.

Prominent among anthropologists in Mexico who have utilized the term *popular classes* in their writings have been Néstor García Canclini and Guillermo Bonfil Batalla. This has allowed them to avoid the use of Marxist terminology now regarded by many as hackneyed, while at the same time giving a populist slant to their perspectives and approaches to formulating innovative cultural theory in general.[10] García Canclini's students and colleagues at the Universidad Autónoma Metropolitana–Iztapalapa have produced several pioneering studies on *clases populares* and urban space (see, among others, Nieto 1998; Nivón 1998; and Safa 1991).

Eduardo Nivón (1998), for instance, has written provocatively about "the substitution of 'the popular' for 'the public'" in his study of the impact of the media, the Church, and dominant classes on mass culture in recent years. Building upon themes raised by Carlos Monsiváis in various publications, Nivón notes that, especially after 1968, the question of how to incorporate poverty and daily life into accounts of culture and society have been at the center of studies on popular culture and Mexican national culture. Critiques of the terms *popular classes* and *popular culture* have run the gamut from the logics of political economy to the droll (e.g., in a commentary on a lecture I gave in 1993 at El Colegio de México, Daniel Cazés criticized me for calling Santo Domingo a *colonia popular,* because, he said, the truly popular *colonias* were those like Lomas de Chapultepec, where the wealthy classes resided, and everyone wanted to live in those communities). Several scholars have opted to downplay people's unequal relations to the means of production and have chosen instead to emphasize questions of inequality as reflected in the spheres of citizenship and consumerism (see García Canclini 1995).[11]

In an insightful paper on political culture, Guillermo de la Peña posits that we should treat the concept of class as profoundly historical. We must cease to use the term *class* as a magic wand for categorizing groups of people so as to predict social behavior. Instead, de la Peña argues, if the term is to retain any of its salience, it must be utilized as a concept alive to the possibility of real people constructing real (and really) complex interpretations of their daily lives (1990, 105). It is no coincidence that this reevaluation of the constitution and consequence of classes is occurring at the same time that angst-ridden doubt and ironic uncertainty are on the rise, and that modernist (meta)truth and teleology are met with unchecked uncertainty and scorn. The key problem for those who would shuffle off to ironic oblivion may be that, like their overdetermining ancestors, they have too little insight and no plan to help resolve mundane matters like poverty, disease, and oppression in the world. Although there remains much to be altered and amended in class analysis, Michael Kearney is correct in writing that class analysis is still the "most powerful theoretical perspective for understanding the differentiation of identities in complex societies" (1996, 7–8).

AWKWARD AND INDECENT PROVOCATIONS

I conclude this preface by introducing three thorny questions that will reappear throughout the study to follow.

One: If everyone is a democrat, what is so great about democracy?

Even if the meaning of democracy were clearer and more unanimously shared, the question remains: After all is said and done, why is this an age in which there is nary a self-professed anti-democracy advocate to be found in Mexico or any other corner of the globe? When women and men of all political stripes and persuasions tout democracy as the goal of humanity, the miracle of modern thought, and the salvation for the ills of this world, can democracy really be so good? When all alike— from community anarchists to capitalist autocrats—peddle democracy as the solution to society's woes and wants, the time might be right to seek loftier ambitions. And, yes, to be clearer about what we mean by "democracy."

In his discussion of the lessons of the Euro-Communist movement for capitalism and democracy in Mexico, Roger Bartra remarks on what he calls "the extraordinarily 'subversive' potential of the struggle for democracy" (1981, 148). The substance of such subversion is surely problematic when those in power are democracy's most visible and strident champions, and when they equate democracy with a singular economic regime, capitalism (see Amin 1993).

I pose this query not merely as a quest for stricter definition, and certainly not merely as a call to choose among the various guises of the democratic creature, whether they be liberal, republican, bourgeois, or proletarian. Instead, I ask the question because today it seems valuable to ascertain whether a definition of democracy in today's world ought to encompass more than periodic trips to the electoral urns. If everyone is a democrat, and if everyone seeks to legitimate political thoughts and actions by reference to democratic instincts and approaches, then we are asking the wrong questions.

Two: What is actually wrong with blaming the victim?

The universal adoption of democracy as the goal of humanity has not resolved the issue of endemic poverty. And if all agree that agency is a wonderful thing to behold and defend, then the implications of agency for situations in which the powerless are less than brilliantly successful must be explored. If we regard *agency* as involving the successful incursion of the poor and powerless into the arenas of power, then we need to know more about agency's opposites. What on earth could they be called? "The system"? "Anti-agency"?! "Negagency"?!! If agency develops, in part, through an understanding on the part of *los de abajo*, the legendary social underdogs (see Azuela 1938), of their plight and how to lessen at least to some degree their misery, then the implications of agency when *los de abajo* misunderstand and misstep are best examined more frankly. We walk a fine line here between responsibility and reproach; yet the intricacies involved in distinguishing margins and avoiding pitfalls are certainly not reason enough to shun complicated social geography.

In contemporary Mexico, the expression "blaming the victim" is not commonly employed, and the debate about poverty is not framed in the same way as in the United States. Still, the fundamental questions are the same: Why does poverty persist? Who is responsible for poverty in the first place? Who is responsible for resolving this monstrous problem? "¡*Viva México, hijos de la chingada!*" (Long live Mexico, children of the damned!) millions of Mexicans shout on September 16th, Mexico's Independence Day. To be Mexican in this context, to be a Mexican who counts herself or himself as among the children of the damned, is to be socially damned *and* a sucker for accepting this state of affairs.[12]

If a majority of the populace in any country wants something, it does not automatically follow that their choices are democratically reasonable. When the rightist PAN candidate won the 2000 presidential election in Mexico, unseating the PRI, which had held the presidency continuously for seventy-one years, the change was quickly hailed as a sign of manifest democracy. But as Miguel Centeno presciently remarked three years earlier, "The possibility of a PAN victory in 1997 or in the year 2000 would provide exactly what technocrats wanted—democracy without the possibility of dramatic social change and with continuity in macroeconomic policy" (1997, 262).[13] The truth of Centeno's prediction surely provides a counterpoint to the overheated declarations of democracy's lasting triumph that followed the 2000 presidential election in Mexico.

Leaving aside older considerations, of Benthamite majorities running amok and Durkheimian solidarities cohering harmoniously, the issue posed in various guises by my neighbors and acquaintances in Colonia Santo Domingo is simply this: whether, when, and how everyday folks will have a chance to significantly change anything substantial in the world.

*Three: Is fascination with resistance a
postromantic substitute for socialism?*

After 1989, any discussion of popular political cultures was inevitably
influenced by what some have called "fall-of-the-Wall syndrome": after
that date, the goals of socialism all but disappeared from activist, scholarly, and populist discourse even for those who all along had been less
in thrall of politics in the former Soviet Union. So it was that the spirit
of negative instance reigned among many former aficionados of socialism, and critiques of actually existing liberal democracies were refash-
ioned with the understanding that there no longer existed a realistic
hope for better societies.

In the 1990s, the predominant framework by which to envision
change in a postsocialist, postromantic age was through theories of resistance—of slow, covert, incremental struggles that, like barnacles,
would accumulate, bit by bit, and eventually transform the world upon
which they depended for sustenance. Nevertheless, in the real world of
Mexico, and Latin America generally, social movements that flowered
in the 1970s and 1980s provided analysts with more overt forms of
struggle to study and debate. Often initiated around basic issues of survival—from water to land to housing—these movements provided real
opportunities for the people most affected by these problems to organize, finance, and direct the political activities and goals of their own
organizations.

Still, hidden resistance and in-your-face popular social movements
were not easily transferable to the political sphere of political parties
and formal political institutions. So it happened that popular politics
became increasingly associated with local politics, with the microman-
agement of general social problems. As a result of declining socialist
fortunes—the near disappearance of Marxist dialogue from political
debate—the political imagination of the Mexican populace became increasingly circumscribed and debilitated in the 1990s and early 2000s.
In intellectual circles, resistance became the sensible substitute for the
earlier quest for a radically better political world, a dream formerly
known to many as socialism.

And so it was in Santo Domingo. In the 1990s, there as elsewhere,
political life often developed in other directions.

CHAPTER I

Compliant Defiance in Colonia Santo Domingo

They have no ready-made utopias to introduce *par décret du peuple.*

Karl Marx

The Romance of Democracy is an ethnographic study of popular politics and official subjugation in the world's most populous city; a detailed, bottom-up exploration of the lives of residents of a poor working-class neighborhood of the Mexican capital; and an examination of how, when, and why they seek to change their political worlds, and how, when, and why they participate in or eschew the politics of politics. This is a book about what these men and women think about national and neighborhood democracy, about their dreams of a better society, and about their sense of themselves as cultural citizens.

During the period 1968–2000, broad socioeconomic and demographic changes were occurring within and without Mexico—changes that repeatedly revealed how the lives, loves, hopes, and fears of my neighbors on Huehuetzin Street were integrally tied to national, regional, and global events in ways both intimate and obscure. By considering contradictory political passions and practices that developed in the neighborhood of Santo Domingo in the course of a series of momentous events, this study seeks to document the antithetical processes of civil challenge, frustration, and accommodation during this period.

The group of men and women who are at the center of this inquiry lived in the 1990s in a *colonia popular* that was founded by land invaders in the early 1970s. Originally, I decided to live and work in Colonia Santo Domingo because I was studying changing gender relations in Mexico. Given the active participation of many women in the *colonia* in social movements for services like electricity, water, sewer systems, and schools, Santo Domingo seemed a good place to assess the modes and extent of changing identities and practices associated with men and women (see Gutmann 1996). In the 1990s the neighborhood was as large as many cities in Mexico. Demographic estimates are notoriously unreliable, but by the year 2000 well over a hundred thousand people called Santo Domingo home. And, despite its tumultuous origins, nearly three decades after the initial squatters arrived in September 1971, most residents characterized their *colonia* as considerably more tranquil and stable than it had been in the early, chaotic years of land seizures and conflicts. Still, if residents of the *colonia* kept alive any of the spirit of those early years, it was in their widespread belief that formal government institutions and officials could not be trusted to provide them with the necessities in life, and in a general feeling that self-reliance was both the cross and the honor they would bear in life.

Michelle, our infant daughter, and I began our year of living in Colonia Santo Domingo in August 1992. As so often happens when doing ethnographic fieldwork, I gradually became an integral if irregular member of the neighborhood, or at least of one block on Huehuetzin Street. For many years afterward, once, twice, and three times a year when possible, I would return for a few weeks to touch base with my friends and acquaintances. They had become, truthfully, my family. The desires, experiences, challenges, and conflicts of the people living on Huehuetzin Street were no more exotic than those of my colleagues at Brown University in the United States. Nonetheless, when in the mid-1990s my neighbors in Santo Domingo began to insist that I pay more attention to the changes occurring in *la política* (the formal political arena) in Mexico, it occurred to me that for the poor people in communities like this one, the machinations of Mexico's ruling elites must have seemed completely unrelated to their daily lives.

Colonia Santo Domingo is a poor but stable bedroom community on the south side of Mexico City. In the 1990s, the sons and daughters of the original land invaders doubted that they themselves would ever own a home. Such opportunities were less possible in 2000 than they had been even a few decades earlier. Most of them had more formal education than their parents, and most limited their own families to perhaps half the number of children their parents had. Some, women as well as men, had found steadier paid employment outside the home than their fathers enjoyed. Gentrification projects in the 1990s had brought expensive condominiums to the outskirts of the neighborhood, which was located near major transportation arteries and upscale shopping districts. Rumor in Santo Domingo had it that the main reason the area was attracting wealthier residents was because the volcanic-rock base of the *colonia* and the surrounding Pedregales was far more seismically secure than the rock underlying the rest of Mexico City, which was largely built on mud left over from four lakes that covered much of the Valley of Mexico before the Spanish had arrived five hundred years earlier. Japanese investors, neighbors in Santo Domingo informed me in the mid-1990s, were especially aggressive in buying up condominiums in the area. After all, the Japanese knew a thing or two about these *temblores* (tremors), people sometimes commented with a smirk.

So Santo Domingo was home to janitors, taxi drivers, maids, *amas de casa* (housewives), factory assembly workers, curtain makers, tiny workshop owners and employees, furniture makers and restorers, secretaries, clerks, radiator and muffler repairers, day-care workers, street peddlers, long-haul and local-route truck drivers, *albañiles* (construction laborers), bookkeepers, welders, schoolteachers, car mechanics, and a few middle-class professionals in need of inexpensive housing. Except for the condominium dwellers, generally in the 1990s one did not live in Santo Domingo if one could afford something nicer than homes made of cinderblock walls and tin-and-asbestos roofing, which were the most affordable construction materials in the *colonia*. So it was that one neighbor, an employee at the nearby National University (UNAM—the Universidad Nacional Autónoma de México), could be seen twice a week in the morning shuffling through the dusty streets with his bucket filled with two plastic bags of government-subsidized milk. Although he had no children of his own, he claimed as a dependent the child of a neighbor, who was in fact breast-feeding, and in this way he was able to supplement his own nutritional needs.

People in Santo Domingo often measured their own standard of living by that of their children. They gauged their ability to satisfy the needs of their children at different ages, and then compared the lives of their offspring with their own childhoods. Neighbors would sometimes mark levels of poverty in households by noting whether infants slept in hammocks or if parents had enough spare cash to buy a new crib or settled for a hand-me-down that was not being used by other relatives. One of the poorest grandmothers in the *colonia* explained to me, a bit defensively, that children who sleep in *hamacas* from an early age are more intelligent later in life.

For the parents in Colonia Santo Domingo, the difficulties of raising

Figure 2. Huehuetzin Street in Colonia Santo Domingo, 1993.

their children did not simply repeat those of earlier generations of poor mothers and fathers who had migrated to Mexico City from the countryside. Parents in the 1990s had to deal with two contradictory elements that had not existed in the 1970s. On the one hand, real income was lower in the metropolitan centers than it had been two decades earlier, and as a consequence, financial expectations for the future were far lower. On the other hand, with the advent of more formal education, television, the Internet, and other global networks of communications, this generation of parents was generally more aware of the consumer goods and opportunities that were enjoyed by the middle and upper classes but were missing from their own lives.

For someone interested in questions of politics, of power relations at a general societal level as well as in the more intimate quarters of families and households, Colonia Santo Domingo and Mexico City as a whole could seem incoherent and bizarre. On the question of who might wield power in particular situations, all my friends and neighbors in the Mexican capital held firm opinions, usually based on their own sometimes painful, sometimes joyous, and sometimes confusing experiences. Clearly, there were some people (individuals and groups) who made more decisions, and more important ones, than others. Sifting through the conflicting opinions and experiences of a group such as the residents of Colonia Santo Domingo does not simply represent the busywork of ethnography; indeed, such work represents the heart and soul of ethnographic work. It helps us to achieve greater clarity about the who's, what's, where's, when's, and how's of classical sociological categories such as class, patriarchy, and racism, as well as more amorphous practical questions involving such issues as parenting, sexuality, and violence.

In this ethnographic field study, I focus on the intimate spaces and fantasies of popular politics in one part of one community over a period of several years in the 1990s. I am concerned more with the experiences of citizens, with the mundane details of everyday political life, than with formal institutional politics. I have tried to chronicle rather than presuppose my subjects' views about what should be considered politically relevant in the first place. For example, some of the people I knew and lived with in Mexico City thought it was a bit absurd to even talk of democracy when there were so many poor people. They were far more concerned about poverty than they were about whether someone had voted or not in the last election, or whether one's ballot was or was not secret, as important as these latter considerations might be. The types of questions that ground this book politically have to do with what my friends and neighbors thought about voting—whether voting was considered the epitome of democratic participation, and whether, given a choice, they would have preferred to have as little to do with the Mexican government and state as possible. Considerations of self-government here are unavoidably practical as well as philosophical.

It might seem odd for an ethnographer to engage the sacred terrain of formal politics in a large-scale society such as Mexico's. Usually, questions about the politics of voting and abstention are considered the bailiwick of political scientists and others well versed in survey research. I examine these questions qualitatively, however, without resorting to questionnaires aimed at teasing out broad tendencies and trends. Neither is the study of such a large-scale society the customary domain of political anthropology, a field that has historically been more concerned with power relations in small-scale, tribal societies. Only fairly recently have scholars in the field begun to examine politics at the direct, face-to-face level of the village, the neighborhood, and the local community in societies of tens of millions of inhabitants.[1]

The Romance of Democracy is a book about the political lives of the men and women of Huehuetzin Street during a specific juncture in their personal and social histories. In particular, I ask in this study what the people of Colonia Santo Domingo themselves think they can change about their personal and social histories—that is, what impact they think they might have in the narrower and perhaps superficially more circumscribed world of children, marriages, families, and households, as well as in the broader and sometimes seemingly limitless world of international geopolitics and affairs of state.

One aim is to expose the links between the apparently routine interactions and conversations of daily life in the *colonia* and developments in the world of national and international politics. I do not pretend to comprehensively capture the cognitive connections made by my friends and neighbors in Santo Domingo, that is, to fully and definitively represent their ideas and motivations when it comes to political questions. Yet neither do I conform with the conclusions of behavioralist scientists and others who insist that such things as motives are wholly unknowable. Similar to the conclusions of certain interpretivist anthropologists, this kind of thinking tends to arrogantly render the comments of the people themselves as worthless, or at least thoroughly suspect. Instead, I prefer to acknowledge the limits of discourse—for instance, the extent to which people's words may obscure some truths—by placing high value on what people say about themselves and others, and by repeatedly returning to similar topics with the same people (it is simply astounding how people may say different things to the same person, depending on how their relationship develops), and always insisting on comparing different comments by different people, always asking people to compare words to deeds.

Bluntly put, and for better or for worse, most of what ethnographers "do" is talk to people. We talk to people about what they think, what others think, and about what they and others say they and others do. We also "observe," and these observations may be important, but I think on the whole many of us rely far more on words about deeds than on the deeds themselves.

The examination of political parties, administrative apparatuses, interest groups, polling, and electoral systems are crucial modes of study. Yet, in this study, like the people of Santo Domingo themselves, I have other political concerns and focuses that are different from, though I hope complementary to, such approaches. Here, my focus is to describe and understand the political perceptions and participation of *los de abajo,* those social underdogs who are compliant in the face of social controls seemingly beyond their ability to resist, and who at the same time remain defiantly enraged at having to accept this very situation.

CONTEMPORARY MEXICAN HISTORY

One way to understand popular politics in Mexico City and contemporary Mexico in general is to note certain key junctures in recent Mexican history, events which for those old enough to have social memories mark turning points in their personal and historical lives. Commemorating unforgettable events and experiences can, of course, obscure processual changes that may lack such narrow temporal referents. The neoliberal decade of the 1980s in Mexico, for instance, witnessed the further bifurcation of income and more important of wealth there: by the 1990s the thirteen Mexican billionaires on the *Forbes* list of the world's richest individuals owned more than 10 percent of Mexico's annual gross domestic product (Castañeda 1995, 216). Still, specific events have come to be associated with specific years in Mexico's recent history, and these, in turn, have come to epitomize signal historical transitions for many of my friends in Colonia Santo Domingo. It is worth enumerating the most significant.

1968   Following months of student demonstrations in Mexico City (as happened in many other parts of the world), and shortly before the Olympic Games were to begin there, on October 2, hundreds of student protesters and onlookers were murdered by military troops in the Tlatelolco housing complex on the north side of the capital. Even three decades after the event, the reference "1968" still resonated for generations of Mexicans. It referred to what was seen as the defining moment in postrevolutionary Mexican history, after which millions of citizens no longer felt confidence either in their government or in the prospect for positive change in their government. In chapter 3 I provide an exegesis of "1968" as it exists in the popular memory of people in Santo Domingo.

1982   Despite rampant poverty and inequality in the post–World War II economy in Mexico, until the late 1970s the country enjoyed remarkably solid and sustained industrial and financial growth. Consequently, even after 1968, when many lost faith in a brighter political and social future for their country, most continued to believe that the Mexican economy would continue to prosper, at least for the middle and upper classes—and if only one could make it out of the working class. In 1982, this dream, too, was dashed, precipitated in the short term by the financial and monetary policies of President José López Portillo, and more fundamentally by severe balance of payments problems, all of which spelled ruin for countless businesses and investors throughout Mexico. The illusion of a stable and inherently sound economy vanished in 1982, just as faith in the political integrity of the government had vanished in 1968.

1985   On September 19, at 7:19 A.M., an earthquake measuring 8.1 on the Richter Scale shook Mexico City for ninety seconds. Thousands died in collapsed buildings, at least 10,000 in all, and perhaps many more. One-quarter of a million people or more were left instantly homeless, and many more lost their jobs. In the wake of the tremor, and in the face of the incompetence of public authorities in coping with the disaster, hundreds of thousands of residents of the city took matters into their own hands. In the following days and months, they organized rescue squads, set up food-collection points, administered first-aid, located housing supplies, and provided shelter and support to as many victims as they could. The 1985 earthquake subsequently became emblematic for many, in Colonia Santo Domingo and throughout the capital, of both governmental ineptitude and the tremendous ability of masses of people to organize themselves—at least under dire circumstances.

1988   What some have termed the most fraudulent presidential vote in Mexico's long history of corrupt electoral politics took place this year. When it appeared that an opposition candidate, Cuauhtémoc Cárdenas, would win the presidency and unseat the PRI for the first time in sixty years, there was a sudden and mysterious "breakdown" of the computer system tallying the vote lasting three days. When the system was again up and running, Carlos Salinas de Gortari, the government-PRI candidate, was declared the victor by a small margin. The election of 1988 became a symbol of political change, or more specifically, of political change frustrated and denied.

1994   This was quite a year indeed. On January 1, the North American Free Trade Agreement (NAFTA in English, and, amus-

ingly, TLC—for Tratado de Libre Comercio—in Spanish)
went into effect, economically tying the United States, Canada, and Mexico together in myriad new ways. That same
day, and not coincidentally, in the southern state of Chiapas,
thousands of masked indigenous women and men carried out
a series of well-planned armed takeovers of strategic locations
for a few days, announcing to the world, including through
the Internet, their intention to fight for liberty, justice, and democracy by whatever means necessary (see chapter 7). Then,
on March 23, Mexico was rocked by yet another political crisis, as Luis Donaldo Colosio, the PRI presidential candidate,
was assassinated, exploding the idea that Mexico was some
how immune to the type of political violence that had long
plagued other parts of the Americas north and south of Mexico. ("You may be used to this kind of thing in Gringolandia,
Mateo," my friend Isabel told me, "but we don't live like that
here.") The presidential race continued, with Ernesto Zedillo
quickly replacing Colosio as the PRI candidate and winning
in the (unexpectedly clean) elections in August. But the year
was not yet over. On September 28, José Ruiz Massieu, general secretary of the PRI, was himself gunned down in Mexico City. Intrigue and plots on an international scale were said
to be involved in both assassinations, the attendant power
struggles were said to involve upwards of 100 million dollars
and among those implicated was Raul Salinas de Gortari, the
sitting president's brother. Fittingly, if disastrously, for my
neighbors in Santo Domingo, the end of the year brought
another massive financial crisis, with the drastic devaluation
of the peso sending many of those who had finally begun to
emerge from the depths of the crisis of the 1980s back into a
downward spiral of underemployment and unemployment.

1997   Cuauhtémoc Cárdenas won the first election for mayor in
        Mexico City, a post some say is the second most important
        elected office in Mexico. Until that year, the city had been
        governed by a mayor who was appointed by the sitting PRI
        president. The implications of Cárdenas's election to the post
        were widely debated in Santo Domingo. Many of my friends
        who are active in leftist grassroots and community organiz-
        ing were convinced that the election represented a fabulous

opening for democratic politics more generally in the country, all the while noting the degree to which Cárdenas was being hamstrung by interference and financial malfeasance at the hands of the PRI. More broadly, however, there was less optimism among most of my friends in Santo Domingo regarding the potential for change under Cárdenas, as if this were a more Pyrrhic than substantive opposition victory.

2000   The presidential election of 2000 was held in July, and for the first time in seventy-one years an opposition candidate won. Vicente Fox of the conservative PAN had carried a clear message to the voters: Out with the PRI! Anything will be better than they are! Among the questions raised by the election results, of course, was whether the former opposition now in power still could be considered the opposition. Despite infighting within the PRI over who was responsible for losing the election (outgoing president Ernesto Zedillo was the target of most *dinosaurio* vituperation), and questions about whether the PAN victory was more symbolic than substantive, leading political pundits were quickly and uniformly assuring the Mexican electorate of the historic significance of the event. (As an aside, there was some consideration that Mexican citizens resident in the United States should be allowed to vote for the first time in these elections. Among other things, this would have involved Mexican candidates campaigning in the United States—as those from other countries like the Dominican Republic do—which, in turn, would have further blurred national boundaries between the two countries. It would also have led to even more votes for the non-PRI parties—not that this proved necessary. In the end, the proposal was quashed by the PRI in 1999, while it still held control of the presidential palace, Los Pinos.)

In this period of contested presidential elections and assassinations in Mexico and, in Chiapas, an indigenous-based revolt against the central government in Chiapas, whose political repercussions were felt throughout the Republic and indeed across the Americas generally, neoliberal economic policies came to dominate in all spheres of political life in Mexico. Neoliberalism quickly bore fruit, at least for some in Mexico:

by 2000, with some $240 billion in commercial exchange, Mexico had become the second largest trading partner of the United States, ahead of Japan and second only to Canada.[2] The United States had long been the major foreign stakeholder in Mexico's economy, of course, but by the 1990s investment was such that a crisis in Mexico could generate shocking repercussions in U.S. markets. Thus, U.S. speculation in Mexico required absolute vigilance of the political as well as economic conditions in that country. So it was that on February 17, 1995 the *Washington Post* reported, "A memo last month by Chase Manhattan Bank's emerging markets group warned that a peaceful solution to the [Chiapas] rebellion was 'difficult to imagine after face-to-face talks with the government one year ago failed to demobilize the rebels'" (see Robberson 1995). The memo quoted in the *Post* continued ominously: "While Chiapas, in our opinion, does not pose a fundamental threat to Mexican political stability, it is perceived to be so by many in the investment community. The [Mexican] government will need to eliminate the Zapatistas to demonstrate their effective control of the national territory and of security policy."

After the memo was leaked to the press, Chase bank officials tried to quickly dismiss it as representing the judgment of a single mid-level analyst. If most of my acquaintances in Colonia Santo Domingo believed that such ideas were without a doubt shared by Chase executives, and indeed executives of other banks as well, should they have been accused of puerile suspicions and naive conspiracy theories?

Commentary on Mexico's financial and governmental crises was the stuff of daily news in the United States in the 1990s. Yet the practical, day-to-day feelings, worries, and experiences of the poor in Mexico City's *colonias populares,* reeling from the impact of sociopolitical and economic catastrophes, were usually ignored, unless they were rendered obligatory objects of concern by virtue of intermittent outbursts of rebellion. It is not my intention to perpetuate scholarly indifference to the poor continuing to ignore their politically dissident moods and activities—for example, the amorphous if nonetheless popular opposition to NAFTA (see chapter 4). Rather, I will consider in detail the muted and sometimes confused opinions of some of my neighbors in Colonia Santo Domingo, as well as certain of their more clearly voiced sentiments, as they related to democratic and not-so-democratic decisions—decisions about street paving, health care, and transportation, for example—that directly affected their daily lives. Moreover, I will also document their efforts to effect change in the larger national and international arenas as they recognized events and activities that also had everything to do with how they lived and who they were.

LOCALIZING THE GLOBALIZING

In January 1997 I was standing outside the corner *tienda* (shop) of one of my closest friends, Marcelo, sipping a Vickys beer that another friend, Marcial, a Yucateco carpenter, had just bought me to celebrate the New Year. Marcos, who lived next door to the *tienda,* stopped by. Having just been on a family vacation to Yucatán, and having endured the thirty-hour bus ride to return to Mexico City, he was tanned, exhausted, and excited to tell us, and especially Marcial, about his trip. Two things stood out in his mind as highlights of the journey: the archaeological ruins he had seen in Chichén Itzá, and the topless beaches he had visited on Isla Mujeres.

Just as Marcos was beginning to describe the details of each encounter, a little boy walked up to him and asked for some coins to buy candy. I looked at the boy, who was around three years old, and asked him his name. He looked me in the eye and replied that it was Ruvalcaba. Ruvalcaba, I knew, was my friend Marcos's last name, too. Marcos prompted him to give his first name. "Marco Antonio," he responded. Quickly, Marcos then asked, "*¿Y cómo se llama tu padre?*" (And what's your father's name?), to which the child answered matter-of-factly, "*Abuelito*" (Grandpa), whereupon Marcos broke out into a big smile.

Marcos's daughter had become pregnant by a gang-banging youth who had long since fled the scene. The daughter and her son continued to live with the (biological) grandparents, and Marcos and his wife Delia and another daughter of theirs were all helping to raise the boy, with Marcos's formal role in this effort perhaps a bit more diversified, given the fact that he was the only man in the household.

Many people who saw Marcos, in his forties, with Marco Antonio no doubt assumed that they were biological father and son. So, in a quiet and unassuming way, Marcos was happy to go along with appearances as if these served the larger purpose of raising the boy well. In addition to playing the anthropological game of fiddling with polysemic kinship terms, Marcos also exhibited a distinctly defiant pose, perhaps to surprise me at the casual way in which he slid between the personae of grandfather and father. In the same way that Marcos referred to himself that day as a father named "Grandpa," he had described himself in the May 1994 street debate with which I opened this book as a *PRDista sin Cárdenas,* a PRDista who wishes the party could get rid of its leader, Cuauhtémoc Cárdenas.

The labels Marcos used for his contradictory experiences, familial and civic alike, were perhaps not so different from those employed by professional political analysts. Discussions of the form and substance of democracy often carry with them similarly confusing, house-of-mirrors descriptions. Democracy is sometimes treated more as a matter of regimes and sometimes seen principally as a question of popular sovereignty; in one version there are recognizable institutions but no people, whereas in the other there are people with ideas but no mechanism for engagement (see Collier 1999). When Marcos commented that he was "a citizen of democratic Mexico," for example, he generally used this declaration to mock Mexico's formal political regime. "We are the *jodidos* (screwed) of Mexico, Mateo," he often told me.

What democracy means in a real, practical sense, and what it means to participate in a democracy, are questions my friends have sometimes asked themselves and each other. Their models for comparison have run the gamut from the formal democratic exercise of the right to vote, to a type of participatory democracy that is at once more fluid and more apparent, for example, that of grassroots feminist efforts in neighborhoods throughout Mexico (see Dietz 1992; Stephen 1997a). Periodically, my friends and I have talked about having been born into a certain life, with a particular political system, and experiencing the frustrations of trying to change that system. In our discussions, I occasionally invoked the formulation of Antonio Gramsci ([1929–35] 1971, 333) regarding contradictory consciousness—the conflict that arises between ideas inherited from dead generations and those that develop in the course of new efforts to transform the world. In response, as often as not, Gabriel would make reference to one or another Aztec deity he admired on the question of change and continuity in society. Marcos might cite a Catholic saint, and Marcelo a musician who similarly talked about rights and responsibilities to make the world better for those who live in it.

At election time, Marcelo, our friend who for years ran the store on Huehuetzin Street, also manned the polls for the PRD—to guard against vote fraud. Marcelo described this activity as helping to guarantee that democracy was respected in Mexico. He did not really believe his presence near the polling booths made a big difference, he said, and he had less interest in catching fraudulent behavior than in lending a veneer of independence to the proceedings. Independence, even if only for the sake of appearance, was terribly important, Marcelo said. Because even a facade got people thinking about running their own political lives. He used to say that he supported the PRD because the other parties seemed to him more concerned with aping Gringo democracy than with building a truly independent Mexico. Sellouts, *malinchistas,* he called them.

COMING HOME AGAIN

For close to a decade I spent as much time as I could in Colonia Santo Domingo, learning about child rearing, as well as chiles, *futbol,* fandangos, and bouts of *flojera,* tequila, and becoming *tomado.*[3] The central intellectual issue was to document and understand change, both the micro- and the macro-transformations in people's ideas and activities. Since I first set foot in the neighborhood in 1991, mystery and curiosity have been constant issues with which I have had to contend—as often as not with *me* as the object of such appraisals. Santo Domingo is simply not on tourist maps, and the only Gringos who are known to live there are two or three evangelists who have a reputation among many of the residents as pushy and judgmental aliens. Not a group with which I ever would wish to be associated.

I was fortunate, and not a little opportunistic, because when I first came to Santo Domingo to live, I arrived with my wife, Michelle McKenzie, and our then seven-week-old daughter, Liliana. Thus, my presence in the *colonia* was associated from the start with my status as a new and basically inexperienced father. That is a condition that has changed over the years, according to my mentors and kibitzers in the arts of parenting on Huehuetzin Street, only insofar as I now have two children and am a bit less inept being a father. The expectation of my closest friends and anthropological family in Santo Domingo was that whenever I returned I would, as often as was possible, bring Liliana with me, because she was of the community in some symbiotic and culturally potent sense that I could never be.

If my relationship to the people on Huehuetzin Street had its constants, including my status as Liliana's father, other aspects of my status as an unusual Gringo indeed shifted over the years, often to my chagrin. On January 1, 1997, a day or two before I bumped into Marcos and Marco Antonio in the *tienda,* neighbors invited me to stop by and tell them about a book of mine on Santo Domingo that had been published the previous summer in English (Gutmann 1996). The women were drinking eggnog-flavored Rompope liqueur and the men were sipping on their *cubas* as they all crowded over my shoulder to look at the photographs in the book and wait for me to find their names in the index and translate the appropriate quotes, comments, and exposés. One young woman noticed herself in the background of a photo and wanted me to translate the caption. Another woman asked why I had not used a photograph I had taken in 1993 of her father-in-law. A man complained that he had grown thinner in the four years since I had photographed him, and made me promise that "the next book" would have an updated, slimmer image to display.

It was a rather chaotic scene, prompted no doubt by my return after a six months' absence, as well as by little sleep and lots of alcohol on the part of my neighbors. But mainly what struck me that New Year's morning was the feeling I had that I would not be able to write another book about Santo Domingo and Huehuetzin Street. People were treating me in a more obviously calculating manner than before—I was not simply an exotic Gringo father but, potentially at least, a means to getting their names and faces published in Gringolandia. The idea that students and others in the United States might actually come to know them, even what they looked like (hefty and svelte versions, no less) produced guffaws and backslaps.

I did not say anything at the time, but later that afternoon, when I met up again with some of my other friends, I voiced my concerns. Gabi and Marcelo, who were among my best friends, listened to me as I explained my fear that from here on out I would just be able to learn what people wanted me to see and hear, and that people would be ever more vigilant at hiding what they feared might end up in print at some later date. Gabi, in particular, was unimpressed by my worries. He pointed out that I was seriously out of touch if I thought that anything different had been the case previously. Sure, now my neighbors had a clearer sense of the possibility of "being published," he said, but people always divulge or hide information—to or from Gringo anthropologists, neighbors, wives, kids, bosses, parents, hell, even to and from themselves. To emphasize the point, he leaned over and with a wink whispered (loud enough for Marcelo to hear, too): "*Cálmate, Mateo. Mira, vamos a tomar un anís ¿está bien?*" (Calm down, Mateo. Look, let's go have an Anise, okay?).

The offer of *anís* was a signal to both Marcelo and me. Many years before, several of us had spent the better part of a Saturday getting *bien pedo* (literally, well farted) on *anís,* and, ever since, getting me to drink the licorice-flavored liqueur had been a running gag. This was Gabi's way of saying, "Look, you're a little different, sure. But you also have a history here in Santo Domingo, and if we can put up with you all this time, then you will have to learn to adjust to us as well." The conversation shifted to what had changed since 1992, when Michelle, Liliana, and I had first arrived to live in the *colonia.* This question led to two topics: the people who were no longer with us, for one reason or another, and others who had only recently joined us. In the context of Santo Domingo, where families do not often move in or out, mostly we talked about who had died, which couples had split up, and what babies had been born.

Gabi and Marcelo mentioned that Enrique, the disabled son of an elderly neighbor, had finally succumbed to whatever disease it was that had afflicted him since birth. They were pretty sure his mother was comforted because she no longer had the burden of caring for Enrique. Another neighbor, a chronic alcoholic, a genuine *teporocho* in Mexico City vernacular—and a man who when he noticed me on the street used to scream, "*¡Griiiiiiiiiiiiingooooooooo!*"—also was no longer among the living. He had drowned in one too many bottles of rubbing alcohol; "96," those in the know call it, because it is supposedly 96 percent alcohol. None of us in 1997 yet knew that Juan, a young man who worked in his family's liquor store at the corner, would be murdered three years later only yards away from where we were talking that day. In January 2000, two drugged-up customers would try to steal a bottle of rum and, when Juan objected, one would pull out a pistol and shoot him dead. Some neighbors later said the gunmen were cops, though most thought this unlikely.

We talked of neighbors, sisters, brothers, and cousins who had gotten married or divorced since I had first come to Santo Domingo. Gabriel himself had separated from his wife. He was still supporting his family financially, but he saw the children far less now that they no longer lived in the same house. Our friend Luciano, on the other hand, a man who had lived with a second wife and family for several years, had moved back in with his first wife and children around 1995. So, we talked about happy reunions, not aware that by 2000 Luciano would be sleeping in a small room he had built outside the main part of the house where his former wife still lived. Regardless of whether he and his ex-wife were sharing a bed, Luciano was worried that if he did not live there on the premises, he could lose his rights to both the property and the house. Marriages and even marital separations, whether sanctified by the church, the government, or just the couple involved, seemed far less enduring than death.

In 1997 Don Timo was still at his spot on a main avenue waiting for customers who needed their wicker furniture repaired. He was still inviting all of us to his little ranch in Río de Bravo—"*Somos gentes humildes y pobres, pero están bienvenidos a mi casa*" (We're humble and poor, but you are most welcome in our home), he graciously offered. And by 2000, Don Timo's son would be angry with me, after having read in the Spanish version of a book I had written (Gutmann 2000) what their neighbors had related to me about his parents. I promised the son that in the next book I wrote about Santo Domingo I would recount his insistence that his father had never beaten his mother.

In our talk that New Year's Day in 1997, Marcelo reminded us of another death in the neighborhood, one that affected me more than the others. On November 13, 1996, Angela Jiménez had died after suffering three massive heart attacks in rapid succession. My treasured friend, teacher, and confidant, Angela had been called *abuelita* (grandma) by numerous children in the *colonia,* including my own daughter Liliana. "There was nothing the doctors could do about it," Angela's brother Héctor later told me. And nothingness was what many of us in her extended family felt after we lost Angela.

Angela had exemplified the spirit of taking matters into one's own hands, from resolving family disputes, to neighborhood problems, to general social suffering. Her death made us all feel less able to cope with life—less capable of taking on the powers that be, large and small. She had asked no mercy from life, yet she had displayed it in abundance. Her role model was St. Francis, she used to tell us, because of his asceticism and humility. St. Francis loved poverty so much, she would smile when recounting his life, that he renounced the money he had inherited from his merchant father. Angela was a true believer, Norma, her daughter, reminded me. When one of her mother's dearest friends, Glafira, was diagnosed with cancer, Angela had commented, "*¡Qué bueno!*" (Fantastic!). This might seem callous, but Angela said it with all her heart, because she believed that Glafira would soon get to meet her maker. Given the holy fervor her mother embodied, Norma could only shudder in slightly scandalized wonder. (As it happened, Glafira's cancer went into remission the next year.)

On my first trip home to Santo Domingo after Angela's passing, I cried and laughed upon hearing Norma recount how her mother had once admonished her, "*¡Mientras tengas madre, chinga tu madre!*" (As long as you've got a mother, fuck your mother!). Typical, a characteristic example of both Angela's spirit and her tongue. In the following pages I have tried to capture some of Angela's spirit, knowing nevertheless that this would have been a far better study if I could have learned more from her about issues like voting, nationalism, blame, and innocence, and most of all about the twists and turns of remaining defiant and unrepentant in the face of authority.

In the middle of our reveries about who had died and who had separated, Gabi's assistant Momo came running up, asking about a brake-drum spring that he had dismantled but lost. We remembered that Momo, "barely off the breast himself," now had an infant daughter crawling and romping around the one-room home that Momo's mother and father had let him and his wife build on their land.

Thus, birth, marriage, and mortality, road signs of what demographers call the life course, and what people in Santo Domingo call simply "life," stood as appropriate symbols of cyclical changes for individuals, families, and neighbors. But both Marcelo and Gabi felt there had been more to the 1990s for them and for others in Mexico, in the way of linear change and transformation.

What, they wanted to know, did I think of the possibilities for democracy in Mexico's immediate future? How might these compare to democratic processes in the United States? I am often uncomfortable in Latin America when I am asked to represent some sort of U.S. position on a question, especially as in this case, when I am asked to rate progress toward becoming more like the United States. I nonetheless listened to Gabi as he explained once again his hopes and frustrations, which were tied to the Zapatista movement in Chiapas, just as I also listened to Marcelo, who still cherished a dream that the left-of-center PRD party would once again lead Mexico in a fundamental redistribution of wealth as had not happened even during the populist presidency of Lázaro Cárdenas, Cuauhtémoc's father, in the 1930s.

Regardless of my views, it seemed that, in January 1997, some eight months before Cárdenas fils would be elected mayor of the Federal District, both my friends were intent on exploring the events of 1968 (Tlatelolco), the elections of 1988 and 1994, and the financial crises in between. And, they insisted, maybe I should start paying more attention to the winds of political conflict in Mexico.

"So you see, Mateo," said Marcelo, "we've figured out your next book already. Now all you have to do is write it."

Figure 3. Progress being a complicated process to chart, a banner hung in 1993 announced that a kindergarten formerly known as Mickey Mouse would henceforth be named for the Aztec and Toltec deity Quetzalcóatl.

CIVIL IMPOTENCE IN MEXICO

A common approach to the study of politics in Mexico is to focus on formal issues of political parties, political representation, political parties, electoral procedures, interest groups, political parties, administrative apparatuses, state–society issues, and political parties. In Mexico the longevity of PRI (the party of *institutional* revolution) hegemony at all levels of federal, state, and municipal government has been a topic of continued interest, as even the habitually out-of-office parties gained the sobriquet of "the institutionalized opposition" (see González Casanova 1970, 13).[4] More recently, scholars have examined popular social movements in urban and rural areas. These groups of citizens, linked locally and nationally, harbor no illusions that the powers-that-be will concede to their demands without a struggle. They have therefore banded together to fight, both for single issues and for a broader array of demands.

For many analysts the heart and soul of politics in Mexico remains the study of electoral parties—their foibles, fortunes, and futures. In particular, in the 1990s most commentators heralded the numerous

PRD and PAN electoral victories, from governorships to the mayoralty of the national capital, as historically significant benchmarks of broader political changes afoot in the land. Many saw the election to major offices of PRD and PAN candidates as proof positive that now Mexico, too, had democracy (i.e., Mexico was finally a real multiparty state), and by extension, that the popular will was being exercised throughout the country. Whether and how these electoral achievements may have actually served to short-circuit fuller discussion and reflection, or even to waylay the continuing struggle regarding the content and strategies of popular sovereignty and democracy, were just about taboo subjects in certain formal political and academic circles. As to questioning the precise textures and configurations of genuinely popular discourse and governmentality, sorry. In the view of many political operatives and analysts, one should not dwell on such abstractions.

When they think about taking an active role in political and social issues of the day in Mexico, when they consider that democracy necessarily should integrate popular power and participation as central factors in the equation, then one critical question raised by many people in Colonia Santo Domingo is: Where on earth are they supposed to find the time and energy to actually assume such responsibilities on a regular basis? Some of my friends, when pushed, ask how democracy can be practically realized, what specifically constitutes popular sovereignty, and why should they regard democracy as anything more than a paper fiction and a trip to the voting booth every few years. Their conundrum is realistically grounded in a demographic problem: population concentrations have long since made the town meeting and equivalent forms of local assembly impossible. Therefore, despite its roots in the practical airing and decision-making of face-to-face congresses, applied democracy in the twenty-first century can clearly not be organized in this fashion. For this reason, one analyst has written of "the wave-like characteristic of democratizations." This, in part, means that "from the moment the term escaped the philosopher's study, 'democracy' . . . has been primarily an actor's term, not an analyst's" (Markoff 1997, 50, 51).

In Mexico it would appear that voting has replaced assembly—or in Tocquevillean language, associational life—as the primary form of democratic participation, the highest manifestation of popular rule, the most realistic opportunity for the citizenry to decide what kind of society they wish to have. The act of voting en masse in Mexico has come to personify the experience described by David Kertzer: "In simultaneity lies political communion" (1988, 23). Participation in the common and simultaneous ritual of voting thus becomes the sine qua non of citizenship and political legitimacy. Where this leaves abstainers is a surprisingly understudied question.

In an oddly parallel fashion to studies of sexuality that seek to neatly dichotomize "active" and "passive" involvement in sex, based on rigid distinctions between penetrators and penetrated, so too in the world of official politics in Mexico, resolute nonparticipation has no place or only marginal significance in most models. That is, by considering electoral politics as the totality of politics in general, analysts often consign abstentionism of any kind to the litterbox of apolitical and apathetic history. But just as one must study teetotalers as well as drunks to understand alcoholism, so too with politics: we gain a far better understanding of why some people participate sometimes in some forms of political activities if we understand why others do not, and in practice if not in theory "active" and "passive" forms of participation—in politics as in sex—are very difficult to neatly separate.

In his famous study of *Democracy in Mexico*, Pablo González Casanova identified the "contemplative and patient attitude" among Mexico's "marginal people" as a prominent feature in the popular political landscape of his country ([1965] 1970, 127). According to González, "the marginal lower classes" are "more patient and *civilly harmless*" than other members of the lower classes who participate in some fashion in organized political activities such as elections, albeit often in exchange for paternalistic favors (129, emphasis added). Questions of co-optation, conformity, and consent have long been a staple of mainstream studies of political regimes in twentieth-century Mexico, and understandably so. Therefore, when political developments occur that are at odds with this pattern, they are all the more noteworthy. This was the case, for example, of a particular middle-class political coalition in the 1990s that proved to have a societywide impact: El Barzón was a debtors' movement formed by small shopkeepers and others who could not pay the money they owed banks. They decided to band together and declare a partial moratorium on their collective debt, and indeed were quite successful through the roughest years of financial insolvency and defaults on loans, 1995–98 (see Williams 1996; Senzek 1997; and Rodríguez-Gómez 1998).

As recounted in the preface, in May 1994 my friends, at least my male friends, seemed intent on thrashing out the possible repercussions of the various elections that would take place in August. In May, there had been enthusiastic street debate over the future of Mexican politics and the role of common citizens in determining this future. By the time I had returned, in September, the elections were over and the political climate in Santo Domingo could not have been more different. There was now widespread civic weariness, due not only to the assassination of Ruiz Massieu, general secretary of the PRI, but also to a more general political melancholy among residents of Santo Domingo. Scarcely one month after the presidential elections on August 21, and in the face of the unambiguous return to the status quo ante, I now witnessed a wave of political disillusionment, apathy, and acquiescence among my circle of neighbors and acquaintances in Colonia Santo Domingo, at least among the men (see chapter 8). There were no more harangues in the streets over the politics of one or another of the candidates, and barely any discussion of formal politics whatsoever within families or among friends. Certainly, I witnessed nothing like what I had seen the previous May.

Following the elections in August, the political regime of the PRI had been annoyingly relegitimized, as people became reconciled to the fact that one had to accept, if not necessarily savor, the results. After all, as the media repeated ad nauseam, the citizenry had spoken. If yet another politician had been assassinated, well then, that just showed that Mexico was going to the dogs, heading in the same direction as the rest of Latin America, where violent social politics predominated. Somehow, in all the postmortem discussions of the elections of 1994, the initial enthusiasm and subsequent indifference of masses of voters was lost. This makes all the more persuasive the line of reasoning advanced by Jonathan Fox about voting and the broader questions of citizenship in Mexico: "Most analysis of the emergence of electoral competition concentrates quite appropriately on high politics, on the pacts which define the rules of contestation and the founding elections which shape much of national politics. But analysis of the effective extension of the full range of citizenship rights *throughout* a society involves studying how most people are actually represented and governed" (1997, 392). The issue of citizenship is both straightforwardly complex and simultaneously old and new, as Fox shows by drawing our attention in particular to the tensions of "high and low politics."

I stopped by a friend's house early one day in January 1997 and found his house full of relatives still enjoying a party that had begun the night before. Over coffee, Rompope, and rum drinks, several women initiated a rather curious conversation about domestic violence. It was an exchange promoted in good measure by concerns about agency, culpability, and acquiescence. Two or three women in the house, relatives of the couple who lived there, began talking about one particular man, who was also visiting, chastising him for beating his wife and trying to be *"muy macho."* I was confused, not sure what had elicited the round of ridicule. Perhaps it was alcohol, or lack of sleep from all-night festivities, or my own presence—several people there knew about my book on Mexican men. Then, rather quickly, the discussion dissipated, as the women turned to the wife of the alleged wifebeater and began to laugh. I wondered whether the whole conversation had been a joke. Or perhaps it was an example, famous in anthropological accounts, of how alcohol (or other means) allows one to play the "fool" and "jokester" and say what no one normally dares reveal (see, e.g., Dennis 1979). There are many theories as to who and what is responsible for domestic violence, both in the social sciences and in Colonia Santo Domingo as well.

Debates about domestic violence among my friends in Santo Domingo revolve around opposing theories regarding human will and human nature. As with conflicts regarding such "natural" phenomena as child rearing and mother–infant bonding (see Gutmann 1998), so too with respect to wife beating and the like, men and women debate the relative merits of concepts of preordained and immutable male-versus-female natures and competing ideas that posit humans' willingness and ability to adapt and change. Nor is religion a safe guidepost, for people on all sides of these discussions can invoke religious scripture in an attempt to enhance their arguments. In an analogous fashion, I think, there is a certain overeagerness within the social sciences to attribute goodwill and good intentions to those who seek small, incremental change (i.e., those who resist), whereas there is a profound reluctance to do the same when it comes to (political) blame for events and ideas that reinforce oppression and social stratification.

Discussions about human will and change are generally concerned as well with the relationship between hope and development. Expectations have everything to do with conformity and control, not only for the most desperate and needy who rebel (i.e., those who can no longer endure), but also for those who have more freedom to realize what they seek to accomplish. Far from looking for simplistic analyses regarding abstentionism, the issue instead should be whether and to what extent different groups of people at different times see themselves as having a stake in one or another political system and form of representation and participation. This, in turn, relates back to the active/passive dichotomy, because one person's passivity may be another's activity—that is, what constitutes passivity in a certain context and from a particular perspective may take on quite different hues in other contexts and perspectives.

Many of my friends in Colonia Santo Domingo express frustration at their lives and living situations. Often this is framed in rather personal terms, such as feelings of being trapped by their families, jobs, unemployment, and the like. Yet I think that these emotions are not unlike those expressed more generally by women and men who feel helpless and complacent or, alternatively, driven and optimistic because of *"el sistema," "la cultura," "la sociedad,"* or simply *"las circunstancias."* [5]

Whatever else may be different about public affairs and active citizenship on the one hand, and child rearing, domestic violence, and other more "personal" matters on the other, they share several features. Not the least of these is recurring discourse about guilt and innocence, about cause and effect, so that perceived power differences are often subjectively implicated in available channels of change. Briefly put, transformation often occurs when those who feel oppressed force change on others.

OVERTURE TO POLITICAL FANTASIES

The point of this study is not to substitute a facile vision of the scrappy underdog who wants his or her voice to be heard for the more conventional top-down version of political history. The book does focus on the choices, voices, and noises of women and men in Colonia Santo Domingo, Mexico City, in the 1990s, for whom a broader audience is rarely even a fantasy. What these residents of Santo Domingo think about the Free Trade Agreement, about issues of sovereignty and class and national allegiances, is not incidental here. Similarly, whether they vote or not, and whether voting is associated with the dream that somehow they might contribute to changing their political worlds, are not quaint or small matters. Whoever my friends think is to blame for political strife and quiescence, however they feel themselves implicated in the processes of world history, are issues that compel ongoing conjecture and debate—in the working-class neighborhoods of Mexico City as much as in the halls of the academy. Our particular goal in this study is to look for class and gendered qualities, characteristics, and goals to politics, as seen in different attitudes and practices in relation to specific political activities, or simply in the more inchoate manner of political sensibilities.

At the dawn of the twenty-first century, it has become commonplace to talk about global connections and transnational associations, the important transformations that have occurred in the last century, whether they be labeled capitalist, imperialist, colonial, neocolonial, postmodern, or simply modern. David Held has written regarding democracy and the global order: "While everyone has a local life, 'phenomenal worlds' are now increasingly interpenetrated by developments and processes from diverse settings." Some feel justified, Held argues, in extrapolating from this understanding "a sense of global belonging and vulnerability which transcends loyalties to the nation-state; that is, to 'my country right or wrong.'" Yet Held inveighs against conclusions that would champion a sudden rise in "a universal political history," insisting instead on "the persistence of a plurality of frames of political meaning" in the contemporary world (1995, 124–25).

Such a conclusion certainly applies in the case of contemporary Mexico. Far from joining in some regional, hemispheric, Latin American, or universal frame of reference, my collaborators in Colonia Santo Domingo evince a sharp sensitivity and awareness to the global movement of both financial and symbolic capital, and they do so within a fairly wide array of viewpoints, eventually arriving at a dizzying panorama of judgments about what it all means and what it all has to do with them. Questions of change, large and small, are of utmost importance to many of my friends—not all the time for everyone, of course, but certainly sometimes, in some ways, for some people, in some places. Offering reasons for and against particular forms of change, and for and against their individual and collective participation in fomenting and/or retarding change, whether it be at the local level of street sewers or at the national level of safeguarding Mexico's natural resources—this is the stuff of daily life in homes, factories, schools, playgrounds, streets, markets, and subways.

Democracy is held by many to embrace self-government of and by the people. What on earth this means and what self-government might look and feel like are the subjects of this study.[6]

CHAPTER 2

The Children of (Oscar) Lewis

Utopian experiences that we will never see in our lifetime
can become real within the time span of a performance,
and underworlds from which no one returns can be visited
in safety.

Peter Brook

BLAME AND CONSEQUENCE

Oscar Lewis (1914–1970) was a North American anthropologist who
lived and worked in Mexico, Cuba, and Puerto Rico, as well as among
Native Americans and in India, for three decades from the 1940s until
his death in 1970. He was the author of such classic studies as *Life in a
Mexican Village* (1951), *Five Families* (1959), *The Children of Sánchez*
(1961), and *La Vida* (1965). Although Lewis is still read by anthropology students in Mexico, few of my undergraduates in the United States
have heard of him, much less studied his ethnographies. Nevertheless,
curiously enough, in the United States many students have heard of "the
culture of poverty" and "blaming the victim," both expressions that for
better or for worse are attributed to Oscar Lewis. In this chapter, I discuss these and related concepts associated with Lewis and reexamine
some of Lewis's scholarship on class, gender, change, and national identity in Mexico and Latin America, more generally.

My reexamination of Lewis's ethnography, as well as various of his
still controversial theories, is part of a broader exploration of popular
politics among the residents of Santo Domingo. In his day, Oscar Lewis
was among the premier chroniclers of contradictory political passions
and practices among the poor in the Mexican capital; in particular, he
documented the inconsistent processes of civil challenge, frustration,
and accommodation in some of Mexico City's most famous *colonias*

populares, like the barrio of Tepito on the northern edge of downtown. By providing graphic portraits of Mexico's urban underdogs, *los de abajo,* Lewis revealed what some in his day regarded as a grossly unflattering, if not necessarily inaccurate, portrait of a society whose political leaders were loathe to discuss poverty and misery among the vast majority of the population.[1]

Following the publication of *Los hijos de Sánchez* (Lewis 1964a), the Mexican Geographical and Statistical Society publicly vilified Lewis and labeled the book slanderous. A news report in *Excelsior,* then Mexico's leading newspaper, quoted an official of the Society, who complained that the book painted the Mexican people as "the most degraded, miserable, and vile people in the entire world and asserts that our salvation would be to have a North American President rule in Mexico with the magnificent laws of that great country. [T]his anthropological treatise . . . is the confession of the life, character, and behavior of the four children of Alberto [*sic*] Sánchez: Manuel, Roberto, Consuelo, and Marta; two discontented bums and two semi-prostitutes" (translated in Halvorson and Moser 1965, 73).[2]

The Geographical Society accused Lewis of being an agent of the FBI and/or the Pentagon, sent to stir up trouble in Mexico. In fact, Gustavo Díaz Ordaz, Mexico's president at the time, fired Arnaldo Orfila, the editor of the government publishing house Fondo de Cultura Económica, for allowing the book to appear in Spanish. Yet Lewis was obviously not a U.S. government agent. As the well-known Mexican writer Rosario Castellanos insisted in *Excelsior* in 1965, *Hijos de Sánchez* was important precisely because it "damages Mexico's decorum" (1965, 8A).

Oscar Lewis's studies of Mexicans on the bottom of society were controversial for a number of reasons: the decorum they damaged directed attention to extreme poverty in Mexico; they took the opinions and actions of the poor seriously; and they implied that if the poor wanted to do something about their situation, they would do best to rely mainly on their own efforts. In addition, the fact that the studies were written in a novelistic style—*poesía de la vida,* the poetry of life, as Carlos Monsiváis described Lewis's style (2000, 40)—made their impact more accessible and intense.

In the United States, Lewis remains an interesting figure in the history of anthropology, and leftist scholarship particularly, because of his focus on what would today be called "agency" and in his day was more commonly described by terms like "human behavior," "action," or "will."[3] Despite his stated concern to place the people in his ethnographies within clear social contexts that would account for factors like political economy, kinship, and demography, the questions Lewis asked were often more psychological in nature. In a sense, his attention to life histories seems to have stemmed from larger concerns with what later social scientists called the relationship between structure and agency—that is, the extent to which people construct their own social worlds and the degree to which they are caught in webs not of their own spinning.[4] In particular, it appears that, for Lewis, questions of structure and system had become overemphasized in writings on the poor, and he sought to redress this exaggerated state of affairs with renewed attention to the less deterministic elements in social change.

Lewis's objectives share something in common with those expressed by Gil Joseph, who wrote in an introduction to a recent volume on the cultural history of U.S.–Latin American relations: "Whereas theories of dependency, imperialism, and the world system . . . promote dichotomies that centralize and reify political-economic structures and processes, and ignore culturally embedded human subjects, we strive to 'decenter' analysis, break down reifications, and restore agency to the historical narrative" (1998, 14).

Besides entering into longstanding debates within anthropology and sociology regarding cohesion and conflict models of human society, Oscar Lewis also published his major work during the period of McCarthyism and Cold War in the United States, at a time when Marxist sympathies, which Lewis clearly shared, appeared in many forms (see Rigdon 1988). Lying beneath Lewis's invocation of many of the research questions and frameworks of the culture and personality school, for example, one may discern equally longstanding debates among Marxist scholars regarding the degree to which the working class must rely on its own efforts to change society. In a sense, too, any discussion of the relation of class to social change inevitably begs the question, does the lower class want greater access to or do they want out of capitalist society—a dilemma-provoking conundrum for the Left that goes back some time.[5]

In the course of developing his "poetry of life," Lewis also developed a rather cavalier approach to many of his informants, and his style and methodology continue to provoke sharp criticism many decades after his death (see, e.g., Díaz Barriga 1994). Notwithstanding these serious questions pertaining to Lewis's methodological and stylistic approaches to ethnography, he was, nevertheless, decades ahead of his time in finding ways to bring the lives of the poor and formally voiceless to the attention of readers throughout the Spanish-speaking and English-speaking worlds—for example, with respect to issues of political responsibility and blame as these were understood by working-class women and men in Mexico City and Puerto Rico. As the editors of the *New Left Review* wrote in 1966, "'The Children of Sanchez' both challenged the conventional notions of what the social scientist could do, and pointed one way forward to a possible revitalization of the realist novel" (1966, 1).

If from the late 1950s through the mid-1960s, Mexico's decorum was damaged by Oscar Lewis's writings, as Rosario Castellanos insisted, anthropology's decorum was also damaged, and needed to be, on both sides of the Rio Grande/Río Bravo. This was true, both with regard to commonly accepted truths about Mexican society—for instance, machismo—and with respect to larger issues of class, in the United States also known as poverty. In part because of his fuzzy pronouncements on class, in the United States Lewis was held responsible for initiating the federal government's War on Poverty in the 1960s, as well as for a resurgent Social Darwinism in academia. To an extent, these charges stemmed simply from Lewis's own baffling formulations about class; yet they also represented contending analyses among academic leftists as to the relationship between class and the root problems and solutions associated with capitalist society.

Lewis himself was disturbingly remiss in his reluctance to more fully develop some of his controversial, and, frankly, too often half-baked, ideas. Though often accused of theoretical temerity, in fact Lewis's timidity in developing his conceptual argument may have ultimately and inadvertently contributed to the longevity of the stigma associated with his work among scholars, especially scholars on the left, in the United States.[6]

In the spirit of Lewisonian naiveté, then, this chapter sketches out a few blunt conclusions concerning the tendency to blame the victim, with a brief exegesis on the relationship between culture and poverty (the infamous "culture *of* poverty"). Mexican machismo serves to illustrate several ongoing points of dispute.[7]

THE PLACE OF MEN IN DOMESTIC DEBATES

In his extensive ethnographies of rural and urban Mexico, Oscar Lewis described family relations in exquisite detail, and Lewis's long-term attention to family affairs, sexual divisions of labor, and daily life have been an important, if too often unrecognized, influence on subsequent gender studies in Mexico. Far from presenting such relationships as emblematic of static, cultural traits inherent to "the Mexican people," Lewis seemed to delight in tracing the changes in families over years and even decades. In what he called his personally most satisfying study, *Pedro Martínez: A Mexican Peasant and His Family* (1964b), for example, Lewis documented the impact of religious conversion on Pedro's family and his attitudes toward parenting. Lewis took seriously the superficially bland interactions of daily life, seeing in them not simply the perfunctory reflections of larger social forces but also a wellspring of new ideas and manners of interacting. In my own fieldwork in Mexico City I have learned much from Lewis in this regard.

For instance, Angela was explaining to me one afternoon what her husband Juan had been like when their four children were small. "When Juan was a *papá*, it was very different.[8] Then, *papás* had nothing to do with babies." Juan interjected that now he loved to play with children and that he rough-housed all the time with his grandchildren. Angela allowed that this was true. Later in our conversation, and apparently apropos of nothing in particular, Angela launched into a disparaging indictment of certain husbands. She began her rebuke by singling out men who do no housework and who do not let their wives out of the house without their permission. "*No les permiten salir ni a la misa*" (They won't let them out even to go to Mass)," she reported to me, slowly shaking her head in mock disbelief. She was even more disparaging when discussing women who tolerated men who restricted them in this way.

Angela was giving me a lecture on how agency was seen and employed in the practical interactions of family and neighborhood life, and especially about how individual strategies are constructed in relation both to particular social fields and to the individual strategies of others.

In the middle of our conversation around the kitchen table, a woman friend of Angela's dropped by for a visit. Juan brought Isabel a cup of coffee. Angela smiled and casually remarked that such service on Juan's part was also something new in the last few years. Isabel agreed, and, to tease Juan, added, "Where did you find him, Angelita?" When they were first married and living with her mother-in-law, Angela confided, Juan's mother had told Juan not to let Angela go out without his permission. She had never accepted such a restriction, she told Isabel and me, clearly proud of this stand, and of the part she had played in changing the way in which Juan treated her and other women.[9]

Figure 4. Angela Jiménez and Juan López in Tepo-
tzotlán, 1992.

Just then, Angela's lifelong bachelor brother Héctor walked into the
kitchen area. He had come for the chicken necks that he fed his cats
twice a day. "Now, Héctor is another story altogether," Angela said as
she waved her hand in her brother's direction. "Men like him can be really macho." Héctor objected, insisting that even though he had never
married, he still went shopping all the time (and therefore could not be
a true macho).[10] Juan then stepped in to offer his opinion: "In the past,
women would not let men do this [go shopping], for fear that they'd be
called—"

"*Maricón!* (Faggot!)," Angela interrupted.

As odd as it might seem, persuading men to talk in their homes in the
presence of women was often difficult in Colonia Santo Domingo, and

not because the men were reluctant to divulge manly secrets to women. Instead, the men were often self-consciously "muted" by their wives and other women in the home. Rather than confront their wives and their wives' friends, they would sometimes wait until we found ourselves outside on the street, away from the women, to explain to me "the true reasons" why they did or did not go shopping, cook, or wash the clothes.[11]

The ways in which people in Santo Domingo use and understand the term *macho* (as well as *maricón* and other expressions related to masculine identities) are clearly related to the frequently reported, and less seldom analyzed, phenomenon of "machismo." [12] When the work of Oscar Lewis is occasionally mentioned in Santo Domingo, it is more because of his portraits of working-class Mexicans than for what he may have written about machismo. Nevertheless, one of the reasons Lewis is even known for writing about poor men and women is that his descriptions of interactions between husbands and wives ring so true for many in Santo Domingo.

In contemporary Mexico City generally, and regardless of the multiple uses and meanings of machismo, it is noteworthy both that some women are known as *marimachas* (or *marimachos*), and that more generally a man's macho qualities are closely connected to his relationships with women. (The term *marimacha*, not coincidentally, also refers to women who have sex with other women.) For older men and women, the term *macho* often denotes a positive quality that is associated with a man who consistently provides for the economic well-being of his family. Younger men are far more reluctant to accept this label for themselves, although they will freely apply it to their friends. The fact that men in their thirties and forties use the phrase *to be macho* as an insult is also closely connected to the recent history of relations between men and women in Mexico.

MORE ON THE ETYMOLOGY OF "*LOS MACHOS MEXICANOS*"

Concerning the terms *macho* and *machismo,* a few words of clarification are in order. As a definition of "sexist," for example, the term *macho* has a remarkably short history. It appeared in Mexico for the first time in the late 1930s and in the United States about a decade later. In Mexico today, the word *machismo* still has a social science and journalistic ring for most people, and it is far less commonly employed in everyday speech than is the case north of the border, despite the fact that many people in the United States assume that machismo has a uniform and long sociolinguistic lineage in Mexico. On the contrary, within Mexico, the terms *macho* and *machismo* have far more divergent meanings for different people than is the case in the United States.

Why the terms *macho* and *machismo* are so associated today throughout the world with Latin culture, and Mexican culture in particular, is a complicated matter. At a minimum, the word *machismo* must be viewed as describing more than simply sexist ideas: in most usages, the expression refers to a whole network of (generally unequal) social relations between men and women, and between men and men—relations that involve far more than mental constructs alone (see Gutmann 1994, 1996).

The international networks engaged in social science typologizing are fascinating to behold, and tracing the etymology of *macho* and *machismo* (in their contemporary sense) reveals as much about the preconceptions and prejudices of researchers, catalogers, wordsmiths, and lexicographers of various cultural stripes and persuasions as it does about the preexistence of pristine cultural traits "south of the border," as we say in the United States. Several sources write that the semantic roots of the word *macho* can be traced to the (vulgar) Latin, *masclu, masculu,* or *masculus,* terms that also are the origins for the Spanish word *masculino* (Gómez de Silva 1988, 427; Moliner 1991, 2:299). The emphasis here is on what is genetically male in animals and plants, not on cultural values. Another theory traces *macho* to the old Portuguese word *muacho,* which originally comes from *mulus,* meaning "mule" (Moliner 1991, 2:300). The emphasis here is on stubbornness, silliness, and sterility, this last meaning relating to crosses between different species, for example, horses and burros.

The authoritative Santamaría *Diccionario de Mejicanismos* (1959) rather incredibly explains the original meaning of *macho* in this way:

> Because of the influence of indigenous tradition in the semantic evolution, this meaning does not refer exactly to [genetic] sex, in relation to plants and things, but rather to superiority of size, condition, force, or other attribute, or serves as a simple sign to distinguish related species. (1959, 677)

Whereas numerous other sources claim that *machismo* was brought to the New World by Andalusian soldiers during the conquest (see, e.g., Mendoza 1962), according to Santamaría, the Indians did it to the Spanish. Interestingly, the term *machismo* did not appear in Santamaría's first edition of *Americanismos* (1942). Instead, the earliest entry

for the term appeared in the 1959 edition of *Mejicanismos*, indicating
that either it was a new term or it was added belatedly. If machismo, or
at least the term *machismo*, has been around since time immemorial,
or at least since the Conquest, why was it not included before the 1959
edition?

A couple of other readings are worth noting. In Costa Rica and other
parts of Central America, the term *macho* can mean blond or light-
skinned, similar to how *güero* is used today in Mexico (Moliner 1991,
299). In Nicaragua, the term has a particular history: when Augusto
César Sandino in the 1920s and 1930s spoke of the machos, he was referring to Yanqui invaders. One historian of Nicaragua traces the etymological roots of *macho* to the verbs *machar* and *machacar,* meaning
"to pound, break, crush, hammer, beat, bruise, screw." The link is then
made between these verbs and the U.S. rape/invasion of Mexico and
Nicaragua (see Hodges 1986, 114).

In the process of compiling a new *Diccionario del Español Usual en
México* (*DEM*) in the early 1990s, Colegio de México scholars received
the following suggestion from one linguist,[13] regarding how they should
define *machismo*:

> Machismo: exaggerated sense of masculinity. This word is in the DRAE.[14]
> There is no dictionary in English which does not have it. Its importation
> into that language undoubtedly was made from Mexico through the United
> States. It must appear in the *DEM*. The definition I suggest is a translation
> of the one which appears in the *American Heritage.*

While the word *machismo* may have come into English from Spanish
originally, and more specifically from Mexico to the United States, it had
to travel quite a circuitous route to get there. This complicated word history led one scholar to recommend to a leading Spanish-language dictionary looking for a good definition of *machismo* that it use a standard
definition from the United States. That is, if the advice had been taken,
Mexicans would literally learn about one of their so-called national
traits from North American definitions.

Without recapitulating evidence provided elsewhere (see Gutmann
1996, 231–32), suffice it to say that Oscar Lewis is frequently cited in
the social sciences by those seeking to affirm the ubiquity of machismo,
in the sense of flagrant sexism, in Mexico, and Latin America generally. In trying to understand Mexican men, especially poor Mexican
men, numerous scholars have utilized details from Oscar Lewis's ethnographic studies—from the early *Life in a Mexican Village* (1951), to

Five Families (1959), to *Children of Sánchez* (1961). More than a few
writers have seized upon particularly salacious and/or prurient passages
in Lewis's work to promote sensationalist generalizations, which, I believe, go far beyond anything Lewis himself wrote or intended to suggest
about Mexican machismo. For example, in one common retelling, Mexican men in general, and modern urban Mexican men in particular, are
cynically presented, by these ostensible citers of Lewis, as perpetual
braggarts and bullies. Thus portrayed, and with the authority of Oscar
Lewis to back them up, Mexican men become the stereotype through
which, as E. P. Thompson might have written (1993, 406), it is easy to
read all subsequent evidence of Mexican machismo.

True enough, "male superiority (machismo)" appears in Lewis's ill-
conceived and notorious "culture of poverty trait list" (see Lewis 1969,
150; Rigdon 1988, 114). Yet there is reason to believe that Lewis himself may have felt ambivalent about using the term *macho,* not simply
because Lewis generally critiqued overgeneralizations about societies
and peoples, but also because he may not have been wholly comfortable
employing the term in his ethnographic writings.

This becomes apparent when we compare his use of the term, in one
article and two subsequent books about the village Tepoztlán, in which
Lewis essentially repeats the same passage dealing with relations between husbands and wives, with only one notable difference:

1. "While women readily admit the superiority of men and tend
   to admire a man who is *macho,* or very manly, they describe
   the 'good' husband as one who is relatively passive and not too
   domineering" (Lewis 1949, 603).

2. "While women readily admit the superiority of men and tend
   to admire a man who is manly, they describe the 'good' husband as one who is relatively passive and not too domineering"
   (Lewis 1951, 319–20).

3. "[Women] readily admit to the superiority of men and tend to
   admire a man who is *macho* or manly, yet they describe the
   'good' husband as one who is not dominating but relatively
   passive" (Lewis 1960, 57).

It appears that the problem for Lewis was not manliness per se, but
rather the utility of the term *macho* and how it explained or detracted
from the overall points he was making.

Nor was Lewis in any manner responsible for first introducing the concept of Latin machos to the reading public in the United States. On the contrary, if anything, he was responding to the man whom Américo Paredes called "the most hallowed interpreter of the *macho*," Ernest Hemingway (1967, 226). Writing about Mexico, Cuba, and Spain, especially in the period between the world wars, Hemingway popularized many ideas in the United States about what he purported were uniquely Latino forms of bravado and stoicism. Through his descriptions and adoration of bullfighting and other "typical" Latin male activities, Hemingway propelled preexisting stereotypes to new heights. Death and virility, as concentrated in the bull's horns and testicles, became internationalized national icons for not only the Iberian peninsula but the entire Latin American continent as well. The quixotic or archetypal hero in Hemingway, writes one scholar, is no stranger to mortal peril: "Not afraid of dying, he will courageously defy death, but if he must die, it is always with great dignity and no remorse" (Capellán 1985, 75). An archetype is thus "discovered" by Gringos and used to categorize Spanish-speaking men generally and Mexican men more particularly. And as we have seen, others, including more than a few anthropologists, have been complicit in the creation of machismo.

The issue of who has a right to speak about Mexican cultural iconography, including with respect to *los machos mexicanos,* is of course a sensitive one. As a Gringo ethnographer living and studying in a *colonia popular* in the Mexican capital, I frequently faced another issue related to the Gringo Oscar Lewis: certain friends and neighbors assisted me in my research, in part because they harbored the fantasy that I might turn them into characters in my books and thus one day they might become as famous as the children of Jesús Sánchez.

To better understand the scheming of these friends and neighbors in Colonia Santo Domingo, I now turn to Américo Paredes, a most original thinker on Mexican male identities and machismo, as well as the ethnographic methods used to uncover them.

AMÉRICO PAREDES, GREATER MEXICO AND MACHISMO

Américo Paredes (1915–1999), the legendary folklorist of Greater Mexico, was deeply concerned with the persuasive power and the conjuring tricks of ethnography, especially with respect to issues as complex and politically volatile as machismo. Concentrating his work in the border zone of south Texas, Don Américo returned often to the image and historical significance of the cowboy and *vaquero*. In 1978, for example, and in contrast to other highly romanticized depictions of the American cowboy, he wrote of "the idea of the cowboy as the American *macho*." In his groundbreaking analysis, Paredes emphasized *inter*cultural issues grounding "Mexican" male identities and machismo:

> My own interest in the cowboy has been a bit more intercultural, I believe, and it has focused on the manner in which an ideal pattern of male behavior has been developed interculturally along the border, subsequently to influence the male self-image first in the United States and later in Mexico. (1978, 22)

Not only is machismo hardly original or essential to Mexico in any narrow sense, but in fact Paredes argues clearly that macho male metaphors in the United States predate such imagery in Mexico. Machismo, it seems, is far from a "national" character trait of Mexico alone. (And if machismo is not unique to Mexico, one may well ask what it even means to call it a national quality in the first place.) The problem for ethnographers is compounded, Don Américo reminds us in another essay (1977), when one works with people who like to joke and kid, since this type of behavior frequently provides an opportunity for what Paredes calls "the outrageous lie" that tenderfoot anthropologists too often swallow whole. Paredes illustrates the outrageous lie with an example reported by one of his students.

It seems that an attractive, thirty-nine-year-old housewife was describing "a grim but standard picture (standard by the Anglo ethnographer's experience) of her husband as a jealous and domineering *macho*. According to her statements, her husband was extremely jealous of her and did not let her go out alone because like all Chicano husbands he was scared she would 'find a better man'" (1977, 103–04). The woman told Paredes's student that she also wanted to attend college (she already had more formal education than her husband), but that he would not permit this lest she hurt his macho ego. Yet when the researcher met the husband, some contradictions were discovered: he appeared "anything but a domineering tyrant." He seemed at ease with all sorts of people and urged his wife to "emerge more into the world," whereas she seemed far more ill at ease in public places. Though the husband had less formal education, he was fluent in both Spanish and English, whereas she was comfortable speaking only in Spanish. The husband did not recall having suffered any overt discrimination in south Texas, whereas his wife had vivid memories of racism. Paredes concluded: "Obviously, the informant was presenting a special persona to the field-worker, dramatizing stereotyped aspects of Chicano male behavior that she felt would interest the fieldworker. The description of her husband in stereotyped terms gave her the attention and the control over the interview situation that are achieved in a successful performance" (1977, 104).

Here, and elsewhere, Don Américo chides those "who like to let their imaginations dwell on the rape of Indian women" (1967, 222), those who through their own narrow preconceptions about Mexico, Mexicans, and Mexican men invent racist characterizations. In their quest to discover allegedly primordial cultural traits like machismo, ethnographers and psychologists may naturally overlook what Paredes calls "a certain influence of the United States" (222). In the final analysis, Paredes asks, "how Mexican is *machismo* and to what degree is it a Hispanic, a New World, or a universal manifestation?" (222).

In his 1999 study of masculinity in Puerto Rico, Rafael Ramírez traced the influence of U.S. psychologists in the 1950s to the development of Gringo notions of machismo, and I have similarly tracked the role of U.S. anthropologists in this regard (Gutmann 1994; 1996). Still, in general, we are not dealing here with simple racist preconceptions passed off as sophisticated social science analysis, and it would be a mistake to minimize the epistemological difficulties inherent in accomplishing what Paredes calls the ethnographer's "attempt to interpret people's feelings and attitudes in actual speech situations" (1977, 76). Interpreting and explaining cultural and individual feelings, attitudes, and practices is a dicey business that takes more than mere linguistic fluency in a language. Rather, it requires cultural fluency to be able to contextualize the words, inflections, and nuances, to distinguish kidding from kvetching.

Américo Paredes, in this respect like Oscar Lewis, was committed to nuanced portrayals of actual people far more than to stick-figure ideal types cast from Weberian molds.[15] More than Lewis perhaps, Paredes was also acutely aware that who an investigator is may greatly influence what information is learned and indeed who will volunteer what information to the investigator in the first place. Implicit in the studies of both these anthropologists is a notion that is perhaps more important: as risky a proposition as it may be to attempt to represent the lives of others, to refuse to even try is not necessarily any more honorable a stand for ethnographers to take.

THE CULTURE OF THE CRITIQUE
OF THE "CULTURE OF POVERTY"

Oscar Lewis published one article that focused on the culture of poverty (1966) and briefly discussed the concept in a half-dozen other writings. Nonetheless, once the term became associated with U.S. federal programs ostensibly aimed at eliminating poverty, anthropologists like Eleanor Leacock (1971) and Charles Valentine (1968) responded with entire books dissecting and dismissing the concept.

"The major assumption made by many 'culture of poverty' theorists," wrote Leacock in the introduction to her edited volume, *The Culture of Poverty: A Critique,* "is that a virtually autonomous subculture exists among the poor, one which is self-perpetuating and self-defeating" (1971, 11). In her essay, which in many respects is a treatise critiquing the "silent majority" in the United States, Leacock allowed that although people from other social strata—teachers, for example—could be "both the victims and the villains" (28), both responsible and not for their lives, in the case of the poor this was not the case. "Poverty," Leacock wrote, "as a structural feature of our society, cannot be changed by a change of attitudes only" (34). This was a point with which, as we have seen, Lewis was in open agreement.[16]

The main way Oscar Lewis continues to be "cited" today, in the social sciences, in Latin American studies, and indeed more broadly in the United States, at least, is with respect to the idea of the culture of poverty. For better or for worse, beginning around 1959 Lewis attached the term to many of his writings. Indeed, the major exposition of the expression is to be found in the prefaces to many of his ethnographies from this period. Perhaps he intended no more than that his studies might have a bit more the cachet of theory, and thus that his work would carry a bit more intellectual weight. The subsequent critique of Lewis's theory of the culture of poverty is thus even more unfortunate because, ultimately, Lewis had no theory—at most, he had a catchphrase.

But what a catchphrase. Before long, Michael Harrington would publish his classic book, *The Other America: Poverty in the United States* (1962), which would popularize Lewis's term far beyond the borders of anthropology. Harrington's book, and Lewis's catchphrase, were mentioned often as Lyndon Johnson launched his War on Poverty, tapping Daniel Patrick Moynihan to head many of the social-welfare programs initiated and implemented through this period in the 1960s. Still, for our purposes, the history of how the expression *culture of poverty* was employed in U.S. government circles is not as pertinent as the closer examination of facile critiques leveled against the concepts of the culture of poverty and blaming the victim, in large part because men in the U.S. government adopted the formulation for their own purposes.[17]

Despite the fact that most of my students in the United States have not heard of Oscar Lewis, it is worth exploring why the expressions *culture of poverty* and *blaming the victim* are still employed and condemned with such regularity and ferocity. Their appeal to leftist intellectuals as the whipping boys of neoliberal (if no longer liberal) policies and programs is of particular interest, and what we might learn from a patient and careful reexamination of the notion of blaming the victim certainly is relevant to long-standing debates over the competing paradigms of political economy and psychology—and more recent manifestations of this argument, in cultural and postcolonial studies—and to Lewis's emphasis on culture. Lewis has much to teach us on how we might include "views from below" in our models of social strictures and individual responsibility, at the level of households and in terms of society as a whole. One related and especially infamous aspect of the culture of poverty thesis is that the culture of the poor is itself impoverished. Excoriated as Lewis was in his lifetime for this notion, I find this hardly more pejorative than what Frantz Fanon also wrote, for instance: "It is my belief that a true culture cannot come to life under present conditions" (1963, 187), or what E. P. Thompson once referred to as the "animalistic culture of the poor" (1993, 405).

At the heart of certain of these debates among Latin Americanists, especially those on the left, are perennial questions related to consciousness, false consciousness, class consciousness, and even that old favorite, brainwashing.[18] These questions are, in turn, directly implicated in the banal replacement of "democracy" for "socialism" as the goal of social struggles (see Fraser 1997). In the final analysis, then, to what extent may individuals (or groups, for that matter) be reasonably held responsible for their ideas, their actions, and their lot in life? Questions of complicity, culpability, accountability, and responsibility surface again and again, and make many of us squirm to this day. Wonderfully unsqueamish in this respect, Micaela di Leonardo provides insights into Oscar Lewis's studies of the poor: "He had fits of middle-class *pudeur* over the poor lying around in despair and wasting money on lottery tickets, but to his credit, he wanted them to quit these behaviors for purposes of their own human transcendence, not so that they would stop being an eyesore and a menace to the elites of their countries" (1998, 119).

Oddly, or not so oddly perhaps, my experiences in Colonia Santo Domingo are rife with discussions and arguments regarding accountability and responsibility, whether pertaining to housing conditions, alcohol consumption, machismo, or domestic violence. Individual psychologies are analyzed and dissected by family members and neighbors as casually as women and men seek a shady sidewalk to avoid the hot midday sun. These personality traits and quirks are compared with generalizations that women and men already have regarding culture, particularly what they understand as "Mexican culture," and "social progress." (It is still quite common in the *colonias populares* of Mexico City to hear talk of social progress, with rather less discussion of modernity and much less of postmodernity.)

Nonetheless, Oscar Lewis was writing for a different audience than my friends and neighbors in Colonia Santo Domingo. Many of his scholarly readers in the 1960s were undoubtedly familiar with a central tenet of modernization theory, which argues that cultural and psychological thought are among the greatest obstacles to be overcome if economic growth is to be achieved. Changing the cognitive orientations of peasants and the urban poor was the goal championed by some theorists, and, superficially, at least, Lewis may have appeared to be raising similar arguments. Yet there are at least two significant strands of Lewis's own cognitive framework that should lead us to conclude otherwise: (1) unlike others whose theories were developed so the poor could "catch up" with modernity, Lewis was explicitly critical of capitalism and what it had wrought in the world; and (2) Lewis took great pains to unwrap simplistic generalizations about social groups like "the poor."

Stereotypes are the lifeblood of many an anthropologist, and Oscar Lewis was no exception. He consistently showed himself unwilling to perpetuate notions of a homogeneous Mexican national culture, emphasizing instead intracultural diversity and questions of class, family, and sexuality. Nonetheless, despite these efforts, more than a few scholars have accused Lewis of creating and propagating national character types and stereotypes, including with respect to machismo.

Still, perhaps we should be more understanding of those who would generalize in this fashion, for, as social theorist Roger Bartra writes, "Mexico is a paradise for psychoanalytic expeditions that set out in search of the sources of the Oedipus complex. Is there anything more fascinating than that peculiar combination of exacerbated *machismo* and fanatical love for the mother in the figure of the Virgin of Guadalupe?" (1992, 147).

By way of example, men who have a history of beating their wives, and sometimes their children as well, often describe themselves as *atrapados* (trapped or caught). I heard one man who was tormented by his observation that "we are here [on earth] for a time, and we spend so much of this time in anguish, unable to solve even the smallest problems." No wonder some men with violent tendencies and histories have such a difficult time distinguishing in their minds and in their lives between the victims and the victimizers of domestic violence.

Rather than dismiss such confusion as the pathetic justifications of violent men, we might acknowledge that in studying these questions of agency we often exhibit a timid refusal to confront the questions Oscar Lewis was attempting to address with respect to what others have later glossed as blaming the victim (to the best of my knowledge, Lewis never employed this particular term himself). In other words, the point is not so much to rehabilitate Lewis's standing among left academics as it is to reexamine certain problems with which Lewis grappled. As to the motives and intentions of Lewis, I find such questions less interesting (and undoubtedly, less answerable) than those raised by his provocative pronouncements and oeuvre.

A crucial if less explicit issue raised by Lewis's work, as well as that of Américo Paredes, concerns a point that Jean Franco makes regarding the perils of "'popular agency,' that is, the potentiality of ordinary people . . . to act on their own behalf. Lurking under the surface is a certain utopian belief in popular power" (1992, 72). Within this romantic promotion of agency—for times when ordinary people take history into their own hands, right wrongs, and settle scores—often lies a solipsistic avoidance of the obvious limits of such actions. As Susan Rigdon writes, Oscar Lewis

> argued that poverty was *caused* by systemic conditions (murkily defined) that prevailed in capitalist systems (something for both the left and the center). On the other hand he said that poverty was *perpetuated* in *some* families not only by governments' refusals to eliminate its causes but also by the complicity of the poor themselves, as they passed on to their children the adaptations they had made to their poverty (something for the right). In saying this Lewis meant to dramatize the consequences of extreme poverty experienced in class-stratified societies and to demonstrate that it could damage people in permanent, irreversible ways. (1988, 88)

The contemporary implications of this contradictory analysis get far more unpredictable when it comes to determining (and sometimes un-determining) differences between men and women regarding questions like women's participation in work outside the home, or, still more, women's participation in social movements in the neighborhood and in the Mexican capital, more generally. These themes are, obviously, the stuff of daily confrontations and of submerged resentments and ill-will in households throughout the area. And, just as surely, a situation in which a woman wishes to work outside the home (or go to a political committee meeting) and is opposed by her *compañero* is far more common than one in which it is the husband insisting that the woman work and she does not want to do this. Nonetheless, how clear are we as to the manner in which gender inequalities and power differences are worked out within the cozy realm of home and family? To his lasting credit, Oscar Lewis was far ahead of his time in this and in other regards, as he sought to document and better understand not only the general economic constraints facing working-class families in Mexico City and Tepoztlán in Mexico, La Esmeralda in Puerto Rico, New York City, and in Cuba, not only the manifest domination of men in a variety of household decision-making situations—but also the collaboration, knowingly and not, of women in their own situation.

Questions of apathy, fatalism, and resignation—in the working class and apart—should more be the stuff of our scholarly contributions today. It is all well and good to learn from new social movements (the so-called Popular Urban Movements) and to think about changing gender relations, power, and autonomy. But such research must be coupled far more with work on immobility and political passivity so as to provide a more general understanding of political and social change. More specifically, it is important not to view apathy as necessarily the opposite of mobilization and participation. As we will see in chapter 8, non-participation in formal political activities like voting is not necessarily the same thing as political passivity. People are fatalistic about many different things in their lives for a variety of reasons.

As Lewis sometimes remarked, if your aim is to change the lives of poor people, it is not enough to talk about economics, economic opportunities, or even "a socialist revolution" (see, e.g., Lewis 1967, 499). Lewis defended himself against critics by repeating that he had always emphasized economic factors as those most responsible for poverty and misery, and not sex, as others had charged. "*La Vida* [1965]," he wrote, "is an indictment not of the poor but of the social system, the middle class, government officials" (1967, 497). Lewis stated explicitly that he believed capitalism itself was the main reason for poverty in modern societies. But he quickly and generally added, "However, this is not the only reason" (499). And it is to these other reasons that Lewis devoted most of his attention.

Lewis, after all, wrote ethnographies, with all their richness of detail, and like most ethnographers, he spent little time explaining the broad outlines of social relations, economics, and political institutions. As Marit Melhuus shows, "the thrust of [Lewis's] argument was nevertheless to emphasise the cultural aspects of poverty and their meanings, i.e. how people make sense of their world on their own terms" (1997, 41). Certainly many ideas that have been grouped together under the rubric of a theory of the culture of poverty coincided temporally with modernization theories of the 1960s, which aimed to change the outlook of the poor as the path that would lead to the elimination of poverty itself. Unfortunately, this fact alone led some intellectuals to counter Lewis with their own rather mechanical, structural models which, illogically, left little for the poor to do about redressing their own situation.

Today, in an age of scholarship still scrambling to appraise the recent history of agency and grassroots popular movements in Latin America and elsewhere, Lewis seems to have become smarter, as many of the questions posed by Lewis in the 1950s and 1960s, albeit it in a more psychologizing form, are once again under careful scrutiny, especially the meanings people attach to their world, and how people seek to change their world—or not.

CULTURAL VIOLENCE

Before I began my fieldwork on masculinity in Colonia Santo Domingo in 1992, I decided that examining domestic violence should be an important focus of my attention. Commentaries on manhood in Mexico have often made violence virtually synonymous with being a man, and to my continuing dismay, the writings of Oscar Lewis have often been summoned to illustrate this imaginary cultural trait (see, e.g., Gilmore 1990, 16; Prieur 1998, 78). Furthermore, my previous experiences in the working-class neighborhoods of Mexico City showed me that this relationship between men and violence continued to capture the attention of many of the people who live there. It was not simply a topic of concern to academics and activists.

Early in my research, however, I received some disturbing advice

from a woman who worked in a center for battered women. "Do not expect women to open up to you about these matters," she warned, "because they are quite reluctant to talk about such things, even with close
women friends." As a man, and especially as a man from the United
States, women would not be forthcoming with me about domestic
violence.

Despite these words of warning, I nonetheless found that women
were far more eager to reveal their histories of being abused than might
have been expected. Even women I hardly knew discussed their experience of domestic violence more readily than all but a few of the men who
became my best friends in the *colonia*. Due to the reticence of most men
to discuss what they personally knew about wife beating and other
forms of domestic violence, I early on resigned myself to the conclusion
that access to information on this subject from men would probably be
severely limited. It is perhaps not so surprising that men might have
something to hide, and that men might lie about domestic violence, and
that women would respond far more often to my expressed interest in
learning about physical and psychological abuse with angry tales of husbands, fathers, and other male relatives who had beaten them or their
mothers. And it is worth noting that the point is not simply to add
women's experiences to those of men, especially when men remain mute
about wife beating, but rather that women play active roles in the construction of gendered practices, including those surrounding domestic
violence. For both these reasons, frequently it took little more than my
evident desire to discuss these questions with them for the women in
Santo Domingo to decide to make their stories public through me.

Perhaps due to the particularities of Colonia Santo Domingo, where
women have long been political and community leaders and activists,
and perhaps due to grassroots feminist efforts more broadly in Mexico
City to expose and challenge domestic violence in the *colonias populares,* many women voiced their hope that I would write and teach about
the experiences they related to me, and that our joint effort might then
be part of a process to help men confront domestic violence more than
they had. Interestingly enough, in my interviews with certain neighbors
in Santo Domingo, I have been asked if my purpose is similar to that of
Oscar Lewis many years ago. "Are you going to do what Oscar Lewis
did, Mateo? Do you want to tell the stories of the common people?" one
grandfather asked me early in my research on families and gender relations. Talking one afternoon with a young woman in the outdoor
kitchen of a neighbor's house, I mentioned that my wife and I had re-

cently received a letter from a friend in Berkeley who explained that she
had been beaten by her husband, and for that reason was seeking a di-
vorce. The young Mexican woman nodded knowingly. Then she told me
that her own father had beaten her mother, and that the beatings had
persisted for many years:

"When he's drunk he fights with half the world and when he's sober,
he wonders why so-and-so won't talk to him. He doesn't remember.
That's the problem. He's very aggressive. He fights a lot, with whomever
he runs into, even with children. I don't know what his problem is. In
the house, on the street, everywhere."

I asked if her father had had problems with the police.

"No, not with them, but with neighbors. It's just that we don't trust
the police around here, so no one calls them when there is trouble. My
mother and I try to calm him down, but often it's counterproductive."

The importance of understanding the relationship between domestic
violence and women is not primarily in order to portray women as the
victims of such abuse. Instead, these female voices better allow us to see
women as instigators of change in gender relationships based on unequal control and power.

Angela once recounted to me the time when the husband of her friend
Susana had come home drunk early one afternoon and beat her badly.
Susana had arrived at Angela's house with a very bloody towel covering
her face. Susana's husband had broken her nose at the arch, and there
were large bruises around her eyes. (I had seen the scars on Susana's face
and now understood how she got them.) They had talked and cried together, Angela told me solemnly. Angela had asked Susana what she
wanted to do, and Susana had replied that she wanted to go back home
to clean up the house before her children got home from school and saw
blood all over the floor and furniture.

I interrupted Angela's story and told her that this seemed crazy to me,
as surely Susana needed immediate medical attention and her children
were going to see her badly bruised face in any case. Angela told me that,
on the contrary, what Susana had proposed made perfect sense. They
had proceeded to clean Susana's house together, and only then had they
gone to a medical clinic. Later that night, Susana had gone to the police
to file charges against her husband. He was hauled off to jail but later
released, Angela told me, after he paid a hefty bribe to the officials.

Certainly women are a constant point of reference in men's discussions and actions regarding domestic violence, as was evident when
those rare men who would talk about their violent histories spoke of

their jealous rages as a particular spark to subsequent violent outbursts against their wives and children. In this respect, discussions by men in Mexico City with anthropologists about domestic violence have changed from the 1950s, when Oscar Lewis conducted his fieldwork in the neighborhood of Tepito. In the 1990s, when I began living and working in Santo Domingo, the men were generally far more reluctant to admit to wife beating, much less brag about it.

In meetings I was allowed to attend that were sponsored by the Mexico City municipal government for men who have battered their wives and children, participants frequently described themselves as incapable of the injustices that they had been accused of inflicting on others. Some of these men articulated a sentiment that they felt like "*instrumentos*" (tools) whose sole purpose was to provide their families with a steady source of income. These men complained that they were "slighted" and "humiliated" by their wives and mothers, and, as one put it, "When I'm angry, I feel especially *vulnerable,* almost naked."

Another prevalent theme among the men was that the "macho culture" into which they had been born was the primary reason they were violent. "*Ideas y valores machistas*" (macho ideas and values) and "*condicionamiento machista*" (macho conditioning) were to blame, they declared. One middle-aged man, however, admitted, "*El hombre llega hasta donde la mujer lo diga*" (Men get away with as much as women let them). Precisely because so many men complain that "women want "*más libertad* (more freedom)," and because such demands for greater independence by women may correlate to increased numbers of assaults on women, women's involvement in everything from social movements to paid work has a great deal to do with changing male identities and behavior in Mexico.

For what I trust are obvious reasons, my work on *ser hombre* (being a man) would have been quite deficient had my encounters been limited to only what men said about domestic violence and about their own agency, as exemplified in matters of wife beating.

My friend Bernardino, who has been a community organizer in the area around Santo Domingo since the early 1980s, talked about his battered aunt and tried to put her suffering in some historical perspective for me:

"There are experiences that make you think there might be cracks. I have an aunt who just got divorced four months ago. But she suffered a martyrdom for sixteen or twenty years. He hit her, he kept her confined, it was terrible. Years and years, maybe more than twenty, since she has children who are older than I am. She suffered a lot. It's a contradictory case, because the children were the ones who told their mama, 'Hey, how long are you going to wait till you get away from him? Do it now! What's the point of staying with him any longer? We're grown now!' They didn't think that the situation had suddenly become unbearable. It had always been unbearable."

Another woman, Dolores, told me that even after more than fifteen years of having endured beatings at the hands of her husband she had never been able to leave him. "Now," she said, "he doesn't dare beat me because my children will stop him if he tries." Dolores was proud of the fact that "my married son is not like his father, and neither is the single one."

With his deep-seated realism, Bernardino has often expressed to me his belief that change between women and men will take a long time in coming. But he is not a cynic. "In the popular groups, in the organized groups, and as part of society, there is a change," he explained in the same conversation. Women today are on a different level than they were twenty years ago, he said. "People no longer look down on the woman who works [outside the home], who takes positions of leadership. To call a woman 'Boss' [jefa] is a more everyday thing; it's more common. And this isn't just because of popular organizations, but it is a change, a transformation that is taking place in Mexican society."

So it was that I came to understand discrepancies in two conversations I had with another friend, César, about domestic violence in his family (see Gutmann 1996, 206). The first time we talked, we barely knew each other. In response to a general query about whether he knew any husbands who beat their wives, César told me that frankly he did not. He added that in his personal case his wife might have hit the girls a little when they were young, but that he himself was a "pacifista." Silences on topics like domestic violence can be just as revealing as commentary. Luz María, César's wife, was not silent on the question of violence in their home. She talked of repeated physical confrontations between them throughout their marriage, until, six years before I met her, she had finally said to her husband, "Hit me, and I'll hit you." Why did she finally reach her breaking point? I asked her. She just did, she told me, even though her mother—who had a remarkably similar "combustible character"—had never been able to bring herself to give her husband, Luz María's father, the same kind of ultimatum.

Several months after I first talked to César about domestic violence, he and I had another informal conversation that started out about gang fights and eventually led to other forms of violence. In that conversation, César revealed that he had indeed beaten his wife on numerous occasions in the past, and that only when his wife had issued an ultimatum to him—to stop or she would leave him with their girls—did César cease his furious eruptions.

"What has been hardest for me is to accept that the person who has to change is me," César finally concluded. He continued, "The time came when my wife got tired of it all. 'Either you stop, or we're leaving the house,' she told me. It was a big blow for me. It made me understand. After this, I began to look after my family better." Oscar Lewis documented the impact on Pedro Martínez's family of his religious conversions in the 1950s. My purpose here is similar: to detail the impact on families like César's of what might be termed a political conversion that is similarly a piece and not simply a product of larger social transformations under way in contemporary Mexico.

THE CULTURE OF AGENCY

The notion of "agency" emphasizes the ability that dispossessed people have—at least some people, some of the time, in some places—to control important parts of their lives. For example, agency may describe the efforts of poor women to organize themselves to demand and receive better working conditions, fairer distribution of goods, and more reasonable living conditions. *Agency* is thus a term invoked to describe underdogs when they take political matters into their own hands and do not succumb to the notion that as poor people they are inherently powerless as a group to improve their lives. In this way agency is often contrasted, explicitly or casually, with opposite concepts like "structure" and "society" and "the system" that limit the ability of the oppressed to rectify their lot in life. The notion of agency is in a real sense a theoretical retort to mechanical understandings, both modernist and Marxist, regarding how societies change, the role of great leaders and great ideas, changing productive relations, and class struggles. Theories of agency represent, in part, attempts to explain what poverty is worth.

Romanticism about people being and becoming agents of change is often couched in the language of people as individual subjects in contrast to collectivities. And there is something to be said for analysis of people as subjects—as willful, contradictory, volatile agents of change. But when agency is used as an analysis of collections of individuals controlling individual destinies, albeit constrained by larger economic and political forces, something quite atomistic can develop in place of a theory of change grounded in analysis of social forces.

We are treading on perilous ground. All the same, it seems to me that if renewed attention to the positive changes that can be brought about by the dispossessed, despite the structural barriers to their efforts, has been justified in recent years, and if we want to label these initiatives agency, then we must also be willing to examine the entire picture more closely. Simply put, to the extent that the poor, subaltern, oppressed, and powerless take history into their own hands and achieve successes, no matter how small, and to the extent that we truly argue that these dispossessed women and men are in some sense in control of their destinies in no matter how limited and brief a manner, then how can we not hold these same people responsible in some fashion for their own failures and defeats? Writing in a different context, Micaela di Leonardo puts the matter cogently: "Protest and victory are not isomorphic" (1998, 21).

Again, this is treacherous territory, especially in the context of neoliberalism in Mexico, Latin America, and the United States, which takes the form of explicit blaming of the poor for their poverty and severely reducing safety nets and diverse forms of government assistance for the most marginalized and powerless people in these societies. Given the currency of neoliberalism today, it may seem folly or simply callous to raise the question of blame and responsibility in this context. The connection between people's beliefs and their actions exists in relation to both larger social forces and to the experiences and understanding of others with whom they share their immediate lives. We can see this in Colonia Santo Domingo in discussions and debates that unfold daily in domestic settings and among friends in the streets.

In part, this is what Oscar Lewis was doing and what got him into so much trouble with other intellectuals in the 1960s in the United States. Lewis was generally regarded more sympathetically by intellectuals in Mexico than in the United States. Intentionally or not, he revealed the existence of extreme poverty in Mexico as few before him had done, and there was never such a big brouhaha over particular concepts like the culture of poverty there.

This is one reason why we need to examine more closely what it means to participate in a democracy. To what extent is it realistic for my friends and neighbors in Colonia Santo Domingo to dream—albeit intermittently—that they might be able to change for the better the world into which they were born and in which they find themselves ever after?

Maybe they are just fooling themselves. Those of us who write books and articles for a living often champion the poor when they stand up to unfair government authorities and win. We are often at a loss when they stand up and lose. Or when they do not even stand up. We are more comfortable blaming the upper classes for social ills—they often seem more in control. And we are understandably wary about finding fault with those who seem to have so little control over their economic and political situation; thus, we prefer to use sociocultural contexts to explain (away?) beliefs and actions on the part of the poor.

Only when I was dragged into the debate in Santo Domingo regarding "Who's to blame for the way men are?"—that is, only when I began to take seriously such questions as they are clearly posed by my friends and neighbors there—did I begin to look more carefully at questions of agency and culpability. The classic case of implicating victims in their own misery that has emerged time and again in research on Mexican male identities and practices has to do with women's role as mothers in rearing little Mexican machos. For biogenetic reasons, blame is constantly assigned to women-as-mothers, less often to men-as-fathers (see Gutmann 1998). Some of the mothers who talk of the "natural" proclivities of their children, along the lines of boys-will-be-boys, also declare with equal certainty that if a boy turns out macho, it must be the mother's fault for raising him that way. More than a few mothers in Santo Domingo have assured me, "I haven't brought up my boy to be a Mexican macho!" Sometimes it is said partially in jest, sometimes not. Still, tracing the origins of Mexican machismo is a regular pastime of more than a few women in the *colonia*.

In recent decades, prompted in part by feminist conceptualizations of family,[19] social scientists in Mexico and the United States have increasingly emphasized that households are important spaces in which gender identities and relations of inequality are confronted, challenged, and, occasionally, transformed in the day-to-day lives of women and men. Issues of accountability lie at the very core of such conflicts. In Mexico, several recent studies have shed light on just such dissonant processes, particularly from the perspective of women in these situations.[20] Yet we have only begun to understand the implications of these investigations for men and fathers. Despite excellent recent work in which men and fatherhood in Mexico are central issues (see Figueroa 1998; Lerner 1998; and Taggart 1992), as well as rich material to be mined in several classic studies of Mexico, including those by Oscar Lewis (e.g., Arizpe 1973,

1989; and Lewis 1961, 1964a), there is work to be done on how men become the kinds of men they are in Mexico.

This new research still grapples with the same questions addressed by Lewis in a variety of cultural settings in rural and urban Mexico of the 1940s and 1950s. Of particular significance, and very much a product of the culture and personality school of anthropology that was so influential in the United States at the time, Lewis approached families as embodied sites of disagreement and adjustment. One contribution of recent feminist scholarship that Lewis would undoubtedly strongly defend is the critique of the stale vision of families and households as simply representing the last bastion of patriarchy, the ne plus ultra of institutionalized fatherhood. Theoretical work by Teresita de Barbieri (1992) and Steve Stern (1995, 1998b), for instance, has questioned the utility of locating causal factors and assigning blame based on cultural models of patriarchy, which both Barbieri and Stern find overgeneralized and unconditionally in need of historical contextualization.

At the same time, although new research has documented what Stern terms a "transition from a patriarchal regime of hierarchical complementarity, to a regime of discriminatory and stigmatized competition among genders" in Mexico (1998b, 61), there is no need to rush to the other extreme and overestimate the "feminine" qualities of family and household. Certainly domestic matters should no longer be neatly relegated to the "private" world of women, any more than should "public" matters of politics and street life be tidily understood as exclusively male realms (see Alatorre and Luna 2000).

As Oscar Lewis implied, fatherhood is continually in need of redefinition and restudy, in Mexico as elsewhere. In the latter years of the twentieth century, as a result of socioeconomic and demographic transformations, of the impact of popular social movements in which women have been active, and of the general influence of feminist ideas during this period, the meanings and practices associated with fathers and fatherhood have undergone rapid modifications as well. In particular, in the context of women working outside the home for money in greater numbers than ever before, of birth rates having fallen by half in the last two or three decades, and of levels of education for girls now roughly being equal to that of boys, men have been challenged in direct and indirect ways to assume more responsibilities associated with children and housework.

Nonetheless, as in the period studied by Oscar Lewis, notable differences persist between classes, so that, in the 1990s, in the wealthier strata of society, parenting for both men and women is less a practical activity than one of managing servants, who continue to carry out these tasks. In the poorer, working-class communities like Santo Domingo there is far less homogeneity in fathering, so that some men have relatively little to do with their offspring, especially small children, whereas for many other men (and women) in the *colonia,* active fathering is a central part of what it means to be a man and of the things men do.[21]

Father-absence may seem a strange way to discuss fatherhood, yet in an eminently anthropological manner, we may find at the margins of this subject clues regarding the phenomenon of households as concentrated sites of changing gender relations as a whole. Are not some of the infamous fathers in Mexico today known as *padres de cheque* (check fathers), men whose paternity is established and maintained primarily through their periodic remittances to households in which they have long since ceased to reside, at least for most of the year? Indeed, often in Mexico fatherhood is defined either by the man's role in the moment of procreation (a fleeting act establishing paternity) or by the man's later absence from the domestic scene. One of the purposes of studying the practices of fathering in Mexico today is to further distinguish between cultural stereotypes about fatherhood—such as those concerning patriarchy or those defining families as eminently private and female—and the lived realities of fathering. With respect to fatherhood in Mexico, the oft-repeated cliché still seems to have the upper hand over the grounded study of the realities of what men do with their children.

THE CULTURAL CONSTRAINTS OF ABANDONMENT

Agency is frequently, if tacitly, given a gendered character in discussions of women who seek to gain more control over decision making, for instance, with respect to the actions of their husbands, including husbands who desert their immediate families. If tying husbands to their nuclear families at all costs is necessary to a household's survival, how can women do anything but scramble just to get by? Certainly, under such conditions, it may appear that women do not have much opportunity to change many aspects of gender relations in their immediate lives, and much less, in society. Yet, in Santo Domingo in the mid-1990s, men of all ages were clearly affected by women's widespread participation in the community's political affairs. Some of the subtle ways by which men and women reveal feelings about such issues may be seen in the stories they tell about childhood abandonment. In a discussion of abandonment, the memories of the now-grown children many decades later of their fathers' actions illustrate well the relationship between blame and agency that Oscar Lewis pioneered: that the fathers are blamed goes without saying; the challenge for many lies more in interpreting the extent to which things could have turned out differently.

After he gets to know you, Alfredo Pérez might tell you about his painful childhood with a wandering father. But he will get angry if someone else—especially his wife—ridicules his father. In Alfredo's opinion, his wife's father was no more accountable to his children, nor were many poor men of that generation. So no one has the right to speak ill of Alfredo's father except Alfredo himself, and Alfredo's bitterness as he approaches his sixtieth year in the spring of 1993 is still palpable.

"My mother was from a village in the state of Mexico. She came to Mexico City because they were mistreating her and because she had a child and they wanted to take him away from her. She had a stand outside some public baths, where she sold stockings, socks, diapers, and so on. That's where she met my father. They spent six years living in *unión libre* [common-law marriage]. I was born, then my brother. But my father was sort of a *mujeriego* [womanizer] . . . and he began going around with another woman. One day, this other woman went to see my mother, and my mother told the woman that if she wanted to take my father, 'Well then, take him away,' so my mother could get on with her life.

"It was during the war, in 1942, and my father was working on the tram lines. That's why he had stored gasoline in the *jacalón* [shed] where we lived—it wasn't a house like this one; it was a shed with a corrugated cardboard roof.

"Well, my little brother was playing with my mother's comb, the plastic caught fire [from the flame of a lamp], and everything burned down. My mother managed to save my brother and a suitcase, but she burned her legs. I was burned, too. I cried a lot, because of the burn and because I was so alone. There were just a few of us in the family, my mother, my brothers, and me."

Alfredo's father was willing to accept some financial responsibility toward the members of his former family, but only to a point. He paid a doctor to operate on his son and former wife so they would not have to cut off their legs, as originally planned—Alfredo showed me the scar on his calf fifty years later. And Alfredo still remembers dragging himself along the ground until his leg more fully healed, because his father would not pay for crutches.

After the fire and until shortly before he died many years later, Alfredo's father had largely dropped out of the boy's life. Though his mother eventually remarried, by then Alfredo had already moved out. There were no other adult men who played a significant role in raising Alfredo. When he became a father, Alfredo tried to not repeat the mistakes his father had made with him, and on the whole, he told me, he thought he had been pretty successful. He saw similarities in the actions of his father and those of other men of that generation, yet his anger was against his father and not his father's contemporaries. If Alfredo acted differently with his wife and children than his father had, however, this was not simply a result of the lessons learned from his own experience and from what his mother taught him. For Alfredo also believed it was generally better for men not to desert their families, and he had reached this conclusion, in part, because he had lived through a period in which the issue of women and children being abandoned by men was widely discussed and debated in the *colonias populares* of Mexico City.

According to many people I know in Colonia Santo Domingo, although men like Alfredo Pérez have changed in comparison to their fathers (who would have been young fathers at the time Oscar Lewis was conducting his fieldwork in Mexico City), the women married to the men of Alfredo's generation have on the whole changed more. Even if being a mother is still the most important part of life for a woman, what "being a mother" means is not necessarily the same today as it was twenty or thirty years ago.

None of these concerns can be addressed, of course, without taking into account a host of historical and economic factors that every day impinge upon the consciousness and actions of women and men in Santo Domingo. To resolve their own bitter memories from the past, for example, many women have simply concluded that everything was a matter of economic necessity, as if little else need to be said. Poverty, they say, keeps some wives obliged to their husbands for far longer than the women might otherwise choose. So, too, a separation between husband and wife often requires children, girls as well as boys, to begin working and earning money for the family at a young age. Nonetheless, in the same way that Oscar Lewis revealed for the children of Jesús Sánchez living in the 1950s, economic compulsion alone does not explain the actions of fathers with their children.

In a 1999 paper on the history of paternity in Mexico City, Katherine Bliss has documented how fatherhood was politicized in the period from 1910 to 1940 by virtue of complaints by social workers, legislators, and legal reformers during this period that through abandonment, physical abuse, and the corruption of morals, fathers in Mexican society were destroying their families, civil society, and the country as a whole. In addition to providing vivid depictions of the official vilification of working-class men in the capital in the early part of the twentieth century, Bliss carefully links these portrayals to particular historical events of the period, especially the Mexican Revolution. Following the tumultuous and revolutionary second decade of the twentieth century, and in the ensuing national deliberations over general social questions pertaining to progress and social reform, Mexican fathers were increasingly challenged in legal proceedings and other public venues when they failed as providers, partners, and protectors.

As has become clear to me after having known fathers in Mexico City like Alfredo Pérez for many years, official, popular, and scholarly notions about men and paternity are always intimately, albeit often imperceptibly, shaded with overarching contemporary mores and social relations relating more generally to gender relations and other forms of difference and inequality. Digging beneath the surface truisms and assumptions about what fathers (or mothers, for that matter) in Mexico do, and not just what men and women might claim that men do, is an ever-present task made all the more difficult by the complexities of teasing out commonplaces that are as prevalent in scholarly tomes as they are in casual conversations in homes and sidewalks about the particular features of paternity, fatherhood, and fathering.

Households are not only the sites of gender conflict. Through these disputes, quarrels, and confrontations, households can also supply the proving ground for challenges to preexisting identities and patterns of fatherhood and motherhood. To be more specific, in the lives of many neighbors and acquaintances in Colonia Santo Domingo, when transformations have occurred in the activities associated with "being a father" (from feeding the children, to providing them with moral instruction, to helping them with their homework), both men and women have attributed these changes to two factors, especially. First is *necesidad*— when, for example, mothers begin to work outside the home for money and men begin to "help" more in the domestic chores, including child care. The second factor is that women have become more directly implicated in these changes, as they wheedle, coax, and threaten men to participate in one or another activity for which they are ill-prepared and initially often less than favorably inclined.

That is, women in households have had a major hand—they have had agency, in the current idiom—in redefining and redirecting the meanings of fatherhood for many men in recent decades in Mexico's capital city. The abandonment of children by fathers and of wives by husbands was ably retold in numerous ethnographies of Oscar Lewis as well. In his accounts, the results of such abandonment for those left behind as often as not were tragic. As was the case for the Mexican Geographical and Statistical Society, some anthropologists in Lewis's time would have preferred not to see such tragedy emphasized in his portraits of the poor. Because he held these poor Mexican men and women partially accountable for their lives, Lewis was accused of blaming them for their own misery. Yet, I do not find that Lewis's fundamental precepts are so different from more recent discussions of agency: in both cases, scholars allow that the dispossessed have some command—dare we say, some possession?—over their fate. With Lewis, as with promoters of theories of agency, accountability counts for something, although it must be seen within a larger context of economic and political forces that are truly beyond the reach of the children of Jesús Sánchez and his metaphorical descendents.

THE POLITICAL PSYCHOLOGY OF CHANGE

Thus, on the one hand, we have the psychologizing of Lewis with respect to individual motivations and frustrations. Some might even concede that there is merit in such ongoing discussions about individual and group (or "subgroup") volition and personal activities that distinguish one individual from another in working-class settings. I have in mind concepts like the mélange of theories concerning everyday forms of resistance. Such theories habitually display a romantic veneration for the poor, their consciousness, and their resolve. They also prove unable to grasp why women and men might dedicate themselves and their lives to the pursuit of "unrealistic" social change. Contrary to currently orthodox resistance theory, popular political cultures exhibit *both* spontaneous and organized resistance and rebellion, and manifest a living refutation of rational choice notions whereby the already-conscious-because-they-are-poor only engage in politics when and as they are sure they will not be sticking their necks out too far.

On the other hand, beyond the controversy Lewis provoked with regard to questions of psychology and consciousness, in the 1960s there was another serious indictment against his work handed down from leftist intellectuals in the United States. The charges revolved around his alleged denigration of one sector of the working class in particular, the so-called lumpen proletariat, and what in the 1960s was called in certain leftist circles "the revolutionary potential" of the lumpen, the most broken and criminal sector of the working class.

Whereas Frantz Fanon championed the Algerian lumpen proletariat as containing the latent leadership for the struggle against the French colonialists (1963; 1967), Oscar Lewis, on the contrary, focused on what he saw as the crippling weakness in outlook and behavior of the Mexican and Puerto Rican lumpen. Lewis found nothing remotely revolutionary about what he called "the culture of poverty," which Gonzalo Aguirre Beltrán notes was really what Lewis termed a "subculture" rather than the working class, much less the poor (urban and rural) in general (1986, 123; see also Higgins 1974). Lewis certainly did not help his theory of the culture of poverty when he sometimes declared that Jesús Sánchez was *not* representative of the culture of poverty, or when he at other times used the term to refer to the Sánchez family. At most, only two of the four children of Jesús Sánchez were so marginalized socially that they could have qualified as members of Lewis's "subculture of poverty." Jesús Sánchez, the father, always held a regular job and enjoyed a relatively stable, if poor, lifestyle.

For Lewis, naively or not, at least at points in his life, a central premise of his political views seems to have been that the poor could not rely on the government to solve structural problems. At best, the government was unreliable. For this reason, as Rigdon concluded, "Consciousness-raising among the poor was, according to Lewis, the first task for anyone who wanted to foment change" (1988, 157). Because of his intuitive and contradictory distrust of the governments of Mexico, the United States, Puerto Rico, and Cuba, Lewis's scholarship remains appealing and useful, if always ambiguously and confusingly so. Lewis's disdain for those who would expect too much from governments is quite different from current notions of "empowerment" and self-help neoliberalism. Thorstein Veblen's formulation regarding the "trained incapacity" of the poor (see Hannerz 1969, 193) is surely relevant to contemporary discussions on how the poor may internalize the "lessons" of their lives quite well. Relationships between elites and the poor, and between governments and the poor, are anything but static.

In his review of liberal political theory and contemporary campaigns for human rights, John Gledhill reminds us that supranational forms of organizations pose fundamentally "the same questions of how 'power inhabits meaning'" as do national states (1997, 71). Gledhill writes, "Individualism and individuation are inscribed in existing structures of domination and those structures shape the kinds of rights movements which appear to be most challenging of their individualistic premises, notably struggles for recognition of the collective legal personalities of indigenous peoples" (71–72).

What often gets lost in the superficial and potshot "critiques" of Lewis, and especially of "Oscar Lewis's so-called 'culture of poverty' thesis," is a question that at one time was more important to leftists and liberals alike, regarding what if any the parallels might be between being poor in different societies and whether cross-cultural comparisons that lead to comparative generalizations based on class are too easily shunned by analysts of change today. Not that we should seek analysis based on class exclusively; rather, we should include commonalities of class as a critical element along with other social divisions of generation, gender, and ethnicity that can cross international geopolitical boundaries.

Throughout his anthropological endeavors, Lewis tried to paint a markedly *un*-uniform picture of the poor in rural and urban Mexico, while at the same time seeking parallels between the experience of poverty in vastly different societies around the globe. He refused to pigeonhole real people into inert classifications: "We have become prisoners of our own categories. In our desire to reduce our materials to their lowest common denominator we have left out some of our most vivid and dynamic material" (cited in Rigdon 1988:vi). At the same time, he sought representative characteristics that would allow generalizations based in significant measure on class across cultures.

The ethnographies of Oscar Lewis have undoubtedly become an important part of this process of cultural identification and definition, from within and without Mexico, yet what Lewis wrote should not be confused with how others since have used Lewis to promote their own agendas and preconceptions. As is the case with citations to Octavio Paz's 1961 well-known essay, *The Labyrinth of Solitude,* the real revisionist effort required has perhaps more to do with the secondary literature that has grown up around Oscar Lewis's work than with the primary texts themselves. That is, both Lewis and Paz wrote texts that have taken on new lives, lives that are sometimes alien to their authors' original intent. Not all interpretations and uses of Lewis's work, any more than that of Paz, are justified, and there has been widespread misuse and misappropriation of Lewis by some scholars who are less concerned with exploring the confounding issues of blame, responsibility, and social change that is required when studying real people and their real lives in Mexico.

CHAPTER 3

1968 — The Massacre at Tlatelolco

What do Díaz Ordaz and Clinton have in common?
Diáz Ordaz doesn't want to hear about '68 or Clinton
about '69.

> Joke told in Colonia Santo Domingo, summer 1999[1]

Gustavo Díaz Ordaz was president of Mexico from 1964 to 1970. On October 2, 1968, he presided over, and many feel ordered, the massacre of hundreds of students and protesters in the Tlatelolco housing complex just north of downtown Mexico City.[2] The reference in the chapter's epigraph to Bill Clinton, of course, recalls the Monica Lewinsky affair that provided front-page titillation to so many people around the world in 1999. Indeed, as I was gathering material for this book, I often asked friends in Santo Domingo about one or another aspect of political life in Mexico City, and they often responded, "Who cares about politics in Mexico, Mateo? You got anything new about *Mónica?*"

If one were to trace similar expressions of indifference in contemporary Mexican politics, the route would inevitably lead back to the events of October 1968, when a large number of people in Mexico lost their political innocence. After 1968, official politics in Mexico were never again given the benefit of a doubt to such an extent by as many of its citizens. The repercussions of 1968 were felt for the next several decades, never more so than in 1999, when students again challenged political authorities in a strike at the Universidad Nacional Autónoma de México.

What began as chaotic skirmishes between students and police in late July 1968, quickly escalated into an epic student movement in the capital city under the leadership of the Comité Nacional de Huelga (the National Strike Committee). As in other student movements at the time in countries like France, Germany, Thailand, Brazil, Japan, Senegal, India, and the United States, the students at elite Mexican universities like the Instituto Politécnico and UNAM protested in the streets to save the world from its leaders. By July of that year, the term "1968" had become linked by youth across the globe with the May Revolution in Paris and the Prague Spring. By early October, it would also become associated around the world as the year of the Massacre at Tlatelolco.

In Mexico, the 1968 student movement was marked by support among broad sectors of the populace. The students considered themselves representatives of "*el pueblo*" and advocates for the democratization of society and government generally in their country. Not since the legendary railway workers' strike of 1958–59 had any social movement challenged the political order in such fundamental ways in Mexico (see Stevens 1974). Nonetheless, although the 1968 student protesters carried banners with portraits of the international icons of revolutionary change of the time, like Che Guevara and Mao Zedong, their aspirations were far more limited, national, and nationalist in scope: rather than global revolt, they sought liberal reform of the political system in Mexico.

That the aims of the students were restricted to Mexico was a reflection both of the nationalist goals of the student movement in Mexico and the fact that before October 1968 political events in Mexico were of little interest to the rest of the world. Thus, despite the self-identification of many Mexican youth with Che and Mao, despite widespread grassroots sympathy for the student protesters within Mexico, and notwithstanding the common cause of students around the globe in 1968, Mexico was in fact surprisingly isolated internationally. Were this not the case, the political price paid by Mexico's leaders for the murder of hundreds of their students would have been far higher. As it was, the isolation made it possible for the government to militarily crush the student movement with relative impunity; the strongest censure from abroad that they received for the massacre was a mild finger-wagging from the representatives of a few foreign governments.

OCTOBER 2, 1968

After that day, Mexico was another country.
    Julio Scherer García and Carlos Monsiváis

Many years after the events of 1968, I was sitting around the table of friends after lunch one day in Santo Domingo. Our discussion about police corruption and the infamous case of Arturo "Negro" Durazo, who had been police chief of Mexico City in the 1970s, eventually developed into a reminiscence about October 2, 1968. At one point in our chat about Tlatelolco, Angela asked Alejandro what he remembered about 1968. Alejandro, who with his wife was renting a room from Angela while he took classes at UNAM nearby, said he had not even been born in 1968, and thus he personally had no memory of the event. He did mention, however, that he had read about what had happened in Elena Poniatowska's book, *La noche de Tlatelolco* (1971), and of course he had grown up hearing his family and others talking about the massacre. Angela nodded and said that she, too, had read the Poniatowska book many years before. And unlike Alejandro, Angela told us, she was old enough to have vivid memories of that horrible day.

In the late 1960s, before she moved to Colonia Santo Domingo as part of the land invasion of the early 1970s, Angela and her husband Juan had lived on the near north side of Mexico City, not too far from the Tlatelolco housing complex. Angela recalled that on October 2, 1968, Juan had gone out to buy a birthday cake for their son Noé. Juan took so long to return that Angela became worried and went looking for him outside the apartment where they lived. There were people running down the street, coming from the direction of Tlatelolco, and Angela stopped a young woman, who turned out to be a schoolteacher, and asked her what was going on. Catching her breath, the young woman told Angela, "If you are expecting anyone, you should prepare for the worst." The teacher said she was not sure how she herself had managed to escape, but by some miracle the troops had not caught her. The woman had no time to talk more; she was scared that if she were caught and identified as having been at Tlatelolco the troops might still kill her. Fortunately for Angela, despite the teacher's dire predictions, Juan did arrive home shortly thereafter.

Late on the afternoon of October 2, 1968, between 5,000 and 15,000 demonstrators (estimates still vary wildly) had gathered at the Tlatelolco housing complex to protest recent government repression against the student movement in Mexico City. There, they were met by between 5,000 and 10,000 soldiers (there is still no consensus on this figure, either), or roughly one soldier for each protester.[3] In his book, which is based on extensive research in the "archives of violence," including crucial Mexican police files and CIA records, Sergio Aguayo Quezada has proved what many have all along held to be beyond dispute: the massacre was orchestrated by the top echelons of the Mexican government

and executed through special elite troops and numerous infiltrators operating from within the ranks of the student activists (see Aguayo Quezada 1998). Aguayo Quezada shows that following the sudden appearance of a helicopter above the plaza of the Tlatelolco complex, two
green flares were dropped above the crowd as a signal to sharpshooters
to open fire. The student protesters, and even many of the nonelite government troops, found themselves trapped in an ambush. Unable to escape, except into the muzzles of more soldiers, hundreds were literally
slaughtered where they stood.

In the days following the massacre, President Gustavo Díaz Ordaz
claimed that the number of dead was something "more than 30 and less
than 40" (*Proceso,* 16 April 1977, p. 8). John Rodda, a correspondent
at the time for the British *Guardian* newspaper, conducted one of the
only careful investigations into the number of people killed that day at
Tlatelolco. The figures he arrived at were at least 267 dead and 1,200
wounded. In most histories of the massacre at Tlatelolco written since
1968, the most common number used is 300 dead.

With the exception of those who were small children in 1968, everyone who lived in Mexico City at the time has a memory of where they
were on October 2 when they learned of the killings. Doña Fili, for instance, told me that although she was not anywhere near Tlatelolco on
that fateful day, and indeed did not learn of the killings until the next
day, she well remembers how the government quickly set about spreading lies regarding the students in order to garner popular support for
its deceit. When I asked Fili many years later what she could tell me
about Tlatelolco, she recounted: "We didn't find out about what had
happened at Tlatelolco right away. But my daughter was in a daycare
center [run by the Mexico City government] and the director called on
us to support the government's position. He told us that if we didn't support President Díaz Ordaz they would throw our children out of the day-
care center."

When I met her in 1990, Doña Fili was a grandmother and longtime
community activist in Santo Domingo. For her and large numbers of citizens, it took something like what happened in Mexico City in 1968 for
them to finally recognize the potential for military repression against the
citizenry when the nation's leaders felt threatened by social movements
from below. As if to provide perspective on the events of 1968, and to
draw common threads of police brutality from one year and situation to
the next, Fili also reminded me about 1966, the year in which she and
her family had participated in a land occupation in the adjacent neigh-

borhood of Colonia Ajusco. "We invaded in '66 and there was a lot of repression. The police tried to throw us out. There was fighting. They destroyed the few things we had in '66. The police were really repressive in '66."

Not surprisingly, the routine brutality meted out by federal and local armed forces on poor people in Mexico, and especially the indigenous poor, has received little notice when compared to a bloodbath involving middle-class students.[4] At the same time, although the cold-blooded slaughter of 300 students in Mexico City had a profound impact within Mexico, official condemnation from the international community never materialized.

INTERNATIONAL CONSPIRACY OF SILENCE

Mexico's quest to host the nineteenth Olympics began in the administration of Adolfo López Mateos, president of Mexico from 1958 to 1964. As proof of the great leaps forward made in the country's march through modernity, Mexico would be the first developing country ever to experience this singular honor. How better to brand a country with the imprimatur of civilization than to sponsor the Olympics in "El Año de la Paz"? And, needless to say, despite the massacre, the Olympics opened as scheduled on October 12, 1968. Barely ten days after students were slain in Tlatelolco, the Olympic torch was lit in Estadio Azteca on the south side of the capital. The scene has been described in this way:

> Outside the stadium troops and tanks were poised beyond the view of television cameras. There were no international protests, no delegations withdrew, and some, notably the Soviets, praised the Mexican government for its handling of the crisis. The Tlatelolco Massacre—the worst bloodshed in the country since the Mexican Revolution—was a fleeting news item in the international press, one more social scare of that turbulent year. To this day, the 1968 Olympics are far more likely remembered internationally for African American athletes' protests. (Bilello 1997, 784)

There was no criticism or call for justice on the part of foreign governments. As for the United States, far from denouncing the actions of the Mexican government, the CIA during this period was apparently collaborating with the Mexican government by providing daily intelligence reports to Díaz Ordaz on topics such as the ties between Mexican leftists and Cuba and the Soviet Union (see Aguayo Quezada 1998, 94). Following the massacre at Tlatelolco, and despite clear evidence today that its embassy in Mexico City was keeping Washington fully apprised of the brutality of the massacre, spokesmen for the United States maintained a stony silence of complicity, arguing that the slaughter was "a strictly Mexican affair."

For their part, the governments of Cuba and the USSR essentially followed the same course: brief coverage implying accidental shootings at Tlatelolco was offered in the Soviet press immediately following the massacre. In Cuba, there was not even a mention of the killings. Indeed, Mexican students in Havana who sought to protest the massacre found themselves censored by the Cuban government and news media. Neither the Soviet Union nor Cuba wished to alienate the Mexican political leadership; they apparently believed their countries had little to gain by supporting the protesters.

The British ambassador to Mexico called it a "conspiracy of silence" (see Aguayo Quezada 1998, 266), and this scheme extended to the International Olympic Committee, which, after brief deliberation, decided that "The games must go on!" After all, in the words of one Douglas Crocker, a museum curator and Olympics visitor from the United States: "People should wash their dirty linen in private. The students wanted to wash theirs in full view of the Olympic contestants, who had come to Mexico from all over the world, and to take advantage of their being there to get them involved in the country's domestic politics" (see Poniatowska 1975, 308)

In subsequent years, many student activists of 1968 who had not been killed, imprisoned, or forced into exile tried to apply their "domestic politics" in the most marginal neighborhoods in various cities around the country. They began a nationwide social movement that Vivienne Bennett has characterized as "the construction of new channels to express the needs of poor urban residents" (1992, 245). Mainly focusing their efforts on nonelectoral political change, thousands of the youth of '68 spread Maoist ideology and organized people around specific demands like those relating to land, housing, and high water rates. A small number of activists launched guerrilla actions such as robbing banks; the majority devoted themselves to more nonviolent efforts designed to improve the immediate living conditions of Mexico's urban underdogs, and were able to take advantage of a more liberal political climate following the 1968 massacre. The policies framed by Luis Echeverría, who assumed the presidency in 1970, thus provided enough breathing room for these Popular Urban Movements to flourish in many cities, including Monterrey, Chihuahua, and Durango in the north, and Juchitán in Oaxaca in the south.

ENDURING SIGNIFICANCE OF 1968

Sergio Aguayo Quezada (1998) pins the decision for Tlatelolco squarely on President Díaz Ordaz. Like other Mexican leaders of his day, Díaz Ordaz refused to brook any opposition to the regime, and he was the person mainly responsible for assigning one soldier for each demonstrator that day. As President of the Republic, Díaz Ordaz was the only person who could have issued the final orders for the bloodbath, Aguayo Quezada argues. To carry out this plan, the rank-and-file soldiers were issued different instructions than were given to the selected, elite units. Other government officials, including Díaz Ordaz's successor, Luis Echeverría, were also implicated in the planning and execution of the carnage, but, according to Aguayo Quezada, Díaz Ordaz was the final arbiter of who would live and die that day in Tlatelolco.

Still, more than thirty years later, the question of who is to blame for the events of October 2, 1968 remains a secondary issue for most people in Colonia Santo Domingo. For them, the greatest significance of Tlatelolco is the recognition that after October 2, 1968, everything in Mexico was changed. It is true that Mexico continued its phenomenal post–World War II expansion, with growth averaging nearly 6 percent through most of the 1970s. One result was that many, if not most, Mexicans sustained the hope that their children would materially prosper more than they had. Nevertheless, after 1968, the legitimacy of the regime, the government, and the PRI, and the people's faith in the promises of the Mexican Revolution were shattered as never before. And even today, despite the excitement generated by the election of a non-PRI candidate to the presidency for the first time in seventy-one years, despite talk that democracy is emerging "once again" in Mexico, a certain cynicism and disbelief, engendered in part by the mass execution of student protesters in 1968, continues to haunt the culture of politics here.[5]

In the decades since October 1968, Tlatelolco remains a constant point of reference for Mexicans. As described in chapter 1, one significant aspect of popular political culture in Mexico is the association of particular dates, like 1968, with particular issues. So it is that, in the popular imagination of Mexico City's residents, the events of September 19, 1985 are often compared to those that transpired in Tlatelolco some seventeen years earlier. Comparisons between 1968 and 1985 take on a particularly macabre undertone, owing to the underlying sarcasm with which people like to recall the government's persistent underestimation of body counts in one or another tragedy. Adding to this scorn is the fact that not only do Mexican officials continue to absolve themselves of responsibility for the massacre, but also that the population is aware that no government leader has ever acknowledged more than a few dozen deaths at Tlatelolco. Similarly, following the September 19, 1985 earthquake, which brought the Federal District to a cataclysmic standstill, when thousands of bodies lay buried in collapsed buildings in several central areas in the Valley of Mexico, federal and municipal officials lied by telling Mexicans and the rest of the world that only a few hundred people had unfortunately lost their lives.

But absolutely everyone else in Mexico City was convinced otherwise. In the undercounts, as in other ways with the earthquake of 1985, people once again experienced a profound loss of faith in the governmental authorities, as they were persuaded anew of the futility of relying on anyone in a position of power. Perhaps the most salient difference between 1968 and 1985 in this respect is that in 1985 this perception was less shocking, representing as it did a compounded knowledge built on the lessons of 1968.

In the summer of 1999, the 1968 massacre of Tlatelolco was once again on many people's minds in Colonia Santo Domingo. The previous winter students had launched a strike at UNAM, and it had now dragged on for months with no peaceful resolution in sight. More and more, my friends and neighbors began to discuss the possibility that troops would be sent in to end the strike, and the possibility that Mexican soldiers might once again be ordered to fire upon Mexican students and protesters. Perhaps tension in the *colonia* was heightened because the University was so close, on the other side of the Metro tracks. But, in reality, I found that the entire capital was gripped by the issues being thrown into relief by the strike (see chapter 9).[6]

The student strike at UNAM effectively closed the campus for most of 1999, and the question on everyone's mind seemed to be, "Will this end up like 1968?" From his perspective, at least, my friend Gabriel argued that this was unlikely: "It's not the same thing to massacre a people now as it was thirty years ago. Public opinion in the world has changed, and today there would surely be international intervention, and that's why the Mexican government has not been willing to use force against this student movement."

Suffice it to say here that at least one aspect of Gabriel's views are shared by others, that is, his view that left to its own devices, the Mexican government would be just as capable of murdering its citizens in 1999 as it had been in 1968. Although specific leaders may have issued the orders for the sharpshooters to mow down as many students as they could in Tlatelolco that afternoon of October 2, 1968, after that day, a trust in the beneficence of political authorities in general was violated and essentially abandoned by millions of Mexican citizens.

"Can 1968 happen again?" was the question that many on Huehue-tzin Street were asking themselves in 1999. In other words, they gauged the possible outcome of the UNAM strike by the events of 1968. Juan had gone out to find a birthday cake for his son on October 2, 1968. As it turned out, he had managed to both find a cake and avoid getting picked up by police or soldiers that night. Now, in August 1999, he told me he was worried again that the only way to end the UNAM strike would be by brute force. He shuddered to think how people would react this time.

Another neighbor, who was only a little girl in 1968, told me about a conversation she had recently had with some students participating in the UNAM strike. They had been drumming up support for their cause earlier that summer: "They asked me what I thought of the strike. I told them that I thought the government was involved somehow. I asked them 'What exactly do you want? Do you want another '68, like when there was a student movement before, and a massacre?' I told them it seemed to me like that's what they wanted."

That same summer of 1999, I asked community organizer Bernar-dino Ramos whether he thought 1968 could be repeated. He thought a second and responded: "I don't think so. I think there might be some use of force, but the conditions are not such that there could be some kind of military operation, a massacre. And the soldiers wouldn't be sent in by the city government. Definitely not. In terms of the federal troops, things are just not ripe for that kind of attack. Maybe they might try it, or threaten it. But there are not the conditions for an assault. The process of democratic transition prevents them from pulling off something like what happened in 1968."

The significance of 1968 has remained constant in subsequent decades, but its meanings have shifted in important ways. In the 1970s, when the spirit of Che and Mao still surged among at least certain youth, for many the moral of 1968 became the demand for socialism and a thoroughly different, egalitarian society. In 1999, many of my academic friends, who identified themselves as products of the "generation of '68," referred to the student strikers as *porra* (thugs). The student strikers of 1999 had nothing in common with the daring, revolutionary activists of Tlatelolco; they were at best pawns in the hands of drug dealers and others posing as radicals. What was more, these friends repeatedly told me, the strike of 1999 was an affront to the lesson from 1968 that should be clear to all: democratization and the drive for a better egalitarian society could best be achieved through legal, peaceful means.

By 2000, then, democracy—as in, "democratization," "transition to democracy," "construction of democratic citizenship"—had become the central lesson of 1968. By 2000, the massacre of Tlatelolco was thus recalled regularly in Colonia Santo Domingo, not simply as an illustration of the still apparent lack of democracy in Mexican society, but even more as the turning point after which Mexicans became less complacent about the rituals of PRI rule and national and local governments. To be sure, widespread displeasure with the Mexican polity has often manifested itself simply in privately verbalized disgruntlement and not necessarily translated into actions aimed at changing the status quo. Still, 1968 has become a common referent for defiant attitudes and complaints in Mexico.

And like so many of the discussions about dissatisfaction with the government that take place in private and public venues in Mexico City, talk of 1968 and democracy can become rather sterile and ambiguous. As I aim to show throughout this book, the nostrum of democracy solves little when it is monotonously invoked. In 1968, at least initially, the demands of Mexican students seemed less radical than those of their counterparts in the United States and France. For instance, the Mexican students merely raised the issue of basic democratic demands for freedom of speech and assembly, that is, the ability to speak out and not fear the repression of the armed forces of the state. Following the massacre, however, among one sector of the generation of '68, demands grew for socialism. In other words, earlier demands for simple freedoms within the context of a structurally unchanged Mexican society were transformed into demands for democracy within a radically new form of organization and governance.

Following 1968, Mexicans witnessed and participated in a tremendous wave of social movements. The subsequent three decades saw the growth of a variety of movements: in the cities, Popular Urban Movements; in the countryside, campesino struggles for land and occasional attempts at guerrilla group mobilization; throughout every social sector of Mexican society, burgeoning women's, gay and lesbian, and green movements; and especially in the last decade of the century among the ten million indigenous peoples in Mexico, struggles for justice, liberty, autonomy, and democracy.[7]

For Gabriel, and undoubtedly for more than a few other Mexican citizens who identify with the left, there has been a corollary lesson from 1968: leftist political parties do not work. One day, on our way back from the Zócalo in downtown Mexico City, where we had gone to look at a photography exhibit of the 1994 uprising in Chiapas, Gabriel explained: "The left works insofar as it raises the consciousness of civil society. Because a lot of folks are not hooked up to a union or a party, yet they continue struggling, they continue supporting the movements, like the student movement, the campesino movement. But they don't need to be affiliated with a party. The ones who put all their energy into political parties do it because they don't care about Mexico, because Mexican political parties only serve to divide public opinion. They're just playing with the people."

When Gabi thought about what had changed, and what had been learned in Mexico since 1968, he clearly had mixed feelings. At the same time as he described what he viewed as a political maturity among many of his generation in their refusal to get too excited by the latest maneuvers of political parties, he also remained rather contemptuous about political culture in Mexico having changed substantially in thirty years. Yet, when it came to the possibility of troops being sent into the National University to violently quell the strike in 1999, Gabi remarked emphatically that this could not happen, and his main reasoning stemmed from the lessons of 1968: "There are a lot of folks who don't know anything about '68. But there are a lot of folks who *do* know about it. If something like '68 were to happen now, it would spell the finish (*acabóse*) for our glorious Mexican Army."

The student movement of 1968 arose in part to protest Mexico's hosting of the Olympics that year. Objecting to Mexico's assertion that it was a modern, democratic society, and to the claim that Mexico was no longer really a third-rate power, the students of 1968 were determined to reveal the realities of poverty and misery and corruption in their country. The UNAM student strikers in 1999, at least according to what they said, were also concerned that the interests of *el pueblo* were being similarly compromised by Mexican obeisance and fawning before foreign powers.

In 1994, some twenty-five years after Tlatelolco, Mexico's leaders were busily reactivating the notion that there could be a quick fix to the country's economic and political woes, this time through participation in the North American Free Trade Agreement (NAFTA). This time, there was no significant student protest. Official dogma had changed surprisingly little in nearly three decades, but unlike 1968 the promise in the 1990s by Mexican business leaders and politicians that Mexico's membership in NAFTA would make it possible for the country to vault from third-world to first-world status virtually overnight was met by little more than compliant defiance in Santo Domingo and other *colonias populares.*

CHAPTER 4

For Whom the Taco Bells Toll

News item, 1992

With CEO John Martin saying "value and quality know no
borders," Taco Bell opened its first outlet south of the border
in Mexico City.

USA Today, 4 June 1992

News item, 1998

According to Rocío Conejo, a spokeswoman in Mexico City
for Taco Bell's new holding company (Tricon Global Restau-
rants, Inc., which also owns Kentucky Fried Chicken and
Pizza Hut), "because Mexican tacos are very different from
Taco Bell tacos no franchises are presently in operation or
planned for Mexico."

Phone interview, 6 January 1998

ANGELA'S BIG FEET

For Angela, the North American Free Trade Agreement (NAFTA) always held the promise of greater access to goods from the United States.[1]
In her case, what she most wanted were size 10½ wide shoes for her
badly swollen grandmother feet. As for Angela's neighbor Toño, like
most men in Colonia Santo Domingo he has had a hard time finding
steady employment in the 1990s. To Toño, the treaty represented the potential for growth of U.S. business investment in central Mexico. Even if
it might mean slaving in a low-wage maquiladora assembly plant, Toño
had high hopes for better job prospects after NAFTA went into effect on
January 1, 1994.

On that fateful day, as we know, thousands of indigenous peoples made clear their very different interpretation and expectation for

NAFTA: they launched an armed uprising in Chiapas to denounce the Agreement and to demand democracy, liberty, and justice for *indígenas* and all people in Mexico. Although no Chiapas-like uprising against NAFTA has occurred in the *colonias populares* in Mexico City or other urban areas to date, and despite the views of some like Toño, among the poor throughout Mexico, disdain and contempt for the accord have been widespread.

No matter how ambiguous and ill-defined popular opposition to NAFTA might be in the Mexican capital and in the countryside, as Chiapas has so well reminded anthropologists, we must not engage in the violence of ethnographic indifference by discounting politically marginalized political views and actions, be they forthright or muffled. By the same token, and for similar reasons, it is important to regularly assess processes such as the individualization of responses to efforts like NAFTA, including as these relate to the periodic waxing and waning of popular political interest in "politics" altogether. And any account of the lived experience of democracy in twenty-first-century Mexico must include a discussion of the part played by the international storm tides of globalization and nationalism.

With the implementation of NAFTA in particular, the lives of masses of working people in Mexico have become ever more inextricably intertwined with the fortunes of the Gringo economy. Yet, amid mountains of important analyses regarding the more strictly economic and environmental aspects of NAFTA, it is also easy to miss critical cultural dimensions that point to equally momentous changes in the lives of millions of the dispossessed on both sides of the Rio Grande/Río Bravo. NAFTA has meant far more than the commercial reorganization of relations between the United States, Canada, and Mexico. While many analyses by political scientists based on survey data showing greater or lesser "mass support" for NAFTA have appeared (see, e.g., Davis 1998), there have been fewer grassroots investigations of this issue beyond occasional journalistic accounts.

The announcement of Taco Bell's arrival in Mexico City in 1992, for example, was seen as beyond absurd by the capital's poor. In the *colonias populares* of Mexico City, the appearance of these franchises "south of the border" was a symbolic tolling, which heralded good times ahead for the upper middle class and elites alone. After all, the only customers who could regularly patronize such establishments would be the youth from these strata. The vast majority of Mexicans simply cannot afford Gringo fast food. Nonetheless, apparently North

American tacos were too much for even these youth to stomach, which resulted in Taco Bell's evident failure to establish a foothold in Mexico. It seems that even the more affluent sectors of society took umbrage at this attempted Gringo-ization of Mexico's national cuisine.[2]

In this chapter, I address certain implications of the Free Trade Agreement for national and class identities and relations in Mexico. I examine how discontent and frustration among Mexico's urban poor are representative of contradictory political dissidence and popular nationalism, and I explore how and why these manifestations of popular political culture are both ardently felt and yet nonetheless dormant in all but exceptional historical moments. The tension between individual and collective strategies to oppose U.S. domination are evidence, I conclude, of a broader chaos and confusion with respect to the meanings of democratic and popular will in Mexico today. In part, this is undoubtedly of a piece with certain broader chaotic transformations in the world that are often labeled globalization and transnationalism—and with the uncertainties provoked by this disorder.

In his classification of the terms globalization and transnationalism, Néstor García Canclini presents the former as a stage subsequent to the latter (1999, 46). *Transnationalism,* for García Canclini, refers especially to the process of internationalization of economies and cultures that has taken place in the first half of the twentieth century. (*Internationalization,* he writes, is a process that began centuries earlier with transoceanic navigation and commercial exchanges.) *Globalization,* on the other hand, is marked by "a more complex and interdependent interaction between dispersed sites of production, circulation, and consumption." Of the four positions on globalization enumerated by Fredric Jameson—that globalization does not exist, that it is nothing new, that it is something new in degree but not kind, and that it represents an entirely new multinational stage of capitalism (1998, 54)—García Canclini clearly would find the fourth most satisfactory. For him, as for Jameson, in fact, there is something brand new under the global sun.[3]

Regrettably, the relationship between globalization and nationalism is understudied, which can deceptively lead us to the conclusion that globalization somehow may spell the end of nationalism's allure and influence. Using the term *globalization* to include international developments of the nineteenth century—and referring to it as *imperialism,* "its old name"—Timothy Mitchell points out that "the rise of nationalism in the non-West was often an attempt to disengage from this system of globalization, or at least to subject it to local limits and controls" (1998,

420). The problem is clearly complicated in important ways for those areas like Mexico that are in so many respects part of the West in Mitchell's sense. Such a globalized state of affairs has even led Claudio Lomnitz to conclude and speculate that:

> Mexican nationalism, for example, is currently undergoing a profound crisis, and yet, in my opinion, the fully antinationalist stance that has emerged as the backdrop of current official policy is unrealistic. Mexico probably will not become part of—or just like—the United States. In that context, to abandon all forms of nationalism is merely to place the country at the unqualified disposal of the market and of United States policy. (1992, 14)

Mexico as the fifty-first state—the very idea seems incredible, though not as much as it did a few decades ago.

Many men and women in the working-class barrios of contemporary Mexico City believe that defending Mexico's national sovereignty has become the duty principally of the poor because, they feel, the elites have surrendered their national allegiances. Among the poor, this is often seen as an individual rather than a collective project. In communities like Santo Domingo, where most adults are able to find work if they want it but few are able to survive on the wages from one job alone, if someone has the temerity to ask a neighbor "How much do you earn?" the reply might be, "Don't ask how much I earn, ask how much I lose!" In Santo Domingo many people would agree that, in practice, the rich have always put their own interests before those of the nation, yet they might also note their perception that the language of elites when talking about Mexico and Mexico's place in the world has shifted in recent years. Now, even the pretense of independence—for example, opposition to U.S. foreign policy—has all but disappeared. Some say it has been replaced with slogans like that of Jaime Serra Puche, the government official who in 1991 called for Mexicans to accept "the challenge of interdependence" between Mexico, the United States, and Canada— that is, to accept NAFTA (García Canclini 1992, 5). The implication is not only that the United States is as dependent on Mexico as Mexico is on the United States, but that this dependence is basically of like proportions and kind.

There is a perception among the poor—at least among those who worry about such matters—that defense of the Mexican nation is now their burden. This insight is related to the spreading conclusion among activists in Colonia Santo Domingo that popular social movements in the last two decades have focused too restrictively on ameliorating practical problems among the poor and in this way may have inadvertently relinquished political ground around international and global issues.[4]

Although many commentators have addressed the relationship of NAFTA to national identity, national sovereignty, and political debate in Mexico, discussion of popular perceptions and responses to the treaty have been largely speculative, if they have been reported at all.[5] Ethnographic material has been sorely lacking, and thus this chapter also seeks to provide initial indications of popular political discourse and activity in response to the first years of the Agreement.

PREFAB CURTAINS AND JAPANESE MELONS

If, during its initial phase, Angela, and especially Toño, looked more benignly upon the TLC (Tratado de Libre Comercio), Marcos had a more typical response: "The TLC is one more blow against the already *jodidos* [screwed]," one more instance of "the Mexican and Gringo rich fleecing *la gente humilde* [the common folks]." Marcos reported that many janitors and groundskeepers at the National University where he worked felt similarly.

Other accounts of NAFTA's impact are more personal. One afternoon in late September 1994, Doña Josefina described to me what had occurred to her husband, Guillermo, following Mexico's entry into the pact:

"Guillermo worked for many years as a *cortinero* [curtain maker] in a curtain shop," Josefina began. "He would go to people's homes to measure their windows and then make them custom curtains. One day his *patrón* told him that because of the Tratado de Libre Comercio he was going to shut down the curtain shop."

"But what did the TLC have to do with shutting down the curtain shop?" I asked.

"I think he talked about tariffs [*aranceles*]. I'm not sure if it was taxes or what. I don't know. But what it did mean was that he could no longer pay what they were charging him, because [with the Agreement] other prefabricated curtains were going to start coming in [to Mexico]. Much cheaper ones. That's what it was. And he declared bankruptcy. He couldn't pay the workers any more, or continue in business. That's what has happened to a lot of other people, too."

"Like . . . ?"

"Like some furniture workers."

"Have your friends who are furniture workers had problems finding work afterwards?"

"Yes, yes. And near here, as well, there was a factory that made plastic bottles. They also closed that."

"And you're sure this had to do with NAFTA?" I pressed.

"Yes. A lot of places shut down. For example, there was an umbrella shop. They also shut that down because umbrellas from Taiwan began to arrive. So more people were out of work. Look, we know little about the Tratado de Libre Comercio. The truth is that we know little about what the Tratado really was, because they're not going to. . . . The patrón tells us, 'We're going to shut because of the Free Trade Agreement.' But really we don't know about free trade. They don't let us in on that."

"Do you have any idea," I continued, "who *is* making money with the Agreement?"

"I think the ones who are importing goods here [into Mexico]. Because if you go shopping, everything is from another country—radios, grills, dishes, pots, batteries, games, like that. If you go to the supermarket, there's also a lot of meat from the United States."

"Are there any Mexicans making money off the Agreement?"

"Well, maybe Serra Puche and his people have gotten something.[6] He was very optimistic [about the Agreement], because they think that it's going to make us better and do well for us. Well, no, not really! So we see how Serra Puche and all are doing very well. Yes, they have made something. We don't aspire to great things like those who have power, so much power, the owners of so much power, even over lives! We don't aspire to all that; we only want what's necessary. That's why there's struggle. Even if we're few in number, that's what we want, that there not be so much injustice."

In late 1996 I also spoke about NAFTA with my good friend Jorge, who spends between twelve and fourteen hours daily operating a small *tienda* (corner store) on Las Rosas Street. Unlike Josefina, who only went through first grade, when he was an adolescent Jorge studied to be a lawyer. NAFTA, Gringolandia, and Mexican national sovereignty are all subjects dear to Jorge's heart.

"So, my old friend, what the hell do you make of this NAFTA?" I asked.

Jorge began his sermon about the impact NAFTA has had among various social strata in Mexico. "For us in the lower middle class, it's of no benefit whatsoever. It doesn't benefit us mainly because in reality, here, in the city, instead of raising employment, it has lowered it. In the countryside, campesinos have little money to export. And let's say they try to get a loan, as I did when I went back [to Tierra Blanca, his natal pueblo (village) in the western state of Guerrero]. I applied for a loan from BANRURAL.[7] I'm sure you've seen the brochures they give out, or seen their commercials on the TV where they say, 'Apply for rural assistance—go to the Bank and . . .'"

"This is connected to NAFTA?" I once again asked.

"Well, yeah. Because if the banks assist campesinos, well, then the campesinos will get ahead. You know, the poor campesinos. There's land for planting and there's the will, too, but there's no money. NAFTA only . . . how shall I put this, it helps the *grandes* [big shots]. Those who plant on a large scale. The rich, those who have money."

"Are Gringos buying up land in Guerrero?"

"Only on the coast."[8]

"Not to plant?"

"No, not to plant. Only on the coast. There are talks, there are rumors that the government is going to build a dam financed by the Japanese. So there are a lot of plans. If you remember, where you entered, at the crossroads, it's all very flat there."

Jorge was referring to an ill-fated attempt I had made several years earlier to drive to the village Tierra Blanca, where at the time he was tending the family cows for a few months. Michelle, Liliana, and I had spent the better part of a day driving over creeks, boulders, and fallen logs looking for Jorge's godforsaken birthplace. To this day I tease him that Tierra Blanca probably does not even exist and that he only invented it to make a Gringo look like a fool. This was why, in the same conversation, I taunted Jorge by saying that I wanted to divulge "the secrets" of the people from Tierra Blanca to my students in the United States.

"Why?" he asked. "Because Christ never went there?"

"No, man, because no one has ever been there," I replied.

"Well, there's no Gringos who go there! And, if you want," Jorge paused before adding in a whisper, "you can become a guerilla there."

"It's that easy?"

"Out there, only the goats could give you away."

Jorge returned to his tale of Japanese-financed dams: "So, they say that the Japanese want to finance the dam and pay a little rent to grow melons (I think that's what they say) on the land. Because the Japanese really like melons and it's a lot cheaper to grow them here [Mexico] than there [Japan]."

"So, are things better or worse for poor folks after the Agreement?"

"Worse. Because, based on what I understand, the small industries used to have more chance of offering work here in Mexico, but now they have to compete with transnational companies. Games, a lot of other things, they used to make here. But no longer. Why? Because they shut down [the plants]. Now the big North American chains, like Home Mart and I don't know what, can offer everything less expensively."

"But people from Santo Domingo can't afford to go to Home Mart . . ."

"Yes, they can. For example, when they have some money, they'll go for the sales and buy more. But for us, for the tiny merchants [*pequeñisimo comercio*], well, folks are just coming to buy sodas from us. And that's what you sell the most of but earn the least from. The other thing is that my business is hurt by the Agreement simply because a lot of people are without work. So, they obviously don't have money to spend in the *tienda*."

In the wake of renewed hopes for improved economic fortunes, as part of broader democratic transformations in Mexico, Jorge and many of his friends in Santo Domingo have been frustrated in the last decade at every turn. It has become increasingly difficult to imagine fundamental changes occurring in the country's domestic economy, much less in its political sphere or in Mexican–U.S. relations with its concomitant emigration of *paisanos* to the United States. Jorge still votes on election days, but as he readily admits, his distrust of political parties signals a more fundamental disenchantment with participation in collective forms of struggle and "politics" in general.

ANTI-AMERICANISM AND NAFTA

Beginning even before the Treaty of Guadalupe Hidalgo was signed in 1848, the United States had become central to debates regarding Mexico's geopolitical borders, the cultural frontiers of *lo mexicano*, and internal "boundary" disputes involving opposing sectors of the populace. So it is no coincidence that in the 1990s NAFTA became generally emblematic of contemporary U.S.–Mexican relations.

Most urban listeners to the new transnational gospel as preached by Mexican government and business leaders in the 1990s—"The purpose of Free Trade today is to allow Mexico to become the first Third World country to vault quickly into the ranks of the First World"—that is, most in the popular urban sectors of the country were more than slightly skeptical that such a transformation would take place. A recurring and rhetorical question asked by those still actively grappling with these issues in Colonia Santo Domingo was: How can we suddenly forget about history, especially that between Mexico and *el otro lado* [literally, "the other side," meaning the United States]? The idea that the Free Trade Agreement would instantly nullify the arrogantly unequal relations between Mexico and *el otro lado* struck more than a few as ridiculous. Only the Gringos were served by such historical myopia, they felt.[9]

The fact that the true origins of the term *Gringo* are unknown to most people in Mexico and the United States suggests more about economic than etymological history. According to many commentators, scholars included, the term emerged during the U.S.–Mexican War of 1846–48, when U.S. soldiers sang a marching song that began, "*Green grow the lilacs.*" Others, noting the green-colored uniforms of the U.S. soldiers, trace the term's origin to the demand of Mexicans that the "Green go!" In contemporary Mexico, even the popular expression *Gringa, Gringa*—meaning, "Watch out, or I'm going to *chingarte!*" (as in, "If you're not careful, I'm going to take advantage of you"), is seen by some as a derivation of both *chingar* ("to fuck over") and *Gringo*, since it evokes the manipulative relations believed to be typical of Gringos.

That *Gringo* is actually derived from the Spanish word *griego* (meaning "Greek") is revealing because it allows us to establish a longer xenophobic cultural history on the Iberian peninsula (see Fuson 1961). As Américo Paredes quips, Mexicans in the mid–nineteenth century often saw their neighbor to the north as "a big-pawed, evil-smelling Abominable Blond-Man, who in kindlier moments might be thought of as a *Gringo*, a gibberish-talking outlander. But you don't call him that to his face. Some people just don't like to be called foreigners" (1961, 289).

Some periods in history have witnessed greater changes and transformations in social relations than others. In the present era and for the foreseeable future, there is great potential for tumult, in no small part because of significant changes associated with global commerce, communication, and migration. But as to the possibility that profound change will impact the vast majority of the poor in Mexico, doubts persist, and they are doubts rooted in long experience with persistent political and social subjugation.

Incredulity regarding the prospects of Mexico leaping to First World status reflects not simply popular cynicism. The California Chamber of

Commerce, for instance, also questions "the basis for Mexico's claim that it will soon be ready to join the group of industrialized nations" (1993, 14). Men and women in *colonias populares* throughout Mexico have decades of experience with and opinions about import substitution, foreign direct investment, so-called austerity measures imposed by the International Monetary Fund, and maquiladoras. Their views on NAFTA also represent oppositional judgments about the merits of *openly* tying Mexico's economic future so completely to that of the United States, as evidenced by the fact that shortly after the Agreement was ratified in Mexico, jokes began circulating in Santo Domingo that the best job prospects in the future would be those offered by the Pentagon.

If it remains the case that today, for "the majority of Mexico's growing army of deracinated urban poor, the general class opposition between *'ricos'* and *'pobres'* has greatest salience to their conditions of life" (Gledhill 1997, 104), this is by no means an automatic product of historical class schisms, any more than it is an inevitable consequence of class position. How people in Santo Domingo and other *colonias populares* today view *los ricos* and *los pobres* is more particularly linked to the three remarkable and turbulent decades in which Popular Urban Movements in Mexico, as elsewhere in Latin America, involved millions of women and men in struggles over housing, social services, indigenous rights, domestic violence, Christian Base Communities, and social movements around feminism, lesbian and gay rights, and ecology. Especially in the 1980s, political cultures independent of both the government and official political parties emerged on a large scale in the popular urban sector in Mexico.

That said, it is important not to exaggerate the novelty of the cultural processes taking place. Arguments about Mexican cultural nationalism have long involved treatments of how class relates to nation, whether different classes share opposing and/or similar interests, and indeed whether and in what contexts it might be possible to speak of *a single* Mexican national culture.[10] Carlos Monsiváis writes with reference to NAFTA, and "Americanization" in particular, that "the process is global, irreversible, and it must be examined from a perspective that does not characterize everything as 'cultural penetration' or presume perennially virginal societies" (1992a, 200).

Besides, as far as many of my friends in Santo Domingo are concerned, the only thing virginal worthy of attention is the *Virgencita* herself. As Héctor remarked to me one afternoon when I asked him who was his favorite saint. "Guadalupe," he immediately replied. When I asked him why, he replied, "Because in the Basilica [of the Virgin of Guadalupe, on Mexico City's north side] there is an engraving which reads: '*Taliter omni nationi non fecit.*'" Héctor then wrote out these words and told me they were Latin.[11] A rough translation, he said, would be, "She never treated all nations as the same." In other words, the *Virgencita* had eyes for only Mexico. In an age in which studies of regional identities have often supplanted those of national cultures, the ongoing relevance of the Virgin of Guadalupe, for Héctor and for other compliant and defiant citizens of the Mexican republic, is in part her significance as a unifying emblem of what it means to be uniquely and essentially Mexican, including with respect to her indigenous cultures.[12]

In 1986, in a preliminary effort to become qualitatively more "integrated" into Washington's market schemes, Mexico entered the GATT (General Agreement on Tariffs and Trade). This action thus occurred while Mexican elites in the mid-1980s were still attempting to resolve the country's 1982 financial collapse and prepare the way for neoliberalism's triumph in the elections of 1988 that were widely believed to be tarnished by fraud. Especially after the fall of the Wall in 1989, and with the subsequent dissolution of the Soviet system, it became a matter of course for business and political leaders in Mexico to locate their country's strategy for achieving "fast track" modernity ever more exclusively under the North American (and NAFTA) umbrella.

In 2000 the average salary for a worker in Mexico was around $200 a month. Thus, real minimum salaries in the 1990s stood at roughly the same levels as they had thirty years earlier, and workers' real earnings in 1990 were less than half what they had been before the 1982 crisis (see Barkin 1991). They were less still after the crisis of 1994–95. There was little certainty, or optimism, that the Agreement boded well in the short term for the poor in Mexico.

In 1993, after helping Don Armando gather hay for his animals in a rural village outside Mexico City, and after fielding his pointed questions regarding the U.S. bombing of Iraq in January of that year (see Gutmann 1996, 7–8), I asked Armando if I could photograph him with his straw hat, deeply tanned wrinkles, and a new and deep cut on one of his fingers. Don Armando shrugged and stared at me with his finger held up for the camera. Two days later, when I was again back in Santo Domingo, Armando's daughter came looking for me. She told me that her father was very worried about the photo I had taken. It had occurred to Armando that I might be with the CIA or DEA (Drug Enforcement

Administration).[13] I had to promise never to use the picture in classes I taught and never to publish it. Why the CIA or DEA might be interested in a photograph of Don Armando, and what they might do with it, were not discussed.[14]

To be sure, three years later, while skimming through my ethnography of Santo Domingo, Don Armando's daughter and others noticed the photos of some family members that I had published. But on that occasion I was chastised for not having including Don Armando's picture, that is, for having taken his earlier accusations and admonitions seriously. My friends and acquaintances in Colonia Santo Domingo are deeply ambivalent as to how to cope with the menace and the real power of the United States.

Although *el otro lado* can be a blessing for individual Mexicans, in the view of many it remains a scourge for Mexico as a whole. Over the course of several years, while wandering both familiar and unknown streets in *colonias populares* in Mexico City, I have, on many occasions, been the target of the insult "*¡Gringo!*" Walking through alleys or even driving down major avenues, men, usually young men, have often yelled at me: "*¡Gringo!*" or "*¡Pinche Gringo!*" (goddamned Gringo). One time the accusation was accompanied by a piece of flying fruit that hit me on the head. Another time, a would-be assailant was wielding a screwdriver as if he meant to stab me. My friends Luciano and Marcos reason that this kind of catcalling stems from simple resentment of Gringos on the part of poor youth and a few adults.

What seems clear is that this kind of insult is not representative of a facile xenophobia. "Gringos" continue to be a popular target of resentment and anger, but they are not always foreigners. As often as not, the epithet "*Gringo!*" is leveled against a *Mexican* who is perceived to be wealthy and is unexpectedly encountered in poor neighborhoods in the capital.

The River Plate *futbol* team was made up of young men from Santo Domingo and the adjacent neighborhood of Los Reyes. Most of the players sported nicknames, including Keé-kair (as in "kicker"), Conejo (rabbit), Calaca (for a wrist cast), and Choco (as in "chocolate," for dark brown skin). But there was also a Japonés (Japanese), Argentino (Argentine), and Francés (French). The name of the squad itself came from the famous River Plate soccer club in Argentina. As is the case for their middle-class compatriots, these young men from the poor barrios of Mexico City, far from feeling a distaste for things foreign, are especially intrigued and attracted to the exoticism of foreignness. Exoticism

Figure 5. River Plate *futbol* squad holding a trophy they won in 1993. Photo by Miguel Armenta.

has its limits, however. No one on the River Plate team has ever been nicknamed El Gringo; such a title would cross the bounds of acceptable humor and verge on gratuitous insult.

NATION BUILDING AND THE THIRD MILLENNIUM

How Mexico's urban poor perceive NAFTA, and whether and to whom such perceptions might ultimately matter, are questions that remain far from clear. Undoubtedly, for the purposes of U.S. commercial and foreign relations, "local" popular sentiments must be taken into account. A 1996 article in the *New York Times,* for instance, examined "dispirited public sentiments" in Mexico with respect to NAFTA and characterized the overall mood among the poor as one in which "grumpiness reigns" (see Dillon 1996). Nonetheless, lack of enthusiasm for the Agreement on the part of the working poor was not by itself a cause for entrepreneurial worries, as long as this discontent was confined to amorphous and individualized "grumpiness."

Perhaps more disturbing to globalizing elites has been an emerging popular judgment that, although it is increasingly easier for the rich to travel abroad, for most Mexicans, journeying to the United States still amounts to illegally entering a foreign country. Globalization and trans-nationalism have not led to the disappearance of the U.S. Army or the Border Patrol. Moreover, whereas the same wealthy visitors are able to keep their money in dollars in Houston banks—or even in Swiss accounts—the greatest accomplishment most migrants ever hope to achieve is regular dollar remittances sent back to home communities that have been wracked by peso devaluations.

The association of globalization with rich *vendidos* (sellouts) on the one hand, and with Mexico's poor *jodidos* (screwed) on the other, is far from casual in the minds of my neighbors in Mexico City. Many remark that the Free Trade Agreement merely confirms what they already knew to be the case: Mexico has long since lost a national sense of self, and that hereafter Mexico will not even feign national autonomy. So, with the thin facade of independence dropped, for many people in Santo Domingo, Mexico's self-reliance has become a political myth that can no longer be sustained.

If my neighbors in Santo Domingo could hear the comments of one Martín Calderón, a large landowner who was interviewed by Judith Adler Hellman in the early 1990s, they would not be surprised at his scorn for those who question the virtues of the Free Trade Agreement:

> The truth is that the only people who carry on about the invasion of Mexico by foreign companies are the Mexicans who are incompetent, who are unable to succeed without exaggerated protection by the government. These are the same people who oppose the free trade agreement because they will never be able to compete, since they're not efficient at what they do. (1994b, 144)

In a parallel set of activities that some in Mexico find bizarre, to say the least, simultaneous with Mexico's 1994 entry into free-trade alliance with Canada and the United States, there were renewed pleas by Mexican government officials for national unity following the uprising in Chiapas that same year. Guillermo de la Peña has written on the relationship between territory and ethnic identity in Mexico, especially with respect to Chiapas: "In fact, the defense of territory also proved useful to certain spokesmen for the government in attacking the demands of indigenous groups which demand recognition of *their* ethnic territories and rights, since it is argued that these demands will lead to the *Balkanization* of the country" (1999, 13).

The abject lesson is not lost on those few who follow events in southern Mexico: just as Mexico is surrendering certain autonomy and independence to the more powerful northern members of this North American alliance, so too are the southern members of the Estados Unidos Mexicanos (as the country is formally known) expected to sacrifice for the greater national good, as they have for centuries. The correspondence between the racial politics of Mexico—wherein darker-skinned members of society are expected to yield to lighter-skinned members— and the racial geopolitics of the unequal partnership between Mexico, Canada, and the United States is similarly hard to miss.

Partially in response to the rupture of popular support for state institutions and to the growing influence of independent urban social movements in the 1980s, Carlos Salinas de Gortari, whose presidency spanned the years 1988–94, decided to launch the Solidaridad/ PRONASOL program early in his administration. As one government functionary put it in 1992, "The intention behind PRONASOL is to create, through public works and services, a new urban base for the Mexican state. By the end of the 1980s the social base of the Mexican state was unraveling" (in Dresser 1994, 148). Solidaridad/PRONASOL was also designed with the Free Trade Agreement in mind. Specifically, it represented what some analysts have called "Mexico's principal entry in the global sweepstakes to create new institutional arrangements and structures to sustain the open, market-oriented economic development strategies" of NAFTA and neoliberalism in general (Cornelius, Craig, and Fox 1994, 4).

Solidaridad/PRONASOL was thus a major federal effort designed to legitimize the Mexican state (and the ruling PRI party) within an atmosphere of transnationalism and popular discontent. So, although some men and women in Colonia Santo Domingo believe that the maquiladoras will shortly ride the NAFTA wave south to the capital, far more fear that the Agreement will lead to elimination of skilled jobs through the importation of less-expensive, prefabricated products. Solidaridad/ PRONASOL's rush to develop infrastructure like roads and electricity, to say nothing of a nation of consensual consumers, itself never offered more than a few solutions to long-term employment problems in urban areas of Mexico, where most of the country's population is today concentrated.[15]

As my friend Roberto contended while he resoldered the dented radiator on my car, "Solidaridad was meant to trick us. It's just like they come around before election time and hand things out. You know, like a bucket with the candidate's name, or a coupon for an extra [plastic] bag of milk. Well, the only difference is that the handouts are all the time. But they still don't really help if you're poor. They don't fool anyone."

Promises aside, there are few who still buy into the nationalist message of former president (1976–82) José López Portillo: "*¡Preparémonos para administrar la abundancia!*" (Get ready to deal with prosperity!). The petroleum fumes that clouded the heads of so many in the 1970s have been swept away by the economic and political debacles that have hounded López Portillo's fateful words. And as petroleum promises were scattered to the winds, many contemporary premises that had anchored nationalist unity suffered irreparable damage as well. It is all the more remarkable, therefore, that in the face of profound failures of economic progress and of even less confidence in the nation-state, evidence of nationalism and nationalist consciousness persists among the poor in Mexico City. What Florencia Mallon has called "the active participation and intellectual creativity of subaltern classes" (1995, 3) in imagining and creating nationalisms cannot be underestimated today any more than in the period in which the Mexican republic was consolidated following independence in 1821.

Nonetheless, in many respects the nationalisms of the twenty-first century will be dramatically different from those of the nineteenth century that Mallon's study highlights. One noteworthy feature of NAFTA-era popular nationalism in Mexico is the heightened conviction on the part of many that they are unable to influence national politics, for instance, by expressing their belief that Mexico is being undermined openly and covertly by the United States. They grow less and less optimistic about Mexico's political future and increasingly disillusioned about the nature and import of democracy in their country.

The reality, most feel, is that only rarely are they able to politically control their own daily lives, and even less frequently can they influence any political process that might conceivably be regarded as democratic self-determination in Mexico. It is no surprise, then, that when they see that their actions can have an effect, either on international relations or on their personal existence, or both, many relish the opportunity.

In 1993 I went with Bernardino and Esther to a meeting to plan the *colonia*'s pre-Christmas *posada* celebrations, sponsored by a local chapter of the PRD. Though only in their late twenties, both were already seasoned community militants. We brought along a roasted chicken and some chiles to share with the others who were gathering in an apartment in a neighboring area.

As we entered through the narrow portal of the *vecindad* (a group of single-room apartments with communal baths and sinks), we spotted two youths still in their *futbol* uniforms. After inquiring about the final score of a game that had been nationally televised earlier in the day, Berna asked where the meeting room was. The youths directed us further down the walk toward some women who were washing clothes (and children) in the sinks and large metal washtubs. The women directed us still further inside the *vecindad*.

Three men were already sitting in the meeting room when we arrived. Another man and a woman arrived while I was being questioned as to my purpose at the meeting, my political affiliations in the United States and Mexico, my relationship with the U.S. government, and how they could be expected to trust in me to "help the community." The group seemed especially concerned about my possible connection to the U.S. government; evidently, there was a strong suspicion that I was a U.S. federal agent of some kind.

I had seen the man who was leading the impromptu inquiry before at collective work days in the nearby Huayamilpas lagoon, where some community activists met on Sundays to clean up the water and surrounding playing fields. He had seen me participating in these cleanup efforts as well. Since it appeared that I would soon be ordered out of the meeting and the *vecindad*—two people opposed my presence from the beginning, while all but Bernardino and Esther seemed to have serious reservations—I decided to argue politics and not protocol. First, I reiterated my ethnographic purpose in Mexico City, my involvement as a community and political organizer in Chicago and Houston for many years, and my desire to respect the wishes of all attending the meeting. Then I told the group that, personally, I would be astonished if the U.S. government were to take such an interest in a meeting of community activists who lived in some of the poorer homes of the poorer neighborhoods of Mexico City as to assign a Gringo agent to investigate. I said I was fairly sure that the United States was uninterested in such meetings.

My approach backfired, and I was unceremoniously asked to leave the premises. Bernardino escorted me to the street, apologizing as we made our way out of the *vecindad* and assuring me that he would not face untoward repercussions for having invited me.

In retrospect, my actions and words that day strike me as having been, at best, naive, and at worst, presumptuous. In the remainder of this chapter, I shall discuss issues that pertain to ideas about Mexican popular nationalism and sovereignty as these have been developing in the late 1990s. In the process, I shall address certain recalcitrant theories of nationalism and class, including within critical theory, that settle for comfortable naiveté and metropolitan arrogance in lieu of creative new approaches to understanding contemporary nationalism. In developing new moral standards with respect to national integrity and autonomy, and in trying to make sense of their place within the widespread processes of globalization and transnationalism, residents of Colonia Santo Domingo often remark that they feel more bewildered and frustrated than in the past, primarily due to the sense of a lack of direction to history. This social awareness seems all the more poignant given the fact that, despite doubts as to their ability to truly effect change in the world at large, my friends in the PRD meeting that day never doubted that in many ways they themselves had to assume responsibility for the sorry state of affairs in their country, and that these duties included guarding against the perceived threat of an unknown Gringo who had been encountered in an unusual location asking unusual questions.

NATIONAL SOVEREIGNTY

It turned out that my not considering the pre-*posada* gathering a threat to U.S. national security was more disrespectful of popular nationalist politics than if I had been sent to spy on the meeting by the CIA director himself. The response of those in attendance that December day cannot be explained away as simply knee-jerk anti-Americanism. Instead, or in addition, I believe, it represented a real frustration and bewilderment on the part of many in the popular movements in Mexico as they tried to make contemporary sense of the Mexican nation and of the United States.

In a process analogous to what Mercedes González de la Rocha calls the individualization and privatization of solutions to Mexico's economic crises of the 1980s and 1990s (1991; 1994; see also Benería 1992), for many in the *colonias populares* the defense of Mexico's nationhood and sovereignty has become a personal rather than collective responsibility. For numerous others, this goal has become illusory in the extreme; discouragement at the possibility of defending the Mexican nation has contributed mightily to a more endemic political malaise.

The individualization and privatization of popular nationalism in Mexico represents, in part, the fruits of two decades of social movements among the poor that have focused rather exclusively on survival and securing rudimentary services. In the *colonias populares,* the debate in the last twenty years has primarily focused on how individuals, or perhaps families and households, have been affected by watershed developments (like NAFTA) that concern the Mexican nation.

My friend Roberto, the radiator repairman, is typical in this respect. "Do you know where the best caviar comes from, Mateo?" he asked me one morning.

"No," I replied.

"Russia. And the best sausage? Germany. The best tuna? Mexico!" It quickly became evident with the last example that he had a bone to pick with the Gringo. "But what is all this about dolphins and protests from U.S. environmentalists?" he asked me rhetorically. "Mexican fishermen catch them by accident," so people in the U.S. should calm down a bit.

Actually, he noted, it was Mexicans who should be upset with the state of world agricultural commerce. "Where does the best Mexican produce go? To the United States, *cabrón!* Do you know, Mateo, that Mexico today imports beans and corn? Corn from Argentina! What the hell do the Argentines know about corn, for god's sake? They know meat, okay. That's true. But corn? This is idiotic!"

Idiotic it might be, but other than grumble to an itinerant anthropologist, Roberto sighed, there really was not much one could do to change the situation.

If grassroots leftist politics in the 1960s in Mexico, as elsewhere, too often neglected the daily needs and realities of the masses of working and underemployed poor, the pendulum in the intervening decades has not infrequently swung to the opposite extreme, as evidenced by the fact that recent popular social movements customarily ignored the current debate on questions of transnationalism, globalization, and nationalism.

Events such as the presidential elections of 1988 and 1994 and the Chiapas uprising in 1994 have generated heated discussion, including on questions of what these events have to do with Mexico and modernity. This was especially true in the period around the 1988 elections. Yet some fundamental Mexican nationalist institutions—like the *ejido* lands formerly held in communal trust, or the state monopolies of basic natural resources and services like oil and telecommunications—have recently been undermined. A recent spate of foreign investment in such resources and services has met with little organized popular protest, much less rebellion. With the demise of the *ejido* and of state ownership of Mexico's patrimony, says Jorge, the *tienda* owner in Santo Domingo, "before long, only tequila, tardiness, and Mexican curios will carry the 'Made in Mexico' stamp" of authenticity.[16]

There is still a certain desire among many ordinary Mexicans in the

Figure 6. A five-thousand-peso coined in
1988 to commemorate the fiftieth anniversary of Mexico's expropriation of foreign
oil companies in 1938.

cities to defend what they used to regard as the collective project of
Mexican sovereignty. Few of my friends and acquaintances are consistent in their feelings and actions in this respect, but most experience at
least periodic bouts of anti-Americanism and patriotic fervor.

Guillermo Bonfil Batalla writes that past "nationalization of oil,
railroads, electricity, and later the banks were historic milestones
which reaffirmed our national sovereignty" (1992, 175). Especially in
the face of repeated economic crises, most recently in the drastic devaluation of the peso in 1994–95, NAFTA is far more than an ideological issue alone. Now, among the other problems heightened by the
Agreement, Bonfil Batalla writes, is that of "cultural penetration, which
translates into the imposition of the *american way of life* as a model for
Mexican society" (1992, 167–68, English emphasis and orthography in
original).

As epitomized by the Free Trade Agreement, domestic elites are selling the country to the highest foreign bidders and making a fortune for
themselves in the process. Despite this popular sentiment, or perhaps in
part because of it, as Claudio Lomnitz notes, in official venues in Mexico during this same period of crippling crisis and the auctioning off of
the national patrimony, the topic of democracy has received "obsessive
attention" (1996, 56). As part of this discussion on democracy, Lomnitz

reports, there has occurred "a rift between state and nation" as the state has become increasingly identified with "a small and unpopular Americanizing elite who parasitically depends on the Mexican nation" (64–66), while nationalism itself has become differentiated between elite and popular versions. And whereas the Mexican upper crust has a program, headquartered in Washington, D.C., for borderless "integration" into a global network, the majority of the population who seek protection from the state against the global market "has not yet devised a political formula that can simultaneously work in a contested democratic field and provide the kind of state protection that revolutionary nationalism provided" (66).

These issues involve new and evolving nationalist images in Mexico and international relationships in the global arena, overnight financial catastrophes and fortunes in Mexico, and widespread opposition to Mexican immigration that continues to grow within the United States. In Mexico itself, as much in working-class neighborhoods like Santo Domingo as along the country's northern border, the future is perceived as closely tied to the fortunes of the United States. A minor example, perhaps, but one I find revealing is the level of familiarity Mexicans have with U.S. holidays and politics; it is remarkable how many people in Santo Domingo have stopped me in the street on July 4th with the comment, "Oh, Mateo, it's your Independence Day, isn't it?" How many people in the United States would be able to locate Mexico on a world map, much less know the date of Mexico's Independence Day (September 16th)? Depending on the year and the politicians involved, the State of the Union address in the United States in January may receive almost as much attention by the media and public in Mexico as the corresponding speech given every year by the Mexican head of state. Of course, this may simply be an acknowledgment by news outlets and their audience that a U.S. president's declarations may indeed be as significant for the lives of Mexicans as those of their own elected officials.

If erroneous beliefs about the United States are widespread among residents in Santo Domingo, the nature of their illusions are nonetheless revealing. In July 1992, along with more than a hundred other friends, neighbors, and acquaintances, we invited Claudio, Lourdes, and their two children, to Liliana's first-year birthday celebration and farewell party. They arrived with Claudio's mother in tow. As he was introducing me to his mother, Claudio commented that she was ready to go back to the United States with us as Liliana's nanny. I tried to laugh politely and dismissed the offer as no more than a pleasant remark. It quickly became apparent, however, that Claudio and his mother were rather serious about the offer. He spoke with assurance when he reminded me that we were surely returning to a large house in Berkeley, one with plenty of room for his mother. I replied that, if we were lucky, we would have a tiny apartment in a married-student housing complex of the University. Claudio was sure I was underestimating the size of our U.S. residence. Well, he continued, then since we had become such good friends, we should at least go down to the U.S. Embassy in Mexico City before we left and tell the officials there that we needed his mother as a nanny, even if we did not, and arrange for a visa for his mother. When I told Claudio that, regrettably, once again I would have to disappoint him, he shuffled back to his wife and children. After the party, I lost contact with him.

We are often made aware of a myriad of ways by which ideas and cultural goods can be reappropriated and reconfigured daily, regardless of their national origins or their original meanings. María Lorena Cook has shown how, on a grand scale, transnational politics have spurred transnational organizing and solidarity in the wake of NAFTA (1997); on a smaller scale, I might use an example the fact that "LP" in Mexico signifies not only a long-playing record but also a *"litro de pulque."* [17] Activities of the state can inadvertently and profoundly impact national identities and people's awareness of international inequalities. Where all of this will lead is by no means certain. In Mexico, to date, working-class nationalism most often has taken on leftist hues, presaging what Gledhill has called a potential popular nationalist backlash (2000). In Europe, in contrast, recent decades have seen a right-wing resurgence among broad sectors of the working class in countries like France, Spain, and Germany (see Stolcke 1995). The issues of immigration and trade are the currency in which these popular nationalist sentiments deal, and to a certain extent the political loyalties of some sectors of the population in Mexico City may at times seem as capricious as the trade in currency. But a yearning for more control over one's political and economic future is evident in all cases.

In the 1990s we saw rapid changes in international alignments following the fall of the Wall in 1989. The dispersed and even detached reaction to the Tratado de Libre Comercio in *colonias populares* like Santo Domingo is indicative of an underlying and all but hidden process of individualization in approaching political problems like national sovereignty and stability in Mexico.

ANGELA'S OIL

In discussing free trade, big shoes, runaway factories, and globalization once again with Angela, I asked her at one point what her overall impression was of NAFTA.

"It's for the U.S. to get more control of our *petroleo*," she replied.

"Well, I don't want your *petroleo*," I said, trying again to distance myself from the generic image of the Gringo.

To this, she responded calmly, "*Ni yo lo tengo, tampoco*" (Nor do I have it, either).

Such class-based resentment on the part of those Manuel Azuela has called *los fracasados* (the failed) is not even particularly novel (1939). Over thirty years ago, Oscar Lewis quoted Manuel Sánchez, one of the famous "children of Sánchez": "And gasoline, even though it is 'ours,' eighty centavos a liter. *Chingao*, we were better off when the Gringos and the English had our oil! And now that the government has nationalized electricity, too, wait and see what those bastards are going to pull on us. And there's no stealing it now . . . you're robbing the nation!" (1966, 7).

In the midst of calls in the 1990s for global trade and international interdependency, there was potential for questioning about transnational democracy and international solidarity. Weary cynicism mixed with periodic and exasperated outbursts on the streets of Colonia Santo Domingo. In the 1990s in the capital city a passionate desire to make sense of the madness of modernity in Mexico was as characteristic of the epoch as ennui.

Shortly after New Year's Day 1997, I asked Doña Josefina, whose husband Guillermo had lost his job as a curtain maker "because of NAFTA," what she thought would happen in Mexico in the next few years. As a local leader of the Unión de Colonias Populares (UCP), she felt it necessary to express optimism about the future. But there was also an angry edge to her political forecasting that I had not noticed before during our six years of friendship.

"We're going to be better off. That's what we want, and that's what we'll get! If it's peaceful, so much the better. But if it's not peaceful, and if there's an uprising, if nothing else, some things will change. The country will get out of this mess, it can't continue as it is. This is too much already."

"Is it much harder to live today than before?" I asked, thinking of Josefina's early participation in the founding of the *colonia*, of her expe-

riences as a domestic servant beginning when she was thirteen or fourteen, of her love for reading despite her lack of formal schooling, and of
how she and Guillermo had eloped after Josefina's stepfather had for-
bade them to marry.

"Yes, it's much harder today. Before, even though we were living in
plastic [homes], using oil stoves, and sometimes . . . well, actually, most
of us had plastic shoes. We didn't have anything, did we? But we pro-
tected each other. If someone was sick, we helped them, or they helped
us. The area was very nice then.

"Even if it was beans, there weren't the pressures as there are now.
You can lose your job at any time now. Before, if they fired you, they'd
still give you some money. Now, no! Now, no contracts, no work, no
nothing!

"So it's up to us, the *pueblo* [people], whether the change comes
peacefully or in another way. But we've got to change. Having a country like Mexico and a legacy of those who struggled before us, how
could we continue with the way things are? Things cannot continue as
they are."

CHAPTER 5

Crossing Borders

Me voy p'al norte, se oye decir
en los poblados y en los ejidos;
corriendo siempre, siempre escondidos
la mayoría van a sufrir.

> Guillermo Velázquez y Los Leones
> de la Sierra de Xichú

BORDERS OF CLASS AND STATE

Not so many years ago, I worked as a waiter in a restaurant in the swanky Galleria mall of Houston, Texas. Among the wait staff there was regular grousing about the Mexican customers who would arrive on a Friday evening for a weekend of shopping at Saks Fifth Avenue, Lord and Taylor, and Neiman Marcus, returning to the restaurant over the course of the weekend to snack and compare shopping purchases . . . and who would leave us 5 percent tips. These were the weekend Houstonians, the Mexicans who flew in to Hobby and Intercontinental airports on Friday afternoon for a bit of R&R, a two-day getaway from Monterrey, Guadalajara, or even Mexico City. They were the tony, globalized jet-setters for whom the world was evidently only a credit charge away, virtually borderless.[1]

Meanwhile, in the kitchen of the same restaurant, as in the kitchens, sweatshops, expensive houses, and well-groomed yards throughout Houston, Mexicans of another kind "worked like burros" (sometimes they described themselves as working *como negros* [like blacks]) preparing food, wiping toilet bowls, and pruning the hedges of their more prosperous transnational *paisanos*.[2]

Felipe, the salad preparer, never tired of telling others how many tomatoes he had eaten on the first night that he had sneaked across the border—he had buried himself under a ton of tomatoes to avoid detection by the Border Patrol. Felipe had arrived in Brownsville, in the Rio Grande valley, looking like a splattered jar of spaghetti sauce, he sometimes added. The first time is often the worst, others would chuckle. Then there was the head busboy, Heleodoro, who following the passage of IRCA (the so-called "amnesty" immigration act of 1986, which had been sponsored by Senator Alan Simpson and Congressman Peter Rodino) finally revealed the secret he had managed to hide for many years: though he had worked not only as a busboy but also as a chauffeur for a wealthy woman in the River Oaks neighborhood, he was also illiterate and could barely recognize his own written name. This, among other reasons, had prevented him from returning to his natal village in Guerrero on the Pacific Coast of Mexico; he had been afraid, not only of reentering the United States after the trip, but also of simply getting lost on the way down. In Houston, he had somehow managed to memorize other visual clues so as to navigate the streets and highways.

As for the others in the restaurant, these Mexican women and men who attended to the needs and whims of tourists from Mexico, Europe, or just Louisiana, often with elegance and submerged wit, could all recount personal or family histories of migrations and deportations—the wasted time they had spent in holding pens at *la migra* in south Texas, the repeated and brazen crossings into Gringolandia. They make up part of the spatially discontinuous communities, in Guillermo de la Peña's formulation, for whom migration to the United States has been as unavoidable as it has been hazardous (1999, 19; see also Mummert 1999).

One reason crossing the border has become ever more hazardous in the 1990s is that, despite the ever-spiraling rhetoric about globalizing and transnational processes, the border has received even more military attention by U.S. agencies assigned to patrol the southern frontier and enforce immigration laws there. In the words of one analyst:

> Even as the North American Free Trade Agreement (NAFTA) promotes a deterritorialization of the economy, U.S. border-control initiatives reinforce state claims to territorial authority. In effect, policymakers are simultaneously building a barricaded border and a borderless economy. The U.S.–Mexico border consequently has the distinction of being both the busiest land crossing in the world and one of the most heavily fortified. (Andreas 1999, 14)

More generally, with respect to globalization and global citizenship, Timothy Mitchell has cautioned that "increasing globalization is not the only direction in which history can move. . . . Not all recent history has been a process of increasing integration" (1998, 417, 421). When thinking about Mexican transnational migrants, in particular, we must consider not only emerging hybrids and global *mestizaje*. We must also understand that Mexicans remain in high-risk categories for diseases like tuberculosis, contracted not in Mexico, nor simply because these immigrants are poor, but more specifically because they are poor immigrants living in a racist society in severely overcrowded conditions in communities such as Houston's Northside or East End. We must recall the hundreds of Mexicans, the officially recorded Mexicans, who have died each year in crossings of the two-thousand-mile U.S.–Mexico border. A University of Houston study released in 2001 reports, "We identify 3,676 vital registration records of deaths from external accidents or injuries of foreign transients in 55 border counties for a 14-year period" from 1985–98 (Eschbach, Hagan, and Rodriguez 2001, 8; see also Amnesty International 1998). The report provides details on the deaths of Mexican migrants caused by train accidents, motor vehicle accidents, drowning, hypothermia, dehydration, and homicide.

On January 25, 2001, the Federación de Organizaciones Mexicanas en Nueva Inglaterra sent out an e-mail which read in part: "We hope that in the year already begun there will be fewer fatalities in the region along the Mexico–United States border. Because unfortunately those who suffer are the majority of those who leave their families to seek a 'BETTER FUTURE HERE IN *EL NORTE*.'"[3] Survival strategies, as we will also see in chapter 6, are not necessarily romantic manifestations of resistance. For those who suffocate to death stuck in railway cars under the Texas sun, crossing the border is immeasurably more tragic than it is defiant and hybrid.

For tens of thousands of Mexican women and men, mestizos and *indígenas*, young and not-so-young, indeed, crossing the international border into the United States in the twenty-first century still amounts to invading, individually and in small groups, a foreign territory. The border is long, and there are millions of *paisanos* (countrymen), *oriundos* (Mexican natives), *compatriotas* (compatriots), *compañeros* (fellow travelers), and *familiares* (family members) waiting on "the other side." To some, the border is merely an imaginary line that marks the boundary between two countries, but for the thousands of Mexicans who attempt to cross the boundary between Mexico and the United States each and every day, "the border" is just as dangerous as it might seem to some to be culturally transgressive.[4]

At the same time, although I am critical of facile notions of hybridity that conjure up overly romantic images of melting pots and the like, in the spirit of 1848 and of Marx's portrait of capitalism's gravediggers, it is important to recognize that the very processes of migration and ethnic conflict, racism and economic exploitation, simultaneously threaten the lives of those who venture across the border illegally, and they also provide the seeds of cross-border and cross-class alliances among those for whom El Norte is as much a means to an end as it is a final goal.

In the early years of the twentieth century, Manuel Gamio, the great anthropologist who wrote pioneering works about Mexican migrants and their journeys to "*el norte*," alerted us to what he called "Yankee *metalismo* [metalism] and the Mexican":

> Ironically we call the United States the country of dollars. By this we refer not to the proverbial riches of that republic, but instead to a way of being among its inhabitants, so that their life's purpose comes to be considered, unjustly, as having little spirituality, as utilitarian, materialist, and "metalized," excluding any altruistic motives. (1916 [1982], 149)

In our descriptions of Mexican immigrants and of the U.S.–Mexico border, of transnationalism, globalization, and diasporic flows across international frontiers, we are increasingly confronted with the necessity to carefully distinguish questions of class, race, ethnicity, gender, and even age in analyzing how, when, where, and for whom the border counts. Here, I discuss aspects of only two features involved in border crossings, class and regional origins, in order to better understand Mexican immigration to the United States and certain implications of this immigration for popular politics in contemporary Mexico in general.

Before proceeding further, it may also be worthwhile to reemphasize one simple point: regardless of the extent to which globalization has succeeded in bringing together a migrating humanity, for most Mexicans seeking entry into the United States, the U.S. Border Patrol is not only alive and well and protecting Gringolandia from swarms of Mexican maids and short-order cooks, but the Border Patrol is today growing at an unprecedented rate in terms of personnel and expenditure. Between 1993 and 1999 the number of Border Patrol agents stationed along the United States–Mexico border doubled (Andreas 1999; on the militarization of the border, see also Dunn 1996 and Heyman 1995). For, just as the state, and the nation-state, may be undergoing dramatic changes and/or reanalysis in this millennial age, the cold fact is that, under late-capitalism, the state and the Border Patrol are hardly withering away.

Early one Sunday morning a few years ago, on the way to a *futbol* (soccer) game with my neighborhood River Plate team in Mexico City,

Figure 7. The wall dividing Tijuana, Mexico, and San Ysidro, California. Behind the wall on the right is a waiting Border Patrol car parked on the beach at the Pacific Ocean.

I was treated to a beer by some of the players. Over the blare of the tape deck in the jitney in which we were riding, I shouted that, to reciprocate, I would invite them all to visit me in the United States. Someone shouted back, asking how much it would cost to fly. I said about $300 to Houston, and maybe $500 to San Francisco. The guy sharing my seat on the jitney looked a little pained as he shook his head and, with a tone of disgust, reported that flying was thus not only faster than getting smuggled across by a *coyote*—it was cheaper, too. The disparity between air and land, between legal and illegal, might be termed perversely ironic by some commentators, but to my friends, for whom passage on a plane to the United States was seldom an option, most of the time it just seemed contemptible.

For those who fly *con papeles* (with papers)—those for whom international boundaries are perhaps a momentary nuisance but no more—the border indeed may hardly exist. For those who risk life and limb to cross this frontier, the authority of the nation-state has lost none of its salience at the dawn of the twenty-first century. The contradictory character of U.S. migration policies toward Mexicans does not necessarily guarantee to those without papers that globalization and transnationalism portend any significant change in the risk of border crossings (see Kearney 1995; Ong 1999). As Joe Heyman has written, with respect to the connections between class and the Mexican migratory experience:

> INS officers judge that entrants such as persons crossing the border as non-immigrant visitors are potentially fraudulent in their intent, seeking illegal work, if they appear poor, and are legitimate in their intent if they appear prosperous. One INS supervisor remarked in a mild critique of his own organization, "to an inspector, you are your clothes, at least until the inspector comes to know better." (2001, 132)

The militarization of the border, complete with vigilante pogroms in certain border areas, has occurred simultaneously with the ongoing and all-but-official pattern of INS complicity with businesses that hire those who do make it over. In this way, as many have remarked, U.S. immigration and border policy is really a disguised form of labor policy, a way of regulating and disciplining the flow of cheap labor. If understanding such a pattern of militarized complicity usually makes little practical difference for Mexican men and women, recognizing this regulatory role of the Border Patrol at least helps make clear that U.S. immigration policy is not simply a smoothly managed, top-down enterprise, but one full of contradictory aims and means.

CHILANGOS IN GRINGOLANDIA

For another interesting twist to the contradictory processes of national and class identities, we may briefly consider the often-maligned and alternately maligning native of Mexico City, the (in)famous *chilango*. Having already mentioned certain differences based on class with regard to the U.S.–Mexico border, it is noteworthy the degree to which regional divisions within Mexico persist among migrants to the United States, and, further, how these regional differences may assume even more explicit, class-toned hues in Gringolandia.

The term *chilango* comes originally from the Maya word *xilaan* (or *xilango*), and according to various sources, was first used by people from the east-central state of Veracruz to refer to the *pelos revueltos* (messy hairs) who lived over the mountains in what was then the Aztec capital and is today Mexico City (see Santamaría 1959, 971; Mejía Prieto 1987, 50). In daily usage, in the Federal District, the term is used to assert native standing in Mexico's seat of economic, political, and cultural power. Elsewhere in Mexico today, it is used in a half-joking fashion, as in phrases like "Be patriotic, kill a *chilango*." In this respect, *chilangos* share something in common with native New Yorkers, who are often the butt of jokes by nonnatives. Much of the commentary is meant in jest, but there is also a sharp edge to most "New Yorker" jokes, which reveals the perceptions that exist on both sides as to questions of courtesy, arrogance, and attitude. In a sense, the term *chilango* illustrates the cultural distinction Luis González had made between *historia patria* and *historia matria* (1987), that is, between a unified (urban) history of the fatherland and a more particularized (rural) history of the motherland.

My working-class Mexican friends in Providence, Rhode Island, have repeatedly commented on the aloofness on the part of *chilangos* in the area, which is illustrated by the fact that many refuse to participate in community events, whether these be the local Mexican *futbol* league, holiday gatherings for Mexican Independence Day, December 12 gatherings to commemorate the Virgin of Guadalupe, or protests against the periodic *migra* raids on local costume-jewelry factories. "Chilangos are simply too rude to be tolerated," I have been told by several acquaintances who are originally from the provinces of Mexico.

The standard *chilango* response to anything, according to some, is "*Ya lo sé*" (I already know that). They already "know" everything, complains my friend Julio Aragón, president of the Asociación Social, Cultural y Deportiva Mexicana in Providence. *Chilangos* feel themselves to be superior to others, so they accuse other people of being nothing but "*pinches indios*" (goddamned Indians). Reports another member of the group, "*Te humillan*" (They humiliate you), or at least they try to, as when they explain to non-*chilangos* that, whereas they might be working alongside everyone else here in the *factorías*, in Mexico they were *profesionistas*, and that is how they still regard themselves—and how they expect others to regard them.

Like the stereotypical middle stratum whose origins they claim as their own, *chilangos* are said by many in the Asociación Mexicana to cling to individual strategies in the United States for getting by. This is cited as the reason why they won't join with other Mexicans and other Spanish-speaking immigrants in efforts to stop the *migra* raids at the factories, or to raise money for water and medicine for hurricane victims (in Acapulco in October 1997, e.g., and in Central America and the Caribbean in October 1998) or for refugees displaced as a result of paramilitary attacks on supporters of the EZLN in Chiapas.

Among my *chilango* friends, it is interesting to note that many concede a certain "stand-offishness" with respect to other Mexicanos in the Providence area, while at the same time denying any pretensions to middle-class status or any lack of solidarity with the plight of their (legal or illegal) *compatriotas* in the United States. Some counter charges of *defeño* rudeness by expressing their displeasure at an equally rude, and utterly unfair, stereotype that is widespread among non-*chilangos*: that people from the Mexican capital are *ladrones* (thieves) and are usually dishonest in their dealings with others.

People's origins are raised again in the stories *mexicanos* tell of how they arrived in the United States. According to some of my friends who trace their roots to *la provincia* in Mexico, *chilangos* are more prone to at least allege that they entered the United States in *aviones*, and legally, and to taunt those who arrived by illegally crossing the Rio Grande. Victoria Malkin, in her research among Mexicanos on Long Island, has documented similar views, as when one *chilanga* boasted to her, "*Me gusta que soy del D.F., que tengo cultura*" (I like it that I come from Mexico City, that I have culture), while at the same time representing non-*chilangos* as "*los machistas mexicanos, traen sus pistolas y puro rancho y luego muchos no tiene nada o poca educación*" (the macho Mexicans, [who] carry pistols and are complete hicks, and then a lot have no or very little education) (1999).

Class, regional, and urban–rural divisions are played out in the diverse implications of being from *la provincia* (i.e., of being provincial), and the implications are still more insulting if the migrant should come from a small *rancho* in some godforsaken rural outpost of Mexican-ness. Northerners look down on southerners, southerners on northerners, and both positively despise *chilangos*. So goes the familiar stereo-typologizing in Mexican regional allegiances.

Class is a key subtext that involves perceived and real differences among the poor from Mexico, differences that are described by a mixture of regional and class terms. To a certain extent, this is simply a matter of specific classificatory schemes that have come to signify a variety of despised categories, that is, they comprise words or phrases that carry some added pejorative punch, despite the fact that they may refer to a variety of qualities and attributes. This is clearly the case with the term *chilango*, whose uses sometimes have more to do with perceived class differences than regional ones. Though even then, the *chilangos* of Rhode Island are not generally rich in any true economic sense. They may be more educated, and they may routinely claim a higher social status than their brethren migrants, but if and when they assert social superiority it is based on cultural more than economic factors. The varied meanings of the term *chilango* depend entirely on context. The same is true of another word with cross-border significance, *mayate,* which also has multiple meanings depending on a speaker's social capital and experience.

Among my friends in Colonia Santo Domingo, *mayate* refers rather exclusively to *homosexuales* (though what homosexual means to different people varies considerably). Among Mexicanos in the United States, and among Mexicanos in Mexico who have lived in the United States, however, the word *mayate* is a disparaging nickname for a different category of people entirely: African Americans.[5] A man from the western state of Michoacán whom I met on a beach in the southern state of Oaxaca told me he had lived "among the *mayates*" in Chicago for many years, near the Howard El stop. Only one of my acquaintances in Mexico, a cab driver in the Federal District who had earlier lived for many years in Chicago, used the term *mayate* to refer interchangeably to either *homosexuales* or *negros.* And even for him, *mayate* mainly was used to refer to African Americans, whereas the word he most commonly employed to disparage *homosexuales* was *maricón.*

The term *mayate* originally referred to what is known in English as the dung beetle. (Evidently, the site of the beetle's foraging leads to guilt-by-fecal-association.) Given the dramatically different referents for *mayate* in Mexico and among *mexicanos* in the United States, clearly the term is consistently one of derision and, in a popular form of *otroismo* (othering), it is applied in a similar fashion to those who are perceived as either racial or sexual outsiders.[6]

MEXICANO MIGRANTS: TRANS- AND BI-

The running debate among scholars who study Mexican migration to the United States revolves around whether "binational" or "transnational" is the more accurate description of the migratory processes in which millions of *mexicanos* are involved. The debate is relevant to the points I am trying to make here. Aside from the fact that some of the differences in usage of the terms are undoubtedly generational in character—with younger scholars more often preferring the terms *transnational* since it captures the international processes as a whole—it seems to me that there are additional reasons to promote the term *transnational* as the one that is more adequate, if still far from wholly satisfactory.

Michael Kearney has shown how an analysis of the economic and cultural aspects of transnational communities allows us to capture "the historical sense of transcending the defining power of the state to impose its categories of identity upon persons who are members of such a community" (1996, 123). The extent to which people can actually transcend these state powers, and their ways of doing so, is a key area of study today. In particular, Kearney argues, only by utilizing such a framework will we be able to view the category of ethnicity as "inherently transnational" in the contemporary world.

In a paper about migrants from Oaxaca, Federico Besserer has described the construction of a new diasporic Mexican nation in which women in particular play a significant role in developing new ideas and practices pertaining to democracy and citizenship. Besserer quotes one woman who was abandoned when her husband went to the United States: "There are a lot of women who've been left behind. The men go off with American women and a lot of times they don't come back. What bastards those men are" (2000, 379; see also Gutmann in press).

In my own ethnographic fieldwork among *mexicanos* in northern California and southeastern New England in the 1990s, as well as in my previous experiences in community and political organizing among Latino/as in Chicago and Houston in the 1980s (in other words, experiences in regions that are distinctly different with regard to historical and migratory patterns and as to their relative concentrations of Latino/as), I have noticed two interrelated phenomena. Even if it were true in decades past that *mexicanos* had only two national frames of reference—that is, Mexico and the United States—today this is simply not the case. In place of such a binary and dichotomous vision, Mexican migrants in the 1990s must deal with a battery of issues, such as racism, employment, housing, musical tastes, and marriage, and these are raised in such a way that additional transnational thematic categories inevitably come into play. Migrants can be characterized as "Spanish-speaking," "Latinos," "Hispanics," "the workers," or simply the dispossessed. Transnational issues, and not merely binational ones, are the stuff of television news and daily life for men and women from Latin America who find themselves resident in Gringolandia today.

Few scholars in the United States would argue any longer that migration to the United States can be adequately understood without reference to national, regional, generational, and historical distinctions within Mexico and within Latin America more broadly. In similar fashion, I have found, it makes little sense to talk about the cultures and societies of Mexico and Latin America without reference to the lives and activities of the millions of immigrants who either were born "south of the border" or who can trace some part of their ancestry to the region, although today these immigrants reside in the United States. Whatever is occurring in the United States in the way of Latino/a "cultures" and "societies" is decidedly not simply a recapitulation, augmentation, or diminishing of "traditional life" as it was known in the countries of origin.

In part, I am arguing for a renewed appreciation of the importance of borders, and in particular of the international border that runs from San Ysidro/Tijuana on the Pacific Coast, through the states of Arizona and New Mexico on one side and Sonora and Chihuahua on the other, and ends at the Gulf of Mexico at Brownsville, Texas, and Matamoros, Tamaulipas. We also need to reaffirm the importance of class analysis in our understanding of borders and border crossings, including class divisions that take on the appearance and style of regional distinctions. In the institutional and private kitchens, yards, and laundry rooms of the United States, and not simply in the supposedly nationless corporate boardrooms and resorts, we can learn a lot about the meanings of borders and class, and about what forces propel women and men every day to knowingly face the perils of possible arrest, injury, and even death.

Yet we must reaffirm the importance of class without losing sight of the centrality of ethnicity and race, to say nothing of anxieties over national integrity, as these labels are given phenomenological shape in borderland areas stretching throughout North America. If *chilangos* in Providence are not "rich" in the usual sense of the term, but are nonetheless perceived to be members of the amorphous group known as *los ricos,* then this too provides a window into the experienced differences of class, race, ethnicity, region, and nation. As there are different ways to be poor and middle class, such labels reflect not simply identities in flux. Rather, they make up even more profoundly critical elements in negotiating class in spatially discontinuous communities.

We should avoid equally absurd extremes, neither idealizing national sovereignty nor heralding the advent of borderless hemispheres. Nation-state borders are not impregnable today, nor have they ever been. At the same time, borders such as that between the United States and Mexico are not simply metaphors of difference.

My friends and customers in the restaurant at the Galleria shopping mall in Houston were all Mexican. They had all made their way, individually, in families, or in other groups across the line that divides the sovereign state of Mexico from that of the United States. But they could not have had more dissimilar experiences. These Mexicans could not possibly view their border-crossing experiences, and how they came to find themselves in Gringolandia, as anything but dissimilar.

Rituals of Resistance, or, Diminished Expectations after Socialism

Intellectuals, frightened and spoiled by the powerful, often persecuted, consumers of quarrels and envy, are being uprooted from history by the same forces they helped illuminate: democracy, technology, the market, and socialist utopias.

Roger Bartra

THE ALLURE OF RESISTANCE

"You must have begun drinking when you were six," I teased Gabriel, as we sat in the warm June sun on a wall atop the extinct volcano Xitle in the mountains ringing southern Mexico City.

"No, even before that," he corrected me. "You know why I began before? Because maybe I've inherited something from my father. Maybe I began when I was conceived. That's when I began to drink. It might be. It might be something inherited."

"Genes?"

"Might be. Maybe an escape; it's the most likely. Sometimes, because of the way I think, I feel like I don't fit, in my family or in society. Maybe I don't have the channels for me to realize my potential. Sometimes I end up saying that only drunk and asleep can I forget how screwed up things are, because sometimes I don't have anyone to talk to about all my experiences, my worries, my traumas, my complexes. Because in my family, I feel. . . . In my marriage, I am not understood."

"And your friends? Can't you talk to them?" I asked.

"Sometimes we clash. I like to talk about everything, and I can't do it with them. Like religion, and when I make them see some mistake in

Figure 8. Gabriel Saavedra in 1998.

their way of looking at it. I figure if they weren't my friends, I wouldn't tell them about their mistakes, I could give a shit. But that's why we fight sometimes."

Gabriel's thirst for knowledge and learning and for engaged debate on questions philosophical and political is largely intellectual. He has participated in some marches to support the Chiapas Zapatistas, and he continues to argue against voting as a means to fundamental change in Mexican society. But mainly, in the ten years I have known him, Gabriel talks. He talks openly, sarcastically, and sometimes vehemently about current events, music, indigenous protests, agnosticism, student politics, snake tacos, the naming of children, and a long-ago-crushed dream of moving to Zihuatenejo on the Pacific Coast. He talks with friends, family, acquaintances, and basically anyone he can stop on Huehuetzin

Street who happens to be wandering by during the twelve- to fourteen-hour shifts Gabriel works six days a week. There, from eight in the morning, throughout the day, and often until nearly midnight with flashlights, a lamp, and even cigarette lighters, Gabriel repairs all manner of cars, vans, and trucks in the street and sidewalk in front of the cubbyhole workshop where he keeps his tools. In 1998 he had separated from his wife, and after this time Gabi saw his children only on Sundays. After the separation, he had begun living with his ailing mother in a small house not far from Huehuetzin Street.

One recurring theme in my discussions with Gabi over the years has concerned the question of significance: the significance of parents and how children inherit certain traits from them; the significance of political events and movements in effecting real change in society, especially as that change might relate to the inequality between rich and poor, Indian and mestizo; the significance of what people say in relation to what they think and what they do; and, perhaps on the grandest of all possible scales, the ephemeral significance of humans in a cosmic universe. This last topic had led us to a conversation that warm spring morning about the television series *Cosmos.*

"I watch Carl Sagan in the documentaries. He seems very good. This is one intelligent guy. Now, I haven't studied what I have learned. [Working] people don't have access to the kind of learning he does . . . there's no information . . . it's a small nucleus [of people who can do this kind of studying]. For people who work and sometimes don't have time or are tired, it's easier to have a documentary to watch. It's more practical and you can learn. I think it would be good to propose to the University [UNAM] something like this for the people.

"I know there exists a book, but I haven't had the opportunity to read it. It's translated into Spanish, and, truth is, I think it's got some really interesting things. It's helped me to understand more. When you understand what we are, well, you learn everything.

"Unfortunately people aren't attracted to the program, at least the youth aren't. How come? Actually, there's a lot of interest. I've read some astronomy books that have fallen into my hands, and everything Sagan says I have read in other books. These are the books they sell over there [on the streets surrounding the National University], and as they're less expensive, I buy them. Sometimes I find them tossed away. I've found really good books in the garbage, and the truth is that a book is a treasure."

Gabriel talked of acquaintances who were employed at UNAM who had argued with him about Sagan. They told Gabi that in the University they had already learned everything Sagan was talking about in his program, that he really had nothing new to offer.[1] Gabriel continued,

"So I know more about Sagan than about the University. The University gives classes at one in the afternoon, at two, and no worker can attend them. So, I told these people I was arguing with, 'Do you know what the value of Sagan is? For me, the value is that he's giving information, that you can learn from him. That's his value, and that's why I defend him.' What's a university worth if it's out of reach? And the truth is that you need a lot, a lot of time to learn, because there's so much to learn. And there's not enough time in the schedules of the workers.

"I have the cassettes" of *Cosmos*, Gabriel told me. "I had them taped. You don't see the picture well, but you can more or less make it out. It's really interesting because at any given moment it makes you feel like a flea, and at the same time it makes you feel important. Because I'm realizing what it is all about. I'm realizing that I'm learning things that I never even thought I was going to learn, learning about the nature of life. And I think, 'Even though it's no more than a passing fancy, I've learned a lot.' We want to have this *capacidad* [ability, knowledge]; I would like to have this *capacidad*."[2]

In Santo Domingo, as elsewhere in the world in the twenty-first century, popular theories of genetic inheritance have become a type of secular cosmology, imbuing those in the know with the capacity to explain the deepest and most perplexing of enigmas about human existence and cosmic infinity. For instance, Gabriel discusses his penchant for alcohol in terms of inherited traits, as a way of linking his proclivities to biological roots and in the process of deriving some sense of absolution for his sins. Although his remarks are often offered offhandedly, half-jokingly, nonetheless Gabi is not alone in attributing drinking proclivities to genes (see Gutmann 1999). In this way, problems like alcoholism may be characterized by those who suffer from this affliction as beyond the reach of rational remedies; if they are caused by "inside forces" that are amenable only to evolutionary mutations, then what is a poor problem drinker to do but accept with equanimity his or her biologically derived fate?

At the same time, Gabriel discusses both his pursuit of knowledge and his anger at those who demean such learning as unsophisticated, insinuating therefore that Gabriel is less truly well informed. What constitutes correct understanding, when has someone achieved a real, conscious grasp on an issue or topic, and how are these things measured?

Far from being confined to epistemological and cloistered scholarly towers, these questions make up the stuff of daily street discussions—at least if Gabriel has anything to say about the course of a conversation.

Indeed, while talking with my friend Roberto as he repaired the radiator of a beat-up old Chevy, I was reminded of Gabriel's fascination with *Cosmos*. As I had been gone from the *colonia* for several months, Roberto politely asked after my family. I said Michelle and the girls were visiting my in-laws in North Carolina. Without taking his eyes off the blowtorch he was using, Roberto nodded, "That's a little above Florida, no?" I expressed surprise that he knew so much about the geography of the United States. He said it came from helping his sons with their schoolwork. Roberto had not had much time to study as a child, but he maintained a keen interest in learning alongside his boys. He expressed real frustration at having to rely on so-called experts for his knowledge of the world. Yet, like Gabriel, his knowledge was a question of individual self-improvement and bore little relation to broader issues of social change.

At the same time, despite the fact that people like Roberto do not often give voice to broader issues of social change, underlying many discussions with him and others, and even more when talking with Gabriel, I have been struck by how frequently my friends find themselves grappling with the relationship between their understanding of events and their activity in trying to shape events. Others might call this connection a matter of consciousness and practice. And questions of consciousness and practice have been central indeed to recent theoretical work that goes under the rubric of "resistance."

In the fall of 1990, in my first semester of graduate school, I wrote a paper for Aihwa Ong's seminar on Resistance, a revised version of which was later published in *Latin American Perspectives* (see Gutmann 1993). The tone of the paper reflected the fact that I had just emerged from fifteen years of political activism, mainly in working-class areas of Chicago and Houston, and I was very disappointed to discover the growing influence of narrowly conceived theories of secret resistance. I was especially concerned with two issues: (1) that openly radical movements (both contemporary and historical) had been blithely relegated to the category of "suicidal" efforts, and (2) that poor people, because they were poor, were necessarily assumed to have far more understanding for their situation and for the solutions (or lack thereof) to their problems than I felt was warranted. The tone of the paper was meant to be one of alarm, and I stand by the basic points made there, while acknowledging that its effectiveness was diminished by the sharpness of the polemical edge in presenting these ideas. The present chapter is meant to expand, improve, and reaffirm my earlier arguments and conclusions.[3]

In the 1980s and 1990s in Mexico, many leftist intellectuals studied and championed the Popular Urban Movements. Instead of relying on the government to change the lives of the impoverished two-thirds of the Mexican population, destitute men and women in urban and rural areas had taken matters into their own hands, forged their own organizations, developed their own leaders, and built broad-based social movements grounded in the principles of self-reliance and self-government.[4]

At the same time in the United States, when many left-leaning intellectuals were licking their wounds in the wake of the antiwar and civil rights movements in the United States and the later collapse of the Soviet empire,[5] theories of resistance emerged that seemed to offer a panacea for those no longer able to believe in capacious theories, much less titanic social change, once known as socialism. Like some of the new social movement analysis, resistance theory represented another theoretical current, often more based on identity than on class categories. In an age and climate of Reaganism, retrenched political conservatism, and a fetishized diminution of expectations for substantial social transformations in the United States, theories of everyday forms of resistance became very popular in scholarly publications in the 1980s. As the new century approached, resistance theory (see, e.g., Scott 1985; 1990) had begun to attract attention in Latin America as well (see, e.g., Coronado Malagón 2000).

Undoubtedly, resistance theory has attracted disenchanted post-socialist converts in part because it speaks to the desire of many intellectuals to maintain their support for social underdogs and their hope that change will eventually come about and greater social equality will be realized. Yet, as we saw in chapter 2 with respect to theories and approaches to agency, much of the allure of resistance is romantic in nature (see Abu-Lughod 1990; Kearney 1996). In developing his analysis of the quixotic qualities of resistance theory, Harry Sanabria suggests that "we center more of our efforts on *ineffective* and *unsuccessful* resistance in order to understand better the contexts in which successful resistance can be achieved" (2000, 57). In other words, as with theories of agency, so too with theories of resistance, we need to account for both successes and failures, both activism and passivity, if these concepts are to be made truly helpful in understanding the twists and turns of social change.

For a variety of reasons, including periodic economic crises and frustrations with electoral politics, to many in Mexico in the 1990s progressive change appeared to be less realizable than in the 1980s, even as inequalities of all kinds seemed only to multiply. Many scholars in Mexico, as elsewhere, began to reconceptualize the question of the working classes and their ability to alter their political worlds. Conceptually, resistance theories complemented newly translated documents fresh from French poststructuralist theory which attributed power (and culpability) to everyone everywhere and not just to dominant groups. Thus, scholars utilizing resistance theories could continue to focus their attention on the poor and oppressed while redirecting their energies to micro-encounters of inequality, conflict, and subterfuge, within the context of greatly diminished expectations for the men and women unburdened by material and intellectual riches.

It is easy enough to support Gabriel and Roberto's personal claims to the right to knowledge. And we may and should admire Gabi's refusal to bow to the snobbishness of those who argue that Sagan dumbed down his program for the masses. If such determination and thirst for learning is not simply a good in itself, then when men like Gabriel and Roberto become more learned, even more self-aware, this can have implications for political life more broadly. And surely they may learn without seeking the permission of condescending saviors. But if this kind of self-awareness is led further than the romantic valorization of poor people and their ability to break through unflattering portraits of themselves, such knowledge must be measured in some sense against ignorance and complicity. Or, as Paul Willis has written, in describing a classic example of the inability of the dispossessed to use education as a tool to social mobility: "The destruction of official myths and illusions and a canny assessment of the world do not stop incorporation into that world" (1979, 178). This is also illustrated in Michael Kearney's (1996) lovely invocation of "*jujitzsu* politics," whereby the efforts of one contestant are used by an adversary to bring that person down. In other words, no matter how loathe theorists of change may be to attribute to the dispossessed any responsibility for their misery, co-optation, and duplicity, the recognition of knowledge in the sense of self-awareness requires nothing less.

If cosmic *capacidades* among the poor are celebrated in resistance theory as showing that the poor somehow "naturally" are able to comprehend a good deal more than leftist intellectuals ("One does not expect *Das Kapital* to come from working-class pubs, although one may get something quite close to the labor theory of value," writes James Scott [1985, 330]), we are less often provided with descriptions, much less explanations, as to what resistance may have achieved through the millennia beyond the "feel good" accomplishments of survival politics. In arguing for an integration of culture and political economy in post-colonial studies, Fernando Coronil suggests that we must avoid "essentialist interpretations that celebrate as resistance any form of subaltern response and adaptation" (1998, xii). It is precisely the "essential" abilities of the poor that concern us here. Although resistance theorists appear to celebrate the poor and dispossessed, and to highlight the significance of classes, of spontaneous consciousness arising from one's class position and the obviousness of exploitation to the exploited, they have dichotomized the world into hidden and open worlds, conscious and unconscious, public and private, resistance and accommodation. Yet mechanical economism to the contrary, class position and social being are not the same units of analysis.

In the guise of showing appreciation for economic contingencies—not unlike Gabriel's point regarding working people not having the ability to take classes at the University during the day, and along the lines of one's economic situation as determinant of one's ideology and understanding of the world—scholars who utilize an economist and mechanical materialist framework demonstrate an insufficient appreciation of more full-bodied class analysis. Gabriel and I have argued for years over the relationship between more strictly economic factors, consciousness, and social change. These discussions have helped lead me to the conclusion that the fundamental flaw in much resistance theory is not that it lacks an account of utopian fancy among the oppressed but rather that so many of these concepts about microresistance leading eventually to monumental transformations are one-sidedly idealistic. Indignant over past overly optimistic predictions of social change brought about by national liberation movements and other large-scale social struggles, resistance theorists too often fall prey to equally romantic versions of hidden and covert activities leading eventually to significant ruptures with the status quo. In concluding her essay on the romance of resistance, Lila Abu-Lughod points to the need to learn from the myriad means employed by those suffering from systems of oppression:

> The problem has been that those of us who have sensed that there is something admirable about resistance have tended to look to it for hopeful confirmation of the failure—or partial failure—of systems of oppression. Yet it seems to me that we respect everyday resistance not just by arguing for the

dignity or heroism of the resistors but by letting their practices teach us about the complex interworkings of historically changing structures of power. (1990, 53)

As long as the poor and oppressed are tacitly treated as instinctual animals whose ignorance and knowledge is an involuntary consequence of their being poor and oppressed, questions of political and social consciousness will continue to be considered inappropriate, and discussion of illusions, delusions, and fantasies will be seen as vulgar.

TWO ARMIES AND CLASS ANTAGONISMS

Among the most important issues for resistance theory is the rather automatic association and attribution of resistant spirits and actions to people because of their income and wealth. Whether they are labeled as subaltern, poor, underclass, proletarian, or working class, the assumption on the part of many advocates of resistance theory is that those in the lower economic stratum understand at least the broad outlines of their immiseration at the hands of the dominant classes. That is why they do nothing, at least nothing visible to one not trained in resistance theory—because they know *too* much. The underdog subalterns are *too* smart to risk what little they have in doomed adventurism of the overt, organized variety.

Strangely enough, for all the value thus supposedly placed on class, the poor are rather ill-served by such a theoretical framework. There is a tendency to mistake class position for class relations, to confuse economics with ideology, as if all who are poor think and act alike. Thus, there is a related penchant to underestimate the importance of religion, gender, age, and other invidious distinctions like "politics" within specific class formations. And if classes are treated homogeneously, the very issue of political analysis may be too often and too perfunctorily relegated to the realm of the involuntary and unavoidable—at least for the poor. For intellectuals, a process of shedding romantic silliness is required to attain enlightenment.

In an effort to reaffirm the importance of class—never easy in the United States, and never more difficult than in the early part of the twenty-first century—it is oddly necessary to emphasize precisely the heterogeneity internal to broad categories like the working class. In short, and to employ military parlance to exaggerate the point, it is simultaneously necessary to highlight the ongoing weight of class antago-

Figure 9. Pro-life announcement near Santo Domingo, 1998: Tubal ligations and vasectomies can give you cancer and diminish your sexual appetite.

nisms in Mexican society that belie notions of class being subsumed by other social hierarchies, and to note that such class antagonisms seldom if ever take the form of two opposing armies, one of the rich and the other of the poor.[6] For the poor and dispossessed themselves in Mexico City, political schisms are characteristic and of tremendous importance. Identifying and discussing political differences within families and among friends is a recurring focus of attention in Santo Domingo. That these divisions exist for innumerable reasons in no way diminishes their relevance to political life in neighborhoods there. In fact, they are very related to compliant and defiant currents, as people debate about which social problems are within their power to change and which they believe to be more obdurate and unchangeable.

In the course of living and working in Mexico City for more than a decade, I have often been asked, "How have people accepted you in Santo Domingo?" An ingenuous question for a Gringo to ask, perhaps, this query has as often as not come from friends who are Mexican intellectuals. As if the more than 100,000 people in Santo Domingo, even if they all knew me, would react to me in a uniform fashion. Partly what is evident here is a common assumption about the social homogeneity of others, all the more exaggerated in reference to those who are less formally educated.[7] Resistance theorists correctly criticize the equation of formal education with enlightenment as merely a manifestation of elite condescension. Yet in a not-so-complicated manner resistance theory argues merely for the flip side of this generalization: poverty equates to some kind of reflexive enlightenment.

How women and men have accepted me or not in Santo Domingo has depended on a variety of factors not limited by the fact I am a Gringo or by my relatively more privileged status, first as a graduate student and then as a professor. Indeed, at least initially, in my relationships with many in the *colonia*, I was regarded and treated in a rather standard way, as a glamorized Gringo exotic. This assumption led some to believe that I was wealthy. Others imputed, purely from my Gringoness, that I lead a sexually libertine lifestyle.

So it seems that my friends, too, also dichotomize the world of classes all the time. They make constant references to *clases altas, clases populares, la clase media, la gente humilde, los ricos,* or *los con lana* (those with money). *Los ricos* are a constant source of comparison, the target of ridicule and the object of defensive self-validation. As with many resistance theorists, with my friends I think there is a need to venture beyond the commonplace understanding that *con dinero baile el perro,* that even dogs will dance if you give them money. Not surprisingly for a country in which one of the classic statements on national identity is an unremitting attack on the poor urban *pelado* ("Why can't they be more cosmopolitan, or at least mestizo middle class?" Ramos [(1934) 1962] seemed to ask[8]), men in Santo Domingo are especially sensitive about the perception on the part of the wealthy classes that men in the working class are *animales* and *brutos.* Basing their class prejudices on social divisions of labor—mental labor (for the wealthy) and manual labor (for the workers), men in the *colonia* sometimes ground their own narrow-minded class analysis in other forms of corporal inclinations. In an inversion of the "animality" image that reveals preconceptions about the links between sexual behavior and "animal urges," some male acquaintances in Santo Domingo have casually informed me over the years that *homosexualidad,* or *homosexualismo,* is far more common in the upper classes. The insinuation they wish to communicate to me is that men from the working class are more cultured: at least they know with whom they are supposed to have sex.

In a sense, such value-ranking is not so different from the insistence of several university professors that the poor in Mexico City drink Bacardí Blanco, whereas they would never touch a Mexican rum, especially, as one psychologist insisted to me, because of the horrible *cruda* (hangover) produced by Bacardí Blanco. In the mid-1990s, for instance, the Nicaraguan product, Flor de Caña, or the Cuban, Havana Club, were the rums of choice at many faculty parties.[9]

Although societies never divide into two neatly composed and opposing armies of the haves and the have-nots, as one might infer from unsophisticated versions of resistance theory, the challenge is to preserve class as a foundational framework for social analysis, to not lose the forest for the trees. Describing and conceptualizing class relations, including how class position is rarely a simplistic marker for one's outlook and behavior, certainly requires accounts that highlight hidden and covert resistance as a rich source of coping and struggle among the dispossessed. The point is not to reduce all social life of opposition to these solitary forms, in the contemporary world, in the past, or in the future.

SURVIVAL

Social Darwinists ask: "Why don't they try to better themselves?" Progressives ask: "Why do they put up with it?" In an effort to explain political drowsiness and inactivity on the part of the poor in the face of truly horrendous living conditions, social critics of various kinds may resort to "survival strategies" as an explanation. In the case of resistance theory, the need to survive is often contrasted with more impractical thinking on the part of some ditzy intellectuals, at least those who share unrealistic dreams of actually changing the world, which resistance theorists hold to be as impracticable as the need to survive is authentic.

As Pedro, Enrique, and I leaned on the car of a friend talking one day in the *colonia,* we were approached by two men who had emerged from "*la casa de los borrachos,*" a house down the street, where very desperate alcoholics come to drink a type of *pulque* that had been fermented with human excrement. We knew them both—as the joke went, they were among the "*borrachos conocidos*" (known drunks) on Huehuetzin Street, as opposed to the "*alcólicos anónimos*" (anonymous alcoholics). So as Jaime and his partner approached, we politely greeted them. When Jaime reached us, he slipped off his Yankees jacket and asked us to buy it from him—any price at all would be "okay." We thanked him but said we already had jackets. He then left, only to return a few minutes later with a small nylon bag that he tried to sell to us for "five pesos."[10] Then Jaime offered his baseball cap for the same price. "Five pesos?" he asked. "No? Okay, then, how about three pesos?" Jaime was mainly directing his sales pitch to Pedro, perhaps because Pedro is known to carry more loose cash than many on the street. Initially, Pedro just smiled and shook his head, declining the exchange. Finally, Enrique reached into his pocket and gave Jaime a two-peso coin, saying something about *cooperación* as he did. Pedro followed by handing over a five-peso coin, and I gave two pesos.

On Huehuetzin Street in Santo Domingo, people often "cooperate" with each other in these and similar ways. The word *cooperación* is invoked to describe activities that some might label "wino panhandling," or a "hidden form of resistance," or "proletarian self-reliance," or simply a popular form of sharing what little wealth there is.[11] The retired grandfather Juan told me one morning in January 1997 that he had visited his sister the day before. (He thought I'd be interested because I had once bought a few hundred tamales from this same sister, in July 1993, for the celebration of my daughter Liliana's first birthday.) But, Juan said, he had not eaten with his sister or brother-in-law. The latter had been unemployed for many months and as a result he and Juan's sister were really feeling financially pinched. Juan told me that until her death in November 1996, Angela had been "cooperating" with her sister-in-law by giving her oil and other cooking necessities every week.

The term *cooperation* describes an important aspect of survival strategies among the poor in Colonia Santo Domingo. But not for all of them. Late one night, restless, I heard muffled footsteps outside and looked through my window to investigate. I saw my neighbor, an older woman who had always declined to talk with me, other than to exchange greetings. I also noticed that she was standing beside a pile of cement blocks that had not been there earlier in the day. They must have just been delivered and left on the sidewalk outside my neighbor's house, because she was now in the process of moving the bricks inside her gate, one or two bricks at a time. I was thinking about going out to offer her my help, when another neighbor, perhaps as sleepless as I, passed by and I saw them exchange a few words. She then waved him off with a worried frown and continued to move her bricks. It would take her hours, but it seemed that she would rather spend her night safeguarding those cement blocks than risk their theft.[12]

If theft is carried out against factory managers, it is considered by resistance theorists to be a good illustration of the covert measures (the hidden transcripts) employed by social outcasts against their oppressors. For the poor, however, theft is most often associated with the worst of what the poor do to each other.

Revolutionaries and social scientists have long debated when and why particular sectors of a population will rebel against their conditions of life—and why, more often, they usually do not.[13] Resistance theory has filled what some regard as an important gap in theories of social change, that is, it attempts to explain what the poor and oppressed do about their situation most of the time. Thus, resistance theorists would say, the seeds of slow, incremental, millennial change may be seen in the micropolitics of life's daily interactions, as exemplified by such phenomena as *cooperación* or theft in Santo Domingo. These types of phenomena are sometimes held to be especially relevant for certain population groups whose options appear to be more restricted than those of other groups. Migrants from the countryside to the cities of Latin America, women, and indigenous peoples were, until the 1980s at least, often discussed in anthropological and other literature as fated to political inactivity because of structural constraints, which in turn led to greater vulnerability, and hence in general to a tremendous reluctance to enter into political challenges to the status quo.[14]

One central tenet of much contemporary theory on social change is that, being more innately insightful than intellectuals, the poor are simply too wise to physically fight the status quo. James Scott, for instance, writes: "The situation for most subordinate classes historically" is one which "surely sets limits that only the foolhardy would transgress" (1985, 247), as if people (a.k.a., "the foolhardy") did not still sacrifice their lives in a variety of overt forms of rebellion each and every day. Others who conceptualize these matters argue less for the inherent good judgment of the underdogs and more for recent changes in warfare tactics that have rendered military conflict between classes anachronistic; in this analysis, the sheer firepower of the ruling classes and the inability of the ruled to defend themselves adequately mean the end to armed utopian movements (see, e.g., Castañeda 1993).

In part because they have historically utilized more pacific forms of struggle, like sit-ins, demonstrations, rent strikes, petitions, and rallies, many in Mexico and Latin America have been attracted to the Popular Urban Movements and new social movements to supply the stimulus and leadership for fundamental change. Yet, questions remain. As Judith Adler Hellman asked in the mid-1990s, "Is there any evidence that the Mexican movements observed by these scholars in the late 1980s subsequently contributed to the institutionalization of democratic expression?" (1994a, 125). Indeed, such movements proved to be no substitute for political parties, in part because they focused so exclusively on questions of immediate needs, that is, survival. The dilemma has been that such problems, no matter how pressing, cannot be genuinely re-solved in a piecemeal fashion. For this reason, Roger Bartra noted that, in the 1980s and 1990s in Mexico, although many people believed that the new social movements would provide the necessary impulse from below for "the great transformation" that would incorporate the na-tionalist and populist social programs first demanded by these move-ments, and notwithstanding the fact that such movements successfully mobilized tens of thousands of citizens to achieve certain reforms, social disparities of nearly every kind continued to grow during this same pe-riod (1999, 70–71).

Elements of this confusion regarding the origins of change, and how to bring about social transformations, were also evident in the conflict that developed among Latin American feminists in the 1990s, namely, whether they should work within or against the state. Among the varied options discussed and debated among feminists throughout the Améri-cas in this period were: (1) maintaining complete independence from government policies and programs; (2) actively becoming involved in such governmental efforts, as representatives of state institutions; and (3) cooperating on specific government programs, but criticizing oth-ers when appropriate and maintaining an absolute autonomy in terms of decision making and leadership (see Alvarez 1998; León 1994; and Molyneux 2001).

In Mexico, the uprising in Chiapas of 1994 has obviously been a case much debated in this respect, especially as to the significance of the armed component of the original rebellion, the significance of the ongo-ing threat of offensive military operations by the Zapatistas, and the goal of armed self-defense, albeit limited, on the part of the indigenous in-surgents. Certainly, the EZLN has provided an implicit counterpoint with respect to methods of struggle when compared to the Popular Ur-ban Movements and other kinds of mass social struggles that have been resolutely pacifist, if occasionally employing civil disobedience to force their demands to be heard.

Perhaps because of their precarious situation, most of the time most of the world's people are able to focus on little else beyond enduring their miserable existence. Perhaps it is only privileged intellectuals who have the luxury to dream about other forms of human sociality and who have actual opportunities to attempt to realize their utopian schemes for alternative futures. In Mexico, in 1995, one in four Mexicans still lived in dwellings without sewage disposal; more than 50 percent of towns in the country were classified as extremely poor; and despite the fact that poverty in Mexico is worse in rural areas and among indigenous peoples, the highest mortality rate in the country was in the Federal District (see PAHO 1998, 356–57). Or, to put the matter more frankly, in the words of a friend, Omar, who grew up in a *vecindad* in downtown Mexico City, "Mateo, do you know what it's like to grow up poor? You can't even take a crap in private, Mateo. You share everything when you have no money."

It appears to many that the poor have little time or energy for political change on a grand scale, and on the face of it, this argument may seem solid, grounded, and reasonable. It is similar, perhaps, to Gabriel's comments cited earlier regarding the difficulties of attending University classes for those who are working all day. Yet, what are we to make of religion and cosmology? Certainly the poor, disenfranchised, and indigent throughout history have demonstrated an ample willingness and ability to seek answers and solutions to the largest, most abstract issues of their times. And religion surely must be understood as more than a mere balm and opiate for the oppressed, as it has also provided a profound source of philosophical wrangling and ethical guidance related to social change. And this, despite the abhorrent living conditions that the vast majority of women and men have had to endure throughout recorded history.

And what about sports? At least among men, there is a fanaticism devoted to sporting events, athletes, and teams, and more significantly for our purposes here, detailed attention is paid to the highly complex nuances in strategy, history, human relations, and political leadership as manifested in sporting events—from the *futbol* games of the National University team, the Pumas, to the neighborhood basketball pickup scrimmages. The sophistication and knowledge required to seriously follow such sports activities undermines the notion that workers are generally so tired and/or so dull that abstractions and mental challenges of any but the simplest kind are beyond their normal abilities, and that at best, those who earn their living from manual tasks are capable merely of irrational convictions and fanciful imaginings.

Rather than succumb in embarrassed silence to charges that religious and revolutionary ideologies both require the same leap of irrational faith, and that, as such, they represent no fitting response to the exigencies of survival, we might seek instead to explore the links between ideas and actions, and to ask what such faith might be worth to the desperately poor (see Lancaster 1988). And as for religious faith, as Graham Greene famously wrote in *The Power and the Glory*, his 1940 novel of a whiskey priest and anti-Catholic repression in postrevolutionary Mexico, it is available to all:

> It was for this world that Christ had died: the more evil you saw and heard about you, the greater glory lay around the death; it was too easy to die for what was good or beautiful, for home or children or a civilization—it needed a God to die for the half-hearted and the corrupt. ([1940] 1962, 131)

Interested in talking more with people in and around Santo Domingo about articles of faith and the role of the Catholic Church in matters of survival, I spoke with Daniel Enríquez, who shed light on this question of the spiritual links between social change and the religious ethos of the Christian Base Communities at the Iglesia de la Resurrección, to which he belonged. Daniel spoke to me about a liberation theology priest he had known:

"I knew this priest, only I don't remember his name. He was with the little chapel called Anunciación. It used to be a little chapel made of nothing but stones and an asbestos roof. *Bien humlidísima* [Really poor]. He was someone who helped. A wild enthusiasm for getting on with the youths. He saw that they were in a little group drinking beer. 'Get over here. Stop doing that.' He was with the people, and I began to get interested in that, in the talks he was giving."

"You weren't with the youths who were drinking a lot?" I asked Daniel.

"No. I've never drunk much. It was the ones he saw. I liked that whole scene with him, because the truth is that here in our Mexico you don't see people who are worried about change too much. It's sad but true. That's the way it is."

Some people in Mexico worry about change more than others, of course. In Santo Domingo, for many, there existed a cultural cachet in associating oneself with certain kinds of change. For instance, some people in the *colonia* claimed to have been among the original invaders of 1971. This was a matter of political prestige, and a means by which people sought to establish their militant credentials and their impoverished background. People could establish these credentials through reference to particular survival strategies, with the most impressive strategies being those that had solved social, and not simply individual, problems. If you had arrived in Santo Domingo after the original invasion, there was a greater likelihood that you had bought your parcel of land, unlike the earliest settlers who had made their claims as squatters.

Laying claim to this kind of cultural capital represented a form of re-verse snobbism among the residents of Santo Domingo.

Nonetheless, not everyone was as eager to invoke personal histories of survival, which is why some balked at using the term *invasion* when they discussed the colonization of the area. Some were most reluctant to refer to their occupation of the *colonia* as an invasion. At a community meeting one evening in October 1992, a man got up to speak about land titles "*antes de la invasión*" (before the invasion), then quickly corrected himself by adding, "*Mejor dicho, antes de cuando tuvieramos la pose-sión de la tierra*" (Or rather, before we took possession of the land).

Survival is not in itself an explanation for activity and inactivity. It is a term employed to suggest material pressures that lead to either action or apathy. As talk of survival strategies often brings into play popular politics and political differences among those "just trying to survive," it is crucial not to underestimate the ability of people like the residents of Colonia Santo Domingo to rise above immediate concerns and, to be sure, even needs. Or, to put it another way, we should not fail to appre-ciate the ability of some people some of the time in the *colonia* to draw connections between their own pressing survival needs and larger fac-tors that shape their material and spiritual lives.

HUMAN RIGHTS AND MENTAL MACHISMO

Daniel Enríquez, from the Christian Base Communities, wanted to make something clear to me in our discussion of faith, survival, and Catholi-cism. "We recognize that the needs of other countries are very different than our own," he explained. "Why? Because, basically, we don't have any wars in Mexico, thank God. In Guatemala there are guerrillas, in Nicaragua there are guerrillas. There are problems. There is hunger. If people from these places don't want to participate in the war there, they escape, they come here. And we help them, we give them support. This is an important change, because it's no longer a question of, 'Oh, that's another country, why should it matter to us?' It is a human being who matters to us because we can also see ourselves in their mirror who knows when.

"There's a lot of support for Central America in the Iglesia [de la Re-surrección]. Just a little while ago, Rigoberta Menchú came to the Igle-sia. It was a tremendous experience. That's why the Iglesia is so impor-tant. For the way it treats the people. Because it is concerned with the people. A total concern. The same priests, with help from other professionals, come to give talks about human rights. There is a human rights group in the Iglesia, because there have been a lot of problems around here, and the police have come, beating people, carrying out searches. But we now know how to defend ourselves, what belongs to us and what shouldn't happen.

"It's a way to help each other, not so much in the material sense, but more in terms of human concerns."

Nobel laureate Rigoberta Menchú had been a prominent figure for several years in the Pedregales, as elsewhere in Latin America and, indeed, other parts of the world. This was undoubtedly one factor that lent fuel to the fires of controversy that now surround her 1984 autobiography after journalist-turned-anthropologist David Stoll wrote a 1999 critique of Menchú and of her image.[15] In a 1992 ceremony that took place at the Templo Mayor, one block from the Zócalo in the historic center of Mexico City, Rigoberta Menchú gave her Nobel Peace Prize medal to "the Mexican people" for safekeeping. Then President Carlos Salinas de Gortari accepted the medal and agreed to keep it "until such a time as conditions in Guatemala change," gratuitously adding several platitudes about "Indian rights" in Mexico being sacred.[16] As we viewed the ceremony on television, one of Angela's daughters told me that she saw her mother as the Rigoberta Menchú of Santo Domingo. Although Menchú was *una indígena* (an Indian)—and therefore not someone with whom a mestiza should be casually equated—Angela's daughter argued that her mother nevertheless resembled Menchú in that she was similarly very articulate and able to voice the concerns of her community.

How one understands and copes with change is regulated, in part, by popular conceptions about spurs and obstacles to such transformations. In Mexico City, it is rather routine to level slights against the rural campesino, as when Daniel Enríquez told me in our conversation in 1993 of his family in the provinces of the state of Guanajuato:

"In Guanajuato people are very much dedicated to their work in the fields. There is little interest in learning, in education and changing work from farm work to something more formal, in a factory, an office, et cetera, et cetera. Why is there still no interest? Because in Guanajuato they still have *la tendencia del campo* [the rural ways], they don't have the vision of getting out of there, of getting ahead. They see it as, 'This is the land that my parents worked, and here's where I am going to work the land, and where my children will have to work the land.' They have ideas so deeply rooted in not changing."[17]

Others might point to Daniel's church affiliation as evidence of a similar conservative traditionalism, which is why he enjoyed comparing his Christian Base Community to the dominant Catholic Church hierarchy. Although both are in a sense defined by faith, with the former, Daniel said, faith referred to the possibility of learning, of raising consciousness and effecting change. With the latter, on the contrary, faith resided in the belief that accounts would be settled only in the afterlife, that one must accept one's lot in life here on earth and devote one's efforts to patiently waiting.

Daniel Enríquez puts great store in what people think, and in the relationship between ideas and actions. In a discussion about parenting, and what mothers and fathers do differently with their children, he offered the common observation that frequently men consider that they have fulfilled their duties once they have financially provided for the family. Then, according to Daniel, when women complain that the men are not earning enough to support the family well, the men too often resort to drink.

"When it comes to alcoholism, there's still no equality [between men and women]; nor does God want there to be any. There are lots of complaints [from women] about money not being enough for this, not enough for that. And [for men] the refuge is alcohol. It's lunacy. This is what happens because machismo still prevails. But it's not a physical machismo; it's a mental machismo."

We might say that for Daniel Enríquez, both men and women in such households apparently employed a certain type of agency, although of course Daniel would not have used just that term. Still, by simply acknowledging that even in the most destitute of circumstances individual women and men have decisions to make, that they have some power within their lives to choose between alternatives, was for Daniel not the same as pretending that people always utilize their agency in helpful ways. Evidently, Daniel believes that the struggle over attitudes and opinions waged by the Christian Base Communities is at heart a matter of promoting progressive change in the face of traditional thoughts and practices and a way to oppose currents of conservative change.

PROTESTAS, MARCHAS, AND PLANTONES

Following the 1994–95 financial crisis in Mexico, a particularly heated topic of debate in Santo Domingo concerned the *marchas* and *plantones* (demonstrations and occupations) that were being carried out by one or another group protesting austerity measures. Invariably, the opinion a person in the *colonia* may have held about the protests that blocked traffic in the downtown Centro area was determined more by his or her general political sympathies than by how much and how often he or she had been personally inconvenienced by the events. Whether or not the protests were viewed with contemptuous scorn or accepted as a necessary nuisance, such political activities were undoubtedly seen as one of the only means that poor people had at their disposal if they wanted to change social policies. Or more precisely, *marchas* and *plantones* were among the few options available for open street protests (*política de la calle*). As such, such street politics are exemplary of a defiant politics, in which defiance "presumes intent," in the words of Susan Eckstein (1989a, 11).

Obviously, marches, sit-ins and other occupations did not begin in 1994. In fact, in Santo Domingo, such protests constitute an important part of the *colonia*'s history, going back to its earliest days after the original invasion. At one of the regular meetings of block-captains in Santo Domingo that I attended in 1992, for instance, the debate was about how the *colonia* could help residents who still lacked proper deeds establishing ownership of their land to "regularize" their plots. A woman suggested they should write an open letter to President Carlos Salinas. A man next to her said they should explore the possibility of paying to publish the letter in the newspapers *Novedades* and *Excelsior*. Another woman reminded those present that in the previous year, rather than writing a letter that would be "ignored by Carlos" (as she referred, scornfully, to the President of the Republic), they had organized a *marcha* and *plantón* at the Zócalo. She insisted that such protests were the only way to get those in authority to really notice. Among other things, the woman's comments confirmed both the importance of open, overt "resistance" and also the difficulty of compartmentalizing resistance into categories of overt and covert in the first place. That is, in such a forum—not open to just anyone, but certainly not as confidential as a discussion in the woman's kitchen would have been—residents of Santo Domingo slid more easily than many resistance theorists would have been able to do from secretive to transparent forms of struggle. Since the first days of the invasion of Santo Domingo in September 1971, when men and women gathered around rock piles and discussed how to contend with municipal authorities and the periodic incursions of police into their makeshift squatter camps, it has been similarly difficult to distinguish between activity that constitutes hidden forms of resistance and that which represents overt kinds of confrontational politics.

In January 1997, on my first visit back to Santo Domingo since Angela had died in November the year before, Juan and Héctor offered to drive me to visit her crypt, which was then located near Metro Río Consulado on the north side of the city.[18] In order to get to the crypt, we tried heading in their car straight through downtown but quickly found ourselves in a traffic jam several kilometers south of the Centro. We never figured out for sure what had caused all the traffic, but as we sat there going nowhere, both Juan and Héctor launched into a spirited condemnation of marches, protests, and occupations in general. It did not matter, Héctor insisted as he leaned over to look at me in the back seat, who might be demonstrating—students, campesinos, workers, or some other trouble makers—the demonstrations were futile, disruptive, and most annoying. Juan, who was driving, added that all I had to do to learn about the ineffectiveness of protests like these was listen to the television news. Weren't the TV announcers correct that so many stopped cars greatly exacerbated the already high levels of wintertime pollution in the city? They explained it all quite clearly on television, Juan said, and he was convinced that the media's analysis of protesters who were out of synch with the population overall was overwhelmingly accurate and fair.

Such diverse opinions about *protestas, marchas,* and *plantones* among residents of Santo Domingo, and their even more varied practical relationship to such activities, are integral to the political processes and struggles in the *colonia.* As Marc Abélès has written, political meetings and street demonstrations are major rituals in many societies. That street demonstrators "brandish symbols of antagonism," such as slogans and banners, amid shouts and heckles, serves to illustrate "an undercurrent of violence." And such rites "punctuate circumstances in which political life takes a more agitated turn" (1997, 324). For those like Juan and Héctor who usually disapprove of marching and demonstrating, these rituals of protest have become a lightning rod spurring them to further resentment. For the protesters themselves, their understanding of the significance of their actions is undoubtedly more varied. For some, participation in these activities is seen as the only option left them. Others, however, may suspect that even the more agitated rituals represent sometimes little more than another means by which to legitimize those whose policies are the target of the protest.

Moreover, odd as it may seem, protest does not always entail actual opposition to the target of dissent. Protests can also be ritualized and used to legitimize the powers of the status quo. Paraphrasing Max Gluckman's (1960) famous discussion of rites of rebellion, David Kertzer has shown that, "in spite of their apparent delegitimating intent, such rites can serve to reinforce existing power inequalities . . . [as] people are able to ventilate their natural resentments of occupying inferior places in society and, in so doing, allow the system to continue" (1988, 54–55). Then, too, as Kertzer notes: "Ritual can provide a basis for resistance and revolt. Indeed, lack of a hierarchically organized political organization and military inferiority are often closely related" (168).[19] Acting as safety valves and sops, protests can validate the powers that be, as Stanley Brandes has shown in his 1988 analysis of fiestas in rural Mexico: insofar as protests actually defy existing social relations, they can upset them. Either way, however, rarely is resistance or protest so one-sided and clearly delineated that it represents some kind of pure political action which is thoroughly absent any significant countervailing impulses and effects.[20] Further, as mentioned, a theory that purports to make covert forms of resistance the sum total of all significant contemporary struggles by oppressed peoples is necessarily disinclined to recognize counterexamples when they do occur. In this respect, Michael Kearney has pointed out that "resistance theory sees no cleavage places, no lines of fissure along which large-scale oppositions might form" (1996, 157).

Among my friends in Colonia Santo Domingo who are more inspired by protests and marches, a recurring reason for their support is an expressed feeling that through these actions they become more aware of how much they have in common with people who otherwise seem to have dissimilar life experiences. Many friends talk about the kindred feelings evoked by allegiances across class, ethnic, and political lines— what some might term "cross-class alliances"—whether the support is for those who favor or oppose a particular *marcha,* or for demands of a specific group of protesters. The community activist Doña Fili was not alone in the 1990s in her admiration for the Barzón debtors' movement. In its own right, and as an indication that people in different social strata may share significant experiences and goals, the Barzón stood as an example for many in Santo Domingo of widespread suffering among people in Mexico following the crisis of 1994–95. Events in Chiapas since that time have similarly drawn together people from a variety of social backgrounds, based principally on their political opinions of the EZLN.

In the view of several friends in the *colonia,* at least the Zapatistas were attempting to protest something—the implementation of NAFTA—when they rose up in 1994. So, three years after the rebellion in Chiapas, on New Year's Day 1997, I sat talking to Gabi and our neighbor Luciano about the Zapatistas and the Agreement. Both Gabriel and Luciano kept trying to get me to tape a performance of a *cómico* (comedian) whose main shtick was ridiculing NAFTA. I tried (only somewhat successfully) to explain that the people in the United States were less interested in what comics might have to say than in what the people of Huehuetzin Street were thinking about NAFTA, the Northamericanization of Mexico, the EZLN, and such issues.

As a way to link these two issues—political struggle and foreign encroachment/control of people indigenous (*naturales*) to the area—Gabriel began talking about the history of Indians from the time of Spanish conquest in the early sixteenth century until the early 1900s, and the relevance of this history for people in Mexico in the 1990s. Among other things, Gabi asserted that the word *México* itself reflected the oppression of the Indians under colonial rule, as, he said, it originated with the Spanish, who had repeatedly declared to the Mexica (Aztec) people they encountered after their arrival: "*Mexica, ¡no! Mexica ¡no!*" This negation of the Mexica people, Gabriel insisted, became the contraction *México.* Thus, the history of Mexico in the last five hundred years constitutes a dismissal of the pre-Hispanic ethnic identity of the people Gabi most closely identified with the ancestral land of the Mexicas.

A couple of years later, in August 1999, Doña Fili was telling me about the prospects of uniting different oppressed peoples to do something about their conditions. There were some lessons to be learned from the Zapatistas, in particular, Fili advised me:

"When something comes up, people get together. If it's important, in any given moment, people unite. You can hand out five thousand leaflets and people won't unite. I think that when it's something spontaneous, people get together. When the Zapatistas came, there was very good support from the people. Really good! Even the organizers expected it."

"When was this?" I asked.

"March 21, 1999," Fili told me.

In March 1999, there had been a Gran Consulta Popular of the EZLN. Throughout Mexico, Zapatistas met with various representatives of social and academic organizations. In Mexico City, they met with anthropologists in academic centers, passersby in the main downtown Zócalo, and thousands of residents of *colonias populares* like Santo Domingo in the neighborhoods themselves. Recounting the Zapatistas visit to Santo Domingo, Fili continued:

"The response was very good. There was a lot of support for the Zapatistas who came here to Santo Domingo. They went all about, and wherever they went people crowded around. Even a little drunk came over from [the neighboring community of] Los Reyes. And he said to them, 'Ah, you are the Zapatistas.' And they told him, 'Yes.' They speak very clearly, very sweet. I had thought they would be more combative [*milicianos*]. But they're really sweet. 'Ah, well, I want you to come to my home. You are going to stay with me. What do you need?' And the Zapatistas told the drunk, 'No, thanks. Really we're just hanging out with the *compañeros*.' At La Resurrección [the Christian Base Community church], we had to get in line, not to cross ourselves to Jesus, but to greet the Zapatistas!"

CONSCIOUSNESS AND CULTURAL COMPLICITY

In an essay on the paradoxes of foreign–local encounters in Latin America, Steve Stern has argued that popular strategies of resistance and survival have "failed to preclude conflicts of interests and values and competing strategies of survival among subalterns" (1998a, 49). One of Stern's chief concerns is to show how resistance theory is hobbled in explaining situations in which subalterns may be "partly complicit" with colonializing powers.

In addressing these questions of consciousness and complicity, contingent concerns about motivation and intent inexorably arise. Without reverting to a discussion of evolutionary psychology and cognitive linguistics, suffice it to say that I take as axiomatic that people are able to express meanings, to give meaning to their own actions and those of others, albeit to a greater or lesser degree, and at certain times better than others. This is true regardless of how fragmentary and partial and processual the route of interpretation of meanings and explanation of actions may have been. That ethnographies are distinguished by the personalities of their authors, we hope, is cause for celebration as much as distress.

Without oversimplifying already overwrought debates regarding scholars' abilities to peek inside the intentions and motivations of other people, I believe that most of my neighbors and acquaintances in Colonia Santo Domingo make claim to understanding the views of others. They think that, at least some of the time, they know why people act as they do. Ethnography is in part a record of this kind of insight.

With respect to learning what people think, feel, and do, as with psychoanalysts, ethnographers are limited by their own ability to listen, empathize, and analyze.[21] The recent attention to agency stems not only from a backlash of simplistic critiques of Marxist theories of false consciousness and from a further delegitimization of socialism, but also, in a more positive vein, from a desire on the part of many social theorists to understand and account for the intentional, subjective actions on the part of nonelites, including in the realm of resistance. The trick, as Herzfeld writes (1997, 23), is not to adopt an overexcited appraisal of either the politically successful or the politically weak.

Héctor once took me to a neighbor's house in Santo Domingo. A girl, around fifteen years old, answered the door after he knocked. She showed us into a dank, filthy hovel. As our eyes became accustomed to the darkness, we walked further into the house, stepping over a child who was asleep on a mattress on the floor. It was a very sad home. As we stood next to the mattress, several small children, no more than three or four years old, silently emerged from another room. I shuddered as I remembered being in an eerily similar setting many years before, that time in the Ozarks of Arkansas. Impetuously determined to put "Easy Rider" myths to the test, in 1972 I had decided to hitchhike from Chicago through the Deep South during spring break. Caught in a rainstorm in the Ozark mountains, a band of small children who saw me walking down the road invited me to escape the downpour in their one-room house. Once inside, I was shocked to discover a woman who appeared to be catatonic slowly rocking in a chair in the corner. Even more disturbing to me, the children seemed as oblivious of her as she was of them. This house in Santo Domingo now reminded me of the Ozark experience. To make the parallel more complete, Héctor informed me that the children here lived without adult supervision because both their parents had died and they had no other known adult relatives to care for them.

Many years ago, in "The Eighteenth Brumaire of Louis Bonaparte," Karl Marx wrote famously that "the great mass of the French nation is formed by simple addition of homologous magnitudes, much as potatoes in a sack form a sack of potatoes" ([1852] 1969, 478–79). Now I do not wish to imply that the children in these two houses, one in Mexico City and the other in the middle of the Ozarks, were entirely without self-awareness. But I am also reluctant to attribute some great source of wisdom to those who evidently suffer in so many material and psychological ways. Theories of resistance display a deep romanticism for the insights that are thought to spontaneously spring from impoverished brows. To believe that these children, because of their misery, for example, might have been privy to special insights into the nature of their condition is similar to the wishful thinking of resistance theorists, who attribute more motive force to impoverished conditions than is reasonable. In particular, I think the relative isolation of the children in both cases stands out as a major factor limiting their awareness of their situation and the possible routes to changing their lives. In the most optimistic interpretation of Marx's potato metaphor, the relationship between isolation and consciousness is, I think, the point he was asking us to consider.

In contrast, Gabriel is convinced that for him the give-and-take of street debate provides the only means to a greater understanding of the limits and virtues of cultural constraints. He is also convinced that most of his friends, family, and customers consider him a bit crazy. When he works on Sundays and people chide him about this, he loves to provoke them: "And does Sunday hold some special meaning for *you*?" For Gabi, quarrels about opposing theological, political, and cultural views are spiritually refreshing. And he is not alone, of course. Norma once told me not to hang the wash on the downstairs lines at her house, but rather up on the roof: she wanted people to see a man doing this. She wanted to tweak the consciousness of certain neighbors, especially male neighbors, about the household division of labor. Small stuff, no doubt, but in just such stuff of daily life may lie a key to understanding contradictory consciousness and compliant defiance. By tracing the subjective understanding and voiced sentiments of people in Santo Domingo, for example, with respect to causal chains of change, we can better understand how ideas and social relations change. By documenting and analyzing arguments in households and between neighbors, we can explore what changing people's minds has to do with changing people's activities and practices. In particular, with such finely grained exploration of beliefs and behavior, we can better gauge popular sentiments regarding the relative virtues of relying on change from without (above) and from within (i.e., self-reliant change).

Unrealistic aspirations and political fantasies must be accorded sufficient weight to explain contradictory impulses and practical actions within and not simply between groups of people. Nowhere are incongruous inclinations better brought to light than in political humor. Riding in a bus full of academics as we returned from a conference several hours outside Bogotá, Colombia, in 1998, I was puzzled by the similarities I felt but could not explain between Mexico and Colombia. Then, without warning, the bus was stopped on the highway and we were told the road was closed and we would have to detour through the mountains. One of the organizers of the event stood up to explain the change in route and then added, "We are going to be passing through a zone where *la guerilla* is said to be strong. In case they stop us, we can offer them a Gringo [there were two of us on the bus]. I think they'll let us pass if we give them a Gringo." Muffled laughter filled the bus and I finally realized that the humor I so loved in Mexico was one thing that attracted me to Colombia as well. More than simply a way to cope with adversity, this kind of humor provides a mechanism of social critique and a means of indicating what might be done about social problems.

Discussions about politics in streets and homes in Santo Domingo, or on buses in Colombia, for that matter, are not mere reflections of broader social debates. They are the debates. Or at least an important part of them, more productive of changing ideas and behavior than sometimes acknowledged. Overly romanticized visions of resistance are as guilty of underplaying such disputes as are theories that relegate popular discourse to the sphere of epiphenomena to economic transformations and elite political decision making. Friends in Santo Domingo sometimes assert, half-kidding, "I drink because I'm Mexican," or "I fight because I was born in Tepito," or "I have beaten my wife because I was born in a macho culture, and aren't I a product of my culture?" Yet caution is required in interpreting these comments, for often these friends are doing more than reproducing cultural truisms or assuaging their complicity; sometimes they are also using ideas from the past to help transform the present in not so subtle ways.[22]

MEXICO CITY CRIME WAVES

Between my trips to Santo Domingo in December 1995 and December 1996, I noticed a dramatic difference: whenever delivery trucks would stop at Marcelo's *tiendita* to restock the shelves with Pan Bimbo, Coca-Cola, or other products, the driver would get out on one side of the vehicle and an armed guard, usually wearing a *chaleco antibalas* (bulletproof vest) and carrying a pistol, would emerge from the other side. The guard would scan the street as the driver conducted business with the store owner. This had been entirely unknown in 1992–93. When I asked Marcelo and other friends who ran small *tiendas* in the immediate vicinity of Huehuetzin Street whether local gangs had been robbing them, they replied that gangs from other neighborhoods, unknown youth, were the real threat. Apparently, we were sending our gang bangers to cross into other, surrounding *barrios pobres* to rob there, and these neighborhoods in turn were sending their best and brightest over to ours to do the same.

Around 1997, I stopped hailing taxis on the streets of Mexico City. I had never had any problems, but too many friends told me they had and warned me strongly not to tempt fate. *Taxis de sitio,* those based at cab stands, were still safe, it was said, which was why they could charge two or three times the rates of other taxis. The *taxistas* in regular and gypsy cabs, however, were said to be involved in robbing their own passengers, supposedly in cahoots with accomplices who would enter the taxi a block or so after the pickup and assault riders.[23]

Although many residents of Santo Domingo commented on a rising feeling of powerlessness in the late-1990s, and despite the fact that many people linked this feeling to the growing incidence of crime, or at least to the growing perception of the growing incidence of crime in the capital, I think these sentiments revealed more than just a knee-jerk response to increased vandalism, muggings, and corruption. In this period, pertinent discussions at kitchen tables, sidewalk drinking parlors, and *tienda* storefronts all focused on the extent to which people in the *colonia* felt they could control events such as crime. But this discussion was a reflection as well of my friends' perceived ability to control social events of any kind in their lives. The conversations were often couched in terms of gaining a realistic assessment as to whether indeed crime was on the rise, as was being reported in the press. But there was more going on. Because regardless of the outcome of this dialogue, there was the matter of controlling events, of defending oneself and one's family and friends from robbery and assault. And, of course, for some, there was the matter of carrying out robberies and assaults on other people.[24]

As to the question of whether crime had indeed risen significantly since the peso crisis of 1994–95, there is no doubt that after the crisis police presence in many parts of the Federal District grew. Especially in commercial areas, both tourist and nontourist, and in well-to-do residential neighborhoods, police on foot, on horseback, and even (in the case of Coyoacán, for example) on bicycles became more noticeable. On the major roadways, the traffic police, the infamous *mordelones* (big

Figure 10. Glass shards are routinely placed on the tops of walls surrounding homes in Santo Domingo and throughout urban Mexico.

biters), so-called for the *morditas* (little bribes) they take out of motorists, became even more ubiquitous.[25]

On television the question of violence was often linked to drug trafficking. In 1997 a public-service announcement showed an anti-narcotics team patrolling, with a voice-over declaring, "The nation is mobilized against drugs." (To my knowledge, none of my friends and neighbors in Santo Domingo has been involved in the flourishing drug trade in Mexico as anything more than a petty dealer or user.) That same year, I accompanied an elderly neighbor to visit his sister in the industrial section of Azcapotzalco in the northwest of the capital. When I asked why he was bringing along a copy of the Bible, he replied, "You'll see when we get there." Once we were safely behind the curtains of his sister's *vecindad* apartment in Azcapotzalco, my neighbor removed the rubber bands from his Bible, opened the volume, took out a pistol from a cutaway space inside, and handed the gun to his sister. There had been quite a bit of street violence recently in the neighborhood around where she lived, he told me, and he was bringing her this family heirloom. Fear of drug dealers and addicts, gangs, and simply strangers had made my elderly neighbor's sister more scared. Whether crime had in fact become more prevalent in her neighborhood and the Mexican capital overall in

1997, compared to an earlier time, was not clear to me or my neighbor; yet this hardly seemed to matter to him, given the climate of fear which hung over Mexico City for several years at the end of the 1990s.

The actual threat of armed assault should not be underestimated. According to official crime statistics, by 2001 Mexico's rate of gun homicide, for example, had risen to world-class levels. That year, there were 10 murders with guns for every 100,000 people; the figure for the United States in 2001 was 6.3 murders per 100,000 people. Thus, only Colombia, South Africa, and possibly Brazil had more gun homicides (see Weiner and Thompson 2001). At the same time, throughout the 1990s I continued to feel safer in most parts of Colonia Santo Domingo than I would have in similar poor neighborhoods in any large city in the United States.

In addition to a growing fear of *taxistas,* the presence of armed and armored guards on soda trucks, and the heightened police presence in some areas of Mexico City, it is noteworthy that several of my friends have taken jobs in the 1990s as security guards. The husband of one woman I knew tried to set up his own home security business. Another complained that he had lost his job as a result of layoffs following the adoption of NAFTA, and now the only work left to him was "*guardando los bienes de los ricos*" (guarding the property of the rich).

In order to gain some perspective on crime and fears of crime, I talked with Daniel Enríquez of the Christian Base Community. He insisted that crime was not as new as everyone seemed to think, implying that these feelings of vulnerability originated elsewhere. "In 1979, when Santo Domingo was still full of unpopulated hills, there was a lot of delinquency. I remember in particular a group of really down-and-out people from [the neighborhood of] Guerrero who'd been up to all sorts of no good [*fechorías*] over there and had to hightail it over here. Well, there was a time when, after seven at night or so, when it got dark, you didn't see anyone walking around, because they'd assault you." In fact, since that time, including in the 1990s, crime has apparently become less of an issue to be confronted on a daily basis for people around Santo Domingo.

Certainly, Daniel noted, where people are poor and forced to go without things they need, there will be theft and other forms of criminal behavior. And people in want did represent a continuing problem, so there would be continuing crime. I told him about an incident in March 1989, when in a fit of Gringo naiveté I had tried to locate and walk along the streets mentioned in *Children of Sánchez.* I had eventually arrived in the Thieves Market of Tepito, where one of Jesús Sánchez's sons had spent much of his time in the 1950s selling *fayuca* (contraband). In my imagination, the poverty in Tepito had become more titillating than terrible, but I was quickly disabused of that illusion, as a man pulled an ice pick on me while his accomplice grabbed me from behind. Fortunately, they were not young men and I managed to struggle free, escaping unscathed except for having been humiliated by my own imprudence. My purpose in seeking causes other than simply a rise in the crime rate for the climate of fear in the late 1990s is not to deny real threats to persons and property. I simply wish to connect these feelings of isolation and frustration to other contemporaneous political currents.

To an extent, as is the case for all metropolitan areas, the crime and violence in Mexico City have always been woven deep into urban mythologies. Ten years after my encounter in Tepito, in late July 1999, I mentioned to a neighbor in Santo Domingo that I was heading over to the Colonia Buenos Aires with some men who needed parts to repair their cars. He informed me, "Well, Mateo, it's true you can get inexpensive car parts there, but I'll tell you, only Tepito is worse" (i.e., more dangerous). The popular mythology concerning Buenos Aires tells not only of *fayuca* but also of muggings, shootouts, and murders. Indeed, guns seem more associated with La Buenos Aires than with any other *colonia* in the capital. As it happens, the most potentially violent encounter I experienced that day in Buenos Aires was with fellow residents of Santo Domingo.

Having dropped Gabriel and Javier off at one chop shop, Pedro and I had continued around the block looking for a place to park his pickup. Heading down a one-way street, we were stopped by another car coming toward us (we were going the right way, they were going the wrong way). After an awkward moment, the other car backed up, and as we passed it, Pedro realized that he knew the man driving and called out a friendly "*¡Hola!*" It turned out that the other driver was a notorious petty thief from Santo Domingo. Together with two compatriots in the back seat, he was no doubt in La Buenos Aires to sell, not to buy stolen car parts. This man had been arrested only the year before and had spent six months in jail, Pedro told me. On release, he had declared to all that he would go clean, but he was too accustomed to having a lot of money in his pockets, and so returned to burglary shortly thereafter. Pedro told me with a smile that the men were certainly packing pistols.

Nonetheless, despite the history, at least as told in stories, of violent men and neighborhoods in Mexico City, a "new crime wave" was declared in the late 1990s. Now, it seemed, the crime was no longer largely

restricted to a few notorious areas of the city and the surrounding countryside. (In Santo Domingo, for example, it is easy to find people who
will attest to the violent appetites of rural Mexicans who, it is often reported, sleep on top of *"un montón de armas"* [a pile of arms].[26]) Yet,
although many Santo Domingo residents in the 1990s told stories of
people they knew and friends of friends who had heard about robberies,
the fact remains that the actual number of assaults experienced by
people I knew in the *colonia* was small. What is more, compared to
neighborhoods where the poor reside in the United States, in Mexico
City in 2000, there were still relatively few guns used in robberies. Certainly, I have been subject to far more break-ins in working-class and
middle-class neighborhoods of the United States than in similar parts of
Mexico.

Still, whether robberies and assaults actually rose in the late 1990s,
and the extent of the rise, is actually less significant than the fact that a
general sense of helplessness did undoubtedly grow in this period. And,
coupled with frustration over elections that seemed to accomplish nothing, an ebbing of organized social movements throughout the country,
and a dramatic decline in purchasing power following the financial crisis in 1994–95, many residents of Santo Domingo had ample reasons to
fear for the future. It is bad enough when one loses faith in the ability
and willingness of an outside power—whether it be religious or governmental—to intervene on one's behalf. But when a sizeable number of
people who pride themselves on having improved their lives through
their own efforts no longer feel capable of such self-reliance and autonomous agency, despair and fragmented solutions to problems can more
easily take hold.

The rituals of resistance are rehearsed with regularity in Santo Domingo, as in other poor neighborhoods of the world. In the minds of
most of my friends in the *colonia,* if covert and hidden forms of resistance are in evidence there, this is not primarily because people know
too much to try anything else, or even because they are too clever to attempt more dramatic transformations. Just as inactivity is not necessarily tantamount to passivity, so too resistance does not automatically represent a corrective measure to organized forms of struggle. The rich and
poor are not facing off in two tight-knit armies in Mexico City, because,
among other reasons, the rich and the poor do not comprise homoge-
nous classes. Certainly, just as in Santo Domingo, the debates and disagreements within the *colonias populares* of Mexico City are manifestations of struggles to survive and to resist. But they are more, too,

because they are component parts of the effort to become conscious of the reasons for oppression and the means to transform societies in fundamental ways. Even in an age of postsocialist pragmatism and diminished expectations of social change, theories that would reduce the aspirations and also the lives of the dispossessed in the name of working-class realism are of limited benefit.

CHAPTER 7

Chiapas and Mexican Blood

Ah, I see; it's life without a break.
                Jean-Paul Sartre

Depending on the myth invoked, Mexico is populated either by three great ancestral cultures or one overarching race—or both. The three cultures, Mexican schoolchildren are taught, are Spanish, Indian, and Mestizo. The one race is mestizo, and refers to a metaphorical hybrid of Spanish and Indian blood that has, through centuries of miscegenation, combined to form something unique: the Mexican. The fact remains, however, that regardless of the fabled power of this folklore, the living indigenous peoples of Mexico—roughly 10 percent of the population overall, or ten million people in 2000—are ignored and/or despised by most of the mestizo people most of the time in Mexican society. As anthropologists of Mexico have long noted, despite the explicit recognition of Indian peoples in the first myth of three Mexican cultural patrilines, the central paradox of ethnicity in contemporary Mexico is that Indian cultures of the past are lauded while those of the present regularly are avoided or trivialized. With the so-called mestizo (mixed race), matters have fared no better. Here the new "cosmic" race grouping is a convenient umbrella concept that all too often obscures significant ethnocultural differences within Mexico, and, more particularly, hides institutional and casual racism behind the guise of national-racial-ethnic unity.

Yet in the final years of the twentieth century, for millions of people in Mexico, including in Colonia Santo Domingo, issues surrounding indigenous identity, suffering, and demands surfaced with breathtaking rapidity and intensity. This was owing especially to the armed uprising by thousands of Maya-speaking men, women, and children on January 1, 1994, in the southern Mexican state of Chiapas. As the product of a combination of forces and a confluence of events, the Zapatista rebellion sought to show "to the rest of the country and the whole world that human dignity is still alive and is located among the poorest of its population" (EZLN 1994, 89). In an interview shortly after the uprising in 1994, Subcomandante Marcos sought to provide an outline of the Zapatistas' rough class analysis and the relationship of these poorest citizens to the rest of the Mexican population. Marcos described three Mexicos: one made up of the powerful, another made up of those who aspire to power, and a third made up of those who nobody cares about (see Collier and Quaratiello 1994, 84). Representing those-who-nobody-cares-about, the EZLN was demanding democracy, liberty, and justice for all Mexicans. It was explicitly insisting that these rights be recognized not simply for the people who had rebelled in one region but rather that they be respected for people living in all parts of the country.

JANUARY 1, 1994

In Chiapas, those-who-nobody-cares-about are overwhelmingly the indigenous peoples, and at 4 o'clock on the morning on January 1, 1994, thousands of them launched an uprising. When the fighting was halted a few days later, dozens of Tzotzil, Tzeltal, Chol, and Tojolabal people were dead, thousands of others were displaced, thousands of federal troops had been sent to occupy and pacify rebel communities and, when they could, to exterminate rebel leaders. The rebels did not seize power and they did not aim to continue the armed struggle in the long term— nor did they have any prospect of militarily defeating the Mexican Army in the short term. But, they contended, only through fighting and dying could the Zapatistas demonstrate to the rest of the world that human dignity was alive in the forests of southern Mexico. Only through fighting and dying could they make their voices heard and effect a national crisis that would put the lie to legends of peaceful coexistence between different ethnic and racial groups in Mexico. And only through fighting and dying could they resolutely place on the political agenda their demand for drastic social, economic, and political changes in the country as a whole. With the uprising, Maya-speaking Indians of southern Mexico announced in no uncertain terms their determination to confront the world of misery into which the poorest are born and then told they must endure. Those-who-nobody-cares-about were taking matters into their own hands.

As elsewhere in the country, in Mexico City the events of Chiapas were followed from the beginning, and their significance was debated broadly. In the first flush of the rebellion, after the initial shock of the boldness of the rebels' actions became apparent, many in Colonia Santo Domingo expressed fear bordering on scorn for the Zapatistas—in particular, some in the *colonia* worried that the Indians' actions would spark unpleasant reprisals against poor people all over the country. A few, like Gabriel, were plainly inspired and delighted at the serendipity of bands of young Maya shouldering wooden replicas of rifles and in the process scaring the wits out of those in power in Mexico City. Initially, the most common response in the *colonia* to the EZLN, however, was patronizing antipathy or even outright condemnation of the rebellion.

Rumors in the press about wild-eyed Maoist radicals stirring up the natives—"They're not even from Chiapas!"—were gobbled up in the *colonia*. My neighbors felt more ambivalence about reports of liberation theology catechists having provoked the indigenes; after all, with so many *comunidades de base* affiliated with the Iglesia de la Resurrección, it was harder to sell depictions of these young followers of a Church of the Poor as deranged zealots. Further, unlike 1968, when student protesters waved banners of Che Guevara and Mao Zedong, in Chiapas the rebels launched their uprising in the name of Pancho Villa and, especially, Emiliano Zapata, the popular heroes of the Mexican Revolution (see Stephen 2002). Even among those who were scornful of the uprising in Chiapas, there was a begrudging acknowledgment that the EZLN had some right to claim themselves as the rightful heirs of the revolutionary tradition of Villa and Zapata.

Poverty and racism were causes of the rebellion in Chiapas. Even friends and neighbors in Mexico City who knew little of southern Mexico and were fairly frightened by the Zapatistas would easily acknowledge this interpretation of the situation in Chiapas. But as poverty and racism had long been basic to the fabric of life in Chiapas, one must also look beyond these afflictions for additional factors if one is to understand why the rebellion occurred when and where it did. And, in fact, in both Mexico City and Chiapas people had felt increasingly helpless to combat programs of the neoliberals which included the dismantling of basic government-run programs that had offered safety nets to the Mexican poor in difficult times. As Stephen and Collier have written:

The central problem confronting the Zapatistas, Mexicans, and by extension all people in our global political economy, is how to construct political and legal regimes for local, regional, and national political cultures that
can restrain or at least ameliorate the human costs of neoliberalism. Given
the helplessness people feel for being able to redress their deteriorating circumstances, it seems no accident that *autonomy* has emerged as a central—
and contested—concept in Chiapas, Oaxaca, and elsewhere in Mexico.
(1997, 11)

The Zapatistas chose January 1, 1994, of course, because the date coincided with the implementation of the North American Free Trade
Agreement between Mexico, the United States, and Canada. This treaty
was for many in Mexico the definitive manifestation of neoliberalism
run amok. Poverty had always been central to the lives of the Maya-
speaking peoples of Chiapas, but it had become even more severe in the
five years prior to NAFTA, when the campesinos of the region had seen
a 65 percent drop in the price of coffee, a livestock farming crisis, and a
drastic reduction in federal government subsidies. In 1992, President
Carlos Salinas de Gortari had won reform of Article 27 of the Mexican
Constitution, which allowed him to halt land-reform initiatives and take
a major step toward legally restructuring the countryside for agribusiness. By thus dismantling the *ejido* (communal) property system in large
parts of the country, Salinas had been practically able to destroy a crucial component of the preexisting land-tenure system, symbolically destroying a cornerstone of the Mexican Revolution—the idea that property should be owned communally by those who till it—in the process.
In the context of such radical economic and political attacks on the indigenous campesinos of Chiapas, said the Zapatistas, the Free Trade
Agreement represented nothing short of a death sentence.

The combination of all of these events—falling coffee prices, cuts in
government safety nets, the change to Article 27 of the Constitution, the
signing of the Free Trade Agreement, and the impact of thousands of
refugees from Guatemala's civil war on the region—had led to increasing emigration of Chiapanecos to other regions of Mexico, and even
to the United States, and had provided the spark for the Zapatista uprising. These were some of the reasons that thousands of indigenous
campesinos from southern Mexico decided they would rather risk dying
than remain silent any longer.[1]

When, in February 1996, the EZLN and government representatives
finally signed the San Andrés Accords in San Cristóbal de las Casas, a
collective sigh of relief could be felt in working-class areas of Mexico

City. A peaceful resolution to the conflict had been achieved, many wanted to believe, and therefore it was hoped that the military skirmishes that had continued in Chiapas over the previous two years would now abate. This respite proved short lived, however, as then President Zedillo subsequently refused to honor the accords. Anxiety returned for many of my friends and neighbors in Santo Domingo. Although the ups and downs of negotiations after 1996 have not been tracked closely by many of my acquaintances in the *colonia,* there continued to be a widespread unease owing to the continued presence of the EZLN as a political force to be reckoned with. If they accomplished nothing else in this period, the Zapatistas ensured that the patently unresolved issues of racism and oppression in Mexico would receive ongoing consideration in the sphere of public opinion.

Not similarly inspired to rise up in arms, in Colonia Santo Domingo some of my friends began to collect Zapatista memorabilia, including cassette tapes of revolutionary songs, stickers, pamphlets, posters, and flyers. On New Year's Day 1997, I went with Gabriel to the main plaza of the upper-middle-class neighborhood of Coyoacán, a short jitney ride from Huehuctzin Street, but in many respects a world away. Gabi had heard rumors of a third anniversary celebration of the uprising in Chiapas that would be sponsored by Frente Zapatista in Coyoacán. He wanted to attend the event in the spirit of protest, to mark the accomplishments of the Zapatistas to date, and even more, he said, to demonstrate solidarity with others in need. He anticipated that there would be a large turnout for the celebration.

The gathering of at most 150 people seemed to us at the time reminiscent of the hippie "be-ins" of twenty-five years earlier. Forty-five minutes after arriving in Coyoacán, and after listening to a string of bad folk songs about the EZLN written by capital city supporters, and a few good songs written for kids (maybe these were composed by others . . .), we decided to leave. We then headed downtown to the Zócalo, the main plaza in Mexico City's historic center. But we found no commemorations of the occasion taking place there. Talking about the Coyoacán event later, I expressed surprise that the EZLN had not received a better celebration that day. Why hadn't there been more popular support, I asked, and why did those in attendance seem such sixties dinosaurs? It seemed to me as if the hippie left of the last two decades had merely gathered to wish one another *Feliz año,* a Happy New Year. Gabi's sense was that the EZLN was no longer combative, and therefore could no longer rally support from *los chingados,* by which he meant poor people who were only interested in protest if they thought it might bring about change. As this would be, I think, their principal celebration in the Federal District that year, I began to think that Gabi was right: the EZLN had passed its prime. Around the same time, the community activist Bernardino Ramos became an elected official in the area. Berna commented to me that by 1999, the Zapatista movement had simply become "one of many issues. It's one of the important ones, but not the main one. In 1994, 1995, 1996, it was the fundamental issue."

Support for the EZLN and Subcomandante Marcos among my friends has generally been difficult to gauge. Some, like Valfre, a Zapotec-speaking carpenter friend who is from Oaxaca, have consistently praised the Zapatistas, and Subcomandante Marcos in particular, since the first day of the rebellion. "Did you know, Mateo, that Marcos speaks four or five languages? He can talk to all kinds of people! And he has such a rich knowledge about indigenous peoples. There has not been a Mexican revolutionary leader like Marcos in a long, long time." Others, like Julia, the mother of two small boys on Huehuetzin Street, initially were quite hostile when they discussed the EZLN with me. "They are provocateurs and, what's more, they're not even real Indians," she informed me in 1995. By 1999, during the strike at UNAM, Julia had begun to comment more favorably about Marcos and was willing to consider other possibilities: "Well, what the hell, Mateo. Maybe they know something we don't, because it sure seems like nothing is going to change in this damned country." A number of people commented to me in the summer of 1999 that Subcomandante Marcos was openly supporting the UNAM strike.

In July 1997, when a variety of elections were being held throughout the country, in Chiapas the EZLN refused to participate in the vote and actively sought to disrupt what they saw as a criminally fraudulent electoral process. In the capital, the attention of most of the people was focused on the contest that would decide the very first *elected* mayor of Mexico City; PRD leader Cuauhtémoc Cárdenas would win the election that day. Even with the new openness in the Mexico City elections, the Zapatistas' de facto message of abstentionism-with-a-purpose came to symbolize a more explicitly politicized opposition to participation in elections as a means of changing society. When neighbors insisted to Gabriel that his abstentionist politics were tantamount to casting a ballot for the PRI, Gabi was finally able to respond with the weight of the Zapatista movement: that not voting can be just as politically significant as voting. Nonetheless, regardless of the propaganda appeal to those like Gabriel far removed from Chiapas, the abstentionist policies of the Zapatistas in 1997 proved catastrophic within Chiapas itself.

The Mexican government was clearly concerned about the influence the EZLN wielded more broadly in Mexico, not only with respect to participation in the electoral process, but also with respect to more fundamental issues having to do with protecting the idea and reality of a unified national territory. As Rus, Hernández Castillo, and Mattiace have written regarding the significance of the uprising:

> In short, in barely 30 years, the economic foundation of Chiapas's indigenous communities through most of the past century has been swept away. In response, indigenous people have been breaking out of the old, carefully managed labor camp communities to find new ways of making a living and even new places to live. Significantly, however, when they talk about these years, they stress not the material changes but the new political self consciousness and sense of ethnic identity that have come from confronting the crisis on their own and finding their own solutions. Lately, it has become common to refer to the entire period as the time of "awakening." (2001, 13)

Fears in government circles of more such awakenings no doubt grew when, in early 1999, five thousand Zapatistas spread out across Mexico to hold a popular referendum on the San Andrés Accords that the government still refused to sign. Excitement over the Consulta was widespread in cities and towns across the country. Despite virtually no television coverage and little newspaper space devoted to the referendum, in Colonia Santo Domingo and dozens of other poor neighborhoods of the capital that have rich and long histories of grassroots social movements, the impact of the Zapatista visitors was remarkable. More than a year later, many friends still prominently displayed photographs that showed them standing next to one or two masked EZLN cadres. The fact that half of the five thousand Zapatista militants had been women was one of many points of significance that my friends related to me about the visit of the EZLN representatives.[2] One Zapatista woman who participated in the Consulta later talked about the importance of women to the resolution of all social problems: "It's true that some customs are not that good, for example, drunkenness, that's not good culture, nor is forced marriage. . . . What we women do is struggle to change things a little so they get better. . . . The way the people greeted us women [in the Consulta] was really great—they loved us" (see Rovira Sancho 2001).

Figure 11. Photograph of Doña Fili and neighbors standing with a
Zapatista in March 1999 together with a poster of the Virgin of
Guadalupe and a basket of flowers.

IS CHIAPAS REALLY MEXICO?

Early on, a key slogan of the Zapatista movement stressed that Chiapas
was part of Mexico. In 1994 in the state that supplied nearly 60 percent of Mexico's hydroelectric power, 47 percent of its natural gas, and
21 percent of its oil, one-third of the inhabitants did not have electricity,
and half did not have access to clean drinking water. So the maxim,
"Chiapas is Mexico," was meant to openly challenge the blatantly unequal distribution of wealth between regions in the country and to en-
list the support of people from other areas of the country who suffered
similar abuse and misery.

To be sure, not everyone agreed with the assessment. "The uprising
is unreal and doomed to fail," wrote Octavio Paz in early January 1994.
"The movement lacks ideological foundations and, in military terms,
strategic thinking," he added. "Its ideology is also remarkably archaic.
These are the simplistic ideas of people who live in an epoch very different from our own" (in Bartra 1999, 18). Mexicans could hardly have
found a more closed-minded explanation for the uprising: the Indians
deserved the blame for their own plight because they refused to accept
modernity.

Others saw more positive consequences in the Zapatista movement. Roger Bartra, for example, connected the Zapatista movement with the broader issue of democracy: "One of the first consequences of the uprising of 1 January 1994 in Chiapas was the indelible inscription on the political agenda of democracy." Far from dismissing the global significance of the Zapatistas, Bartra instead insisted that Chiapas was very much of a piece with late-twentieth-century political developments. In particular, he maintained, "the vertigo provoked by the abyss brought on by the fall of the former Soviet Union and Central European states" was an important aspect of the general context of what he termed "the Chiapas conjuncture" (1999, 23).

In the years after the uprising, around one-third of Mexico's standing army was stationed in Chiapas at any given time. Altercations in the relatively isolated hamlets of the mountains and jungles of Chiapas became commonplace. In late 1997 the simmering confrontation between Zapatista regulars and their supporters on one hand, and the armed forces of the federal government on the other erupted in the town of Acteal. On December 22 a paramilitary unit affiliated with the PRI in the area slaughtered forty-five Tzotziles, overwhelmingly women and children. Condemnation of the massacre was immediate, both nationally and internationally, yet the principal outcome of Acteal was an increased military presence in the highlands of Chiapas (see Stephen 1999). The reality of such overpowering military power directly or indirectly connected to the government party was a palpable warning for both Chiapanecos and anyone else who might be contemplating rebellion in Mexico that dire consequences would be suffered by any groups who challenged the military authority of the Army.

A widespread demand of the indigenous poor in Chiapas was that the state needed to be considered an integral and important part of the larger national polity. But although Chiapanecos went to great lengths to justify their message that "Chiapas is Mexico," it does not necessarily follow that "Mexico is Chiapas." As anthropologists and historians have insisted in recent decades, regional differences within the Mexican republic are profound and often quite relevant when discussing questions of politics. Thus, an underlying ideological issue in the election of Vicente Fox to the presidency in 2000 concerned popular perceptions of regional differences, and specifically the differences between Mexico's dynamic, capitalist, agribusiness north, an area that has become increasingly integrated with the U.S. economy, and its southern states, characterized by smaller campesino land parcels that are farmed by impoverished, isolated, indigenous peoples. In part, what is evident in popular debates in Colonia Santo Domingo for and against the Zapatistas is that opposing views often reflect larger disagreements regarding regional inequalities, as well as different views concerning the extent to which the impetus for social change can originate among those-who-nobody-cares-about in the population.

CAMPESINOS AND *INDÍGENAS*

Bernardino Ramos described to me his own views about the political significance of the EZLN and its base of social support in Mexico City:

"I see the Zapatista movement as a demand that's come to light after being hidden for a long time. The existence of indigenous peoples and their problems has never been recognized. They've been the subject of simple studies aimed at showing that indigenous people are among our ancestors, something for the history books and academic references about Mexico. But not as a present day problem. I think the Zapatista movement has sparked the conscience of Mexicans, made them notice the inhuman conditions in which the indigenous peoples live. It has touched the conscience of all sectors of society, not just the popular ones. Of course in the popular sectors there is a solidarity that's undeniable. And today [in 1999, more than five years after the uprising], there's still this feeling."

Casual discussions among residents of Colonia Santo Domingo about living indigenous peoples, and not just dead ancestors, were certainly more common following the uprising than before. Many men and women even seemed to take a certain pride in displaying knowledge of particular indigenous groups in Mexico. Several years after the Zapatista movement was born hundreds of miles to the south, I talked about poverty, indigenous peoples, and rebellion with Marcos, the shop steward at the National University:

"There's a lot of poverty and the government hides it," Marcos reminded me. "We see it now in Oaxaca, Chiapas, among the Tarahumaras, the Huastecas, the Potosinas, the Hidalgüenses [other indigenous groups from other regions]. There are places of great poverty and you don't know how they're living. Why? Because the government doesn't reveal this poverty. It talks about what makes them proud and that's power. They oppress these people, take away their riches. The world says, 'Mexico is the ideal country. It doesn't have any political, social, or economic problems.' That's what the world thinks. They say that there's always been peace in Mexico. And when they heard about the rebellion in Chiapas: 'What's happening in Mexico?!' It was the model for Latin America. But we see that, on the contrary, the government has been hiding it all."

"Look what happened in Chiapas," I interjected.

Marcos continued, "The government tried to tell the people, the campesinos in Chiapas, 'Well, why did you rise up?' 'Because we're hungry!' So if I act like a *cacique* [local boss], I just come in and take over lands, cattle, harvests. Campesinos are fed up with all this and that's why the conflict in Chiapas happened. And it's not only in Chiapas that it can happen, but in [other states like] Guerrero, Oaxaca, San Luis Potosí."

"Can something like the rebellion in Chiapas happen here?"

"There can be rebellions, there can be rebellions. We're already suffering. The demonstrations that are occurring show this. Monday in Naucalpan and Tlalnepantla [poor northwest suburbs of Mexico City], LICONSA raised the price of milk two pesos [around 25¢ U.S.]. People were furious. So it's going to be twelve pesos that I've got to pay, two or three times a week. And how am I going to eat afterwards? You might say that two pesos is nothing, but it's a lot!"

"When you're only earning forty pesos a day," I added, referring to a wage equivalent to around $5.00 U.S. a day, which was slightly above the minimum wage in Mexico at that time.

"Imagine!" Marcos affirmed as he shook his head slowly in sad recognition of how a seemingly small price rise would impact millions of Mexico's poor.

Periodically, there was talk in the *colonia* of other guerrilla groups. In the late 1990s the press reported on isolated instances of attacks, on a remote police outpost or on a power pylon, for instance. A middle-aged man was waiting with his four-year-old son one day as Gabi repaired his car on Huehuetzin Street. He described to me how only recently several *dínamos* (electric switching stations) had been blown up in the mountains of nearby Contreras. This attack had been carried out by the Ejército Popular Revolucionario (EPR), he told me. Members of the EPR were said by the authorities to be based in the state of Guerrero, he added, and they had been known to attack in Oaxaca and around Mexico City as well. Mainly regarded as a sideshow guerrilla faction, the EPR had earned the bemused attention of some in Santo Domingo, more for their outlandish assaults than for the future prospects of their strategy.

Of greater long-term significance, no doubt, has been the emergence in areas like Oaxaca and Chiapas of strong regional indigenous and campesino organizations, which in the wake of the Zapatista rebellion, have begun to articulate at a national level in spaces such as that of the National Indigenous Congress (see Stephen 2002).[3] Although my friends in Santo Domingo know far less about these organizations—for news of Chiapas, they are largely dependent on their ability to read between the lines of television and newspaper reports—through efforts like the March 21, 1999 EZLN referendum, there is general evidence that the centrality of indigenous peoples and problems to Mexican society is more than ever before on the minds of many who do not consider themselves Indian in any respect.

In addition to the Zapatista uprising, there have been other significant developments in Chiapas in the 1980s and 1990s that parallel transformations under way more broadly in Mexican society. The rapid spread of Christian evangelism is one of them. It should be said that there is no direct correspondence between the rise of evangelism and the Zapatistas, nor is there a direct connection between Catholicism and the Chiapaneco elite. Yet, the religious turmoil in Chiapas has undeniably struck a chord elsewhere in Mexico among some evangelicals and some disgruntled Catholics; and political differences in Chiapas have often mirrored religious schisms between Catholics and Protestants.

Nonetheless, in contemporary Mexico City the main significance of the EZLN uprising and of what Carlos Monsiváis calls the "moral persuasion of the Zapatistas" rests on the indigenous character of the rebellion. In part this is because, contrary to what many in Mexico believe, in addition to the two million Maya-speaking peoples in Chiapas, there are another two million indigenous inhabitants of Mexico City who are living in wretched circumstances. The poverty and marginalization of Indians, then, is hardly just a problem of the southern provinces alone; for citizens of Mexico City ethnicity and the oppression of Indian peoples is a matter of daily life.

OPTIONS FOR CHANGE

During an era in which the prospect of utilizing the ballot to effect social change has seemed more real than ever in Mexico, the Zapatista uprising of 1994 served in part as a defiant counterexample to raise the possibility of other means to change. In particular, Chiapas raised the specter of armed struggle, of resorting to violence and forsaking peaceful routes of change. Obviously, the language of violence was far more prevalent than actual bullets—at least with respect to the EZLN. After the first few days, officially, the Zapatistas did not fire a shot. The case of the Mexican government is different: Chiapas in 2000 resembled an occupied territory, with military maneuvers, actions, and checkpoints a constant part of daily life for citizens and even visitors to the region. Although the massacre at Acteal may be the most horrific instance, it is by no means the only example of an assault on innocent civilians by government and government-affiliated paramilitary troops in the post-uprising period.

At a time when prominent scholar-politicians were writing of "utopia unarmed" and the end of armed struggle in Latin America (see Castañeda 1993), Chiapas did indeed come as a surprise. It is one thing to note the stubborn resilience of the remaining members of Peru's Sendero Luminoso, or the anachronistic success of the FARC in Colombia, but the sudden emergence of the EZLN in one of the supposedly most pacific zones in the continent was truly unanticipated. And as easy as it may be to dismiss the claim that the Zapatistas never had any serious military aims or prospects, again they have nonetheless succeeded in raising alternatives to the electoral process, which, it could easily be argued, they could not have accomplished had they not initially resorted to arms. They opened a dialogue of national and to some extent international dimensions with respect to the way to bring about social change. In a letter to Subcomandante Marcos, Carlos Fuentes wrote, in part:

> You have come to remind us that our modernity includes you. Did you have to take up arms in order to achieve all this? Not as an imitation of us but as yourselves, as what you are. The indigenous cultures of Mexico might be destined to disappear in the larger process of *mestizaje*. But until that happens, if it does happen, and while it unfolds, we must respect cultures that are ours because they live with us, proffering values that are possibly superior and doubtless necessary, to enrich our diminished ideas of modernity and progress. (1996, 125)

In the same letter, Fuentes subsequently asks the Subcomandante:

> Did you have to take up arms in order to achieve all this? I insist that you didn't. I insist that legal channels must be pursued until they are exhausted; and when they are, new political options must be sought. If exercised imaginatively, politics and law are inexhaustible. (126–27)

The question of how to effect fundamental social change was reintroduced in Mexican society following the Chiapas rebellion, at a time

when such queries were considered obsolete by the intellectual and political leadership of Mexico. In a seemingly innocuous discussion one
day with Alma, the friend of a friend, the Zapatistas made their presence
clearly felt. Alma was disparaging another neighbor:

"There's a young guy around here named José María who is very
mixed up in politics. He's a PRIista. He's very mixed up in it, but he
doesn't do a thing to solve the problems we have even on this street. We
don't have any light on these two lampposts. It's really dark. They don't
fix them for us. Neighbors have to take care of these things ourselves."

I responded with a couple of leading questions: "Are you saying
that the only way is to depend on yourselves? Is that what they did in
Chiapas?"

"Those guys [the Zapatistas], look, they had balls. Right now, you
don't hear so much about Marcos. You can see that he's hooded and hiding. But they were really able to move a lot of people."

"Not just indigenous people or folks from the south [of Mexico]?" I
asked.

Pausing for effect, perhaps, Alma then confided to me in a conspira-
torial tone, "I think they were able to, yes. The solution to all this might
be a second revolution. Then, for real, we'd arm ourselves against the
government."

As ever, playing the role of conciliator, Bernardino Ramos also took
inspiration from EZLN demands for autonomy and linked these with
broader goals of self-governance and sovereignty for the poor and dispossessed in Mexico. Berna encouraged me to see the convergent goals,
if not the common methods, of the Zapatistas and the PRD. In the
largest sense, he said, regardless of the particular means to bring about
change that they employed, the PRD and the EZLN were both dedicated
to bringing about fundamental change for the poor people in Mexico:

"As to the defense of sovereignty, I think that the roots are still there.
Utopia still exists. What you were saying about the Zapatista struggle,
Mateo, is an expression of that, of an integral project for the nation. We
can talk about converging without it being necessarily the Zapatista
model or the PRD model. Zapatismo has manifested itself in diverse
forms of struggle, from the armed one with which they emerged, to the
electoral one and pacifist struggles of civil resistance. I think this is all
going to converge and that we can bring it all together in one project for
the nation."

It was all a matter of knowing how to utilize mixed methodologies
to achieve comparable objectives, according to Berna. Or maybe, I re-

flected, it was a matter of recognizing, as Miguel Centeno perceptively has written, "that civil society may just 'bite back' even the most powerful state" (1997, 249), and that this biting might take a variety of forms.

In Gabriel's case, biting back was invariably flippant:

"What are we celebrating Wednesday [January 1, 1997]?" Gabi needled me on Monday, December 30, 1996.

"New Year's Day?" I responded, uncertain what he was fishing for.

"*No, pinche cabrón, ¡La Revolución Zapatista!*" (No, you damned fool, the Zapatista Revolution!)

In the case of the Zapatistas, from deep within a region the Mexican government had long regarded as among the most politically secure, the soundness of their oratory was hard to ignore. As Subcomandante Marcos stated early during the peace negotiations in San Cristóbal de las Casas:

> If neither weapons or armies are necessary any longer, and blood and fire are no longer necessary to cleanse history, then alright. But if not? If all doors are closed again? If words are unable to climb the wall of condescension and disbelief? If the peace is not honored or real? Then who, we ask, will deny us the sacred right to live and die like dignified and real men and women? Who will stop us then from clothing ourselves again for war and death so as to walk with history? Who? (EZLN 1994, 165)

CHAPTER 8

Engendering Popular Political Culture

My mother used to tell me: "Don't piss in my face and tell
me it's raining."
'Cause then you show me you think I'm ignorant, and that
makes me hostile.

Earl Henry Hydrick (cited by Carol Stack)

Many studies of women and politics in Mexico and Latin America have
documented women's recent participation in formal events such as voting, as well as in more rough-and-tumble activities involving women as
militantes in popular social movements in neighborhoods like Colonia
Santo Domingo. In part because women were ignored in earlier mainstream political science research—or, if addressed at all, gender was
treated as simply one more variable in multiple regression analyses of
voting patterns—these new studies on women have sought to reveal
some of the engendered qualities of political culture.

Using the presidential campaigns of 1988, 1994, and 2000, as well as
the 1997 mayoral election in the capital as a backdrop, in this chapter I
examine certain experiences of my friends in Santo Domingo with respect to social change, especially as this relates to electoral politics and
popular social movements.[1] A central part of my argument is aimed at
illustrating the salience of interactions between men and women regarding politics, democracy, and change. The aim is to examine how the
prism of gender helps us to understand the value of voting, how in Mexico as elsewhere in the world electoral participation is often casually
considered equivalent to democracy. If men and women, as groups, approach elections and other methods of social change in somewhat different ways, surely a gendered analysis is required of popular political
cultures.

As we will see, the gendered aspects of popular politics are not necessarily those best captured in survey research. They involve more than
simply the fact that women vote more than men and that women represent 63 percent of all registered voters in Mexico (Kapur 1998, 364), or
that rural, less-educated women are said to vote more conservatively
then urban, high-school-educated men. Nor is it enough to decry the
fact that fewer women are elected to office at all levels, and especially at
the local level, than men. As important as it is to analyze quantitative information regarding voter registration and polling data, these alone
might lead us to believe that women are more involved and enthusiastic than men in electoral politics. In this chapter, I provide evidence
that points to the importance of going beyond even complex tabulations of election results. Despite the fact that my study is based on a
smaller group of people than would be considered statistically significant for survey research, ethnography is especially well suited to show
that, in the ambiguous opinions and practices that are often glossed as
political apathy, such lack of interest or participation in particular political activities may not necessarily signify a lack of knowledge or political alienation.

WOMEN AND POLITICS IN MEXICO

As to gender differences with respect to voting and formal political involvement more generally, some feminist commentators have concluded
that women are far less committed to electoral politics as a means of
changing Mexican society than are men. Anna Fernández, for example,
has argued that women have been "largely absent from formal politics"
in Mexico. Nonetheless, while compared to men women demonstrate
less "interest in institutionalized politics," they do seek resolution of
daily problems through social movements and popular organizations in
far larger numbers than men (1996, 307–8). In a parallel fashion, Victoria Rodríguez has noted that despite the fact that women made up
17 percent of the 1997–2000 Mexican Chamber of Deputies (85 of 500
seats), "measured in terms of political efficacy . . . Mexican women appear to have gone considerably farther in the informal than in the formal sphere of politics—at least to date" (1998). Yet, if Mexico is re-
puted to be the land of perpetual machismo, and if the percentage of
women in federal legislatures is any gauge of the level of democracy and
gender equality in a society, then what are we to make of the following
figures? In 1998, in the 106th U.S. Congress, 56 of the 435 representa-

TABLE 8.1. WOMEN IN FEDERAL ELECTED OFFICES,
MEXICO AND UNITED STATES, 1998

	Women in office	Total in office	Women as percentage of total
Mexico			
Chamber of Deputies	87	500	17.4
Senate	19	128	14.8
United States			
House of Representatives[a]	56	435	12.9
Senate	9	100	9.0

SOURCES: Mexican data: Rodríguez (1998, 12); U.S. data: http://www.emilyslist.org/el-newsstand/
vpp/women106.asp.
[a]In addition to the fifty-six women representatives, there were two women delegates to the 106th
Congress—from the Virgin Islands and the District of Columbia; if they are included in the total figures for 1998, the overall number of women representatives rises to fifty-eight and the percentage becomes 13.3.

tives were women, or 12.9 percent. That same year, 9 of the 100 sena-
tors were women (see Table 8.1).

There is a connection between divergent strategies for political
change and engendered forms of popular politics in Mexico that is
worth considering here. As Nikki Craske has noted, often the different
political views and practices associated with either men or women revolve around "the ways in which women have been perceived as political actors [in Latin America]: conservative, influenced by the Church,
motherhood constructed as the predominant political identity, and apolitical" (1998, 44; see also Craske 1999).[2] Yet, at the same time, many
(other?) women constitute the majority of rank-and-file members of
popular social movements and organizations. Thus, although the heart
of this chapter centers on the views and activities of men-as-men in popular political culture—including how men are influenced by women in
this sphere—the work of feminist scholars on women's participation in
various forms of political activity must necessarily provide a contingent
backdrop to the present examination, including with respect to what
Díaz Barriga (1998) has noted is the markedly ambiguous and contradictory character of living in an area formed by land invaders.

Of special interest are the shifting concepts of public and private
realms in relation to political forms and goals in Latin America. Maxine
Molyneux's now widely employed studies (1985; 2001) on the distinc-

tion between "practical gender interests" and "strategic gender interests" have been utilized by numerous scholars as a way to discuss issues pertaining to gender inequality while accounting for very different interpretations of the political significance of their activities on the part of the women actors involved. Among the strategic interests noted by Molyneux are the abolition of the sexual division of labor, removal of institutional forms of discrimination, and attainment of political equality in general (2001, 43–44). Practical gender interests, in contrast, revolve around issues formulated by women's own "immediate perceived need." As such, practical interests do not challenge overall gender subordination, although they certainly are a product of these conditions.

In a similar vein, Temma Kaplan's 1982 article on "female consciousness" paved the way for a generation of writings on the links between women's (public) political activism and their (private) roles as mothers. Added to this is the more recent recognition of contradictory consciousness (and interests) for women from different social strata; the idea of homogeneity among women has long been recognized as an artificial construct. Men, too, share in the ambiguities of practical and strategic gender interests, and the understanding of men and their involvement in political activism is also influenced by a variety of factors, such as their roles as fathers. Yet, to date, these issues remain largely unexplored.

Lynn Stephen's analysis of women and social movements in Latin America is especially pertinent in bridging the categorical chasms between practical and strategic, private and public, in conceptualizing politics.

> If women's work is labeled as "practical" and as outside the center of organizational politics, then their political work remains at the margins. In addition, the equivalence of "practical" demands with women's participation in the "private" sphere begs the question of how practical demands can be asserted, if not in the public sphere—a point avidly made by those who point out how "practical" demands become public. (1997a, 12)

In the hidden spaces of families and households in Colonia Santo Domingo, for example, women and men discuss and debate many extradomestic concerns, including practical political beliefs and actions. This chapter addresses how women and men in contemporary working-class Mexico City may share goals of self-rule and corresponding concerns regarding class-based popular political will, yet may act on these goals and concerns in manifestly different ways.[3]

1988 AND BEYOND

In 1988, for the first time in modern Mexican history, Mexican voters were presented with a real choice among the candidates for president. Many commentators believe that the PRD opposition candidate, Cuauhtémoc Cárdenas, and not the PRI nominee, Carlos Salinas, won the election. But irregularities in the vote count, including a faulty tabulating machine and a computer breakdown due to an extended interruption of electricity during the vote count, conspired to push Salinas over the top, and the PRI candidate, as had always been the case, was once again declared the winner. Pundits and proletarians uniformly look back on 1988 as a watershed year that literally opened the floodgates to subsequent opposition victories in gubernatorial races and other key contests, such as that for Mexico City's mayor in 1997, in which the same Cuauhtémoc Cárdenas was the victor.

After the debacle of 1988, many friends and neighbors in Santo Domingo looked ahead to the presidential election of 1994 as the next chance for significant change in the country as a whole. As that election neared, and in the midst of an unusually chaotic political climate following the Zapatista New Year's Day uprising and the assassination of the official PRI candidate in March, a certain resignation to anxiety and chaos began to take hold among Mexicans generally, as many felt the PRI dinosaurs would undoubtedly rule forever. Nonetheless, in the final months leading up to the summer election there appeared a renewed enthusiasm, especially among my male friends, as if the proximity of the vote made prospects for a better future seem more real.

As for the mid-*sexenio* elections of 1997, after the fact, the general consensus among my acquaintances in Santo Domingo was that little had changed for better or worse after Cárdenas became mayor of Mexico City that year. Cárdenas's defenders have often hastened to add that his hands were severely tied after having assumed office, as the civic problems of Mexico City were as outsized as the financial coffers left him by the previous PRI administration were bare. Interestingly, when Cárdenas stepped down in the fall of 1999 to once again run for the presidency of the Republic, he was replaced by his deputy, Rosario Robles, who, according to some of my friends, was able to swiftly bring about dramatic changes—for example, in reducing crime in the city through her attempts to clamp down on police corruption.

The change to a PRD administration in Mexico City also brought additional changes in the local political administration. When we first met

Figure 12. Slogan on a major boulevard bordering Santo Domingo, 1994: "A man [*hombre*] without work is not a man, he is hunger [*hambre*]. Vote for Cuauhtémoc Cárdenas."

in the early 1990s, my friend Bernardino Ramos was leading demonstrations against the office of the *subdelegación* (roughly, the subdistrict chief's office). Following the election of a PRD mayor in 1997, Bernardino suddenly found himself in a jacket and tie, seated at a bank of phones, after he was appointed to the position of *subdelegado* in the Pedregales district of Mexico City (which included Santo Domingo and other *colonias*). In August 1999, understandably defensive about his new position of power, Berna nevertheless described to me the new opportunities that he felt had been opened to progressive community activists because of the PRD mayoral victory in Mexico City two years earlier.

When I returned to Santo Domingo in May 2000, some two months before the presidential election that year, the most noticeable change I observed among male or female friends in the *colonia* was an utter lack of interest in the upcoming vote. As one friend summed it up, "We finally have democracy, just as you do in Gringolandia, Mateo: now we, too, get to choose between two or three candidates!" Then he added, with more than a trace of sarcasm, "Yeah, some choice, huh?" With Cárdenas running a distant third, the horse race had come down to a contest between Francisco Labastida of the PRI and Vicente Fox of the PAN, neither of whom inspired prospects for the desired social change among any more than a few of my associates in the neighborhood.

Writing about this roller coaster ride of electoral enthusiasm followed by sincere disillusionment with formal politics on the part of many Mexicans in the 1990s, Roger Bartra noted that "after more than half a century of modernity, the Mexican political system has ended up in a *cul-de-sac*." And on the matter of democracy,

> Modern myths, such as national unity, institutionalized revolution, etc., have deteriorated. Many Mexicans now believe the train of modernity has stopped. Yet this disenchantment and delegitimization seems to be precisely what is opening the door to democracy. (Bartra 1995, 144)

More precisely, in what way the popular political culture of disenchantment and delegitimization might actually help open doorways to democracy in Mexico is of general concern. Among other things, Bartra argues, it is in the tension between legitimate public politics, especially elections, and other more subterranean expressions of political frustration and discontent that doors to democracy may become passable. In a similar vein, David Kertzer has written of "perhaps the most important ritual of legitimation found in modern nations . . . the election" (1988, 48–49). Nor, we hasten to add, is Kertzer's use of the term *ritual* meant in any way to denigrate these activities; his point is precisely that ritual plays as large a part in the political lives of people in the metropoles as in smaller-scale societies. For these reasons, rather than regard the vote as the highest much less the sole expression of participatory democracy, with Bartra and Kertzer we should instead explore electoral involvement on the part of people in Santo Domingo as one element in the larger constellation of actions and events constituting citizenship there. In their paper on the Mexican presidential election of 1988, Lomnitz, Lomnitz, and Adler described what they term "democratic rituals":

> The insistence upon democratic forms permeates almost all of the stages of the campaign. The use of these forms generally serves to legitimate decisions that have already been made and at the same time are indispensable for the legitimacy of the traditional process [of appointing/electing a new president in Mexico]. (1993, 364–65)

The ritual of voting underwent significant changes in Mexico in the period between 1988 and 2000, both in terms of the defeat of the PRI in multiple elections and with regard to efforts, beginning in the early 1990s, to reduce vote fraud, for example, through issuance of voter identification cards with photographs. Perhaps most significant has been the ritualization of electoral indeterminacy, so that the mere fact that the

PRI was not necessarily destined to win has become confirmation of the legitimacy of democracy in Mexico overall.[4]

LEARNING FROM ENGENDERED
POPULAR POLITICS IN MEXICO

The engendered component of popular politics in Mexico City must be viewed still more profoundly as a *process* grounded in comprehensive inequalities on a societal level, as well as even more complex and varied relations between men and women, and among women and men, at a more intimate level. Further, if Vivienne Bennett is correct in stating that "in Mexico, social activism has become a part of the everyday life and the everyday struggles of poor urban women" (1998, 129), then engendering popular political culture in Mexico is far more than a matter of persuading women to vote in less-conservative patterns. In charting the chaotic character of emerging popular politics in Colonia Santo Domingo, we see that gender differences and complementarities are core issues to be explained and not simply quantified in exit polls or electoral surveys (see McDonald 1997).[5] When one neighbor told me in 2000 that women who got involved in politics of any kind were *las prófugas del metate* (fugitives from the grinding stone), he was not distinguishing between elected officials and community activists.

There is much that women's involvement in nonelectoral political activities may teach us about popular political culture in general, both those of us living in Mexico and those living in other, more distant parts of Latin America. As Sarah Radcliffe and Sallie Westwood have written,

> Latin America, with its great diversity and resilience expressed in popular cultures and through civil society, also has the possibility of re-visioning notions of democracy that draw in questions of ethnicity and gender in ways that are only beginning to be part of the discussion elsewhere. (1996, 44)

In the seemingly simple and innocuous dialogues that occur daily in households in Colonia Santo Domingo, conflicts and cajoling between women and men over everything from birth control to electoral choices reveals elements of the complex psychosocial efforts of women to challenge and change what men are and what they do. There has seldom been any doubt as to the efforts of men to change women, for instance, with respect to voting choices and participation in community protests and organizations. But the influence of women on men in political matters has certainly been underemphasized and little studied. Perhaps discussions and debates in Santo Domingo might provide examples of how women and men there are re-visioning notions of democracy by drawing in questions of gender, including the emerging process of negotiation between women and men as to the relative merits of voting and popular movements as mechanisms of social change. As the Comité Unico de Damnificados demanded after the 1985 earthquake in Mexico City: ¡Democracia en la ciudad y en la casa! (Democracy in the city and the home!).

In the period from 1988 to 2000, there was a convergence, in time if not necessarily in space, of at least three distinct historical trends. First, there was significant popular engagement with national political currents, including presidential elections, although this commitment varied tremendously from one moment to another and among different social groups. Second, questions of self-rule and popular political will in Colonia Santo Domingo were recurrent themes in discussions of politics of all kinds, which was something to be expected in a neighborhood in which for three decades women and men have had to live by their own devices and could seldom count on immediate or long-term assistance from the government. Third, there were significant linkages between popular political culture, the growth of grassroots feminism in social movements, and daily life in *colonias populares* like Santo Domingo.[6] In particular, it is noteworthy that women in Santo Domingo and elsewhere increasingly played the role of catalysts in the transformation of popular political culture generally, and that through women's participation in political life in working-class areas, issues like local autonomy and self-rule became, in diverse ways, some of the central crucibles of democracy in contemporary Mexican society overall. In fact, there was a "sea change in attitudes about women's political participation and representation" in Mexico in these years (Jaquette 1998, 221).

Talk about gender and democracy does not necessarily lead to a modernizing quest in which the position of women is used as a simple test of social progress. Instead, what needs to be highlighted is how, and whether, women in Mexico City, as elsewhere, have intentionally, or not, played an initiating role in fomenting consequential social change in the past several decades, and what are some of the implications of these activities for broader popular political trends.

Families and households are not always the last refuges of scandalous patriarchy and oppression. They are also, at some times and in some cases, embryonic sites of change with respect to gender identities and relations and social life more broadly. This understanding necessarily requires a return to notions of public/private dichotomies, which are perhaps tediously overdetermined in gender and Latin American studies.[7] Bringing the personal and the everyday into politics implies a reconsideration of what constitute political spaces, political debate, and indeed political life—the politics of politics—especially where the borders blur between overt, covert, organized, and spontaneous outbreaks of resistance, skepticism, rebellion, and apathy.

Alejandra Massolo has been among the most lucid commentators in documenting how women have utilized "the public world with which they are most familiar," that is, the neighborhood, and how, since the dramatic presidential election of 1988, there has occurred a "transfer of women activists in urban popular movements and community organizations to the electoral arena" (1998, 193). In the process, issues of strategic and practical gender interests were invariably given more formal voice in multiple political arenas throughout the country. For virtually all men and women in Mexico, the elections of 1988 provided the possibility of electing a non-PRI candidate to the presidency, and for many, the post-1988 period has brought renewed promise of societal change through voting some politicians in and others out of office. Still, and especially in *colonias* like Santo Domingo, an undercurrent of debate has centered around a troubling phenomenon. Kathleen Bruhn, in a paper on neoliberal and left politics in Mexico, has noted: "Popular movements that become involved in elections often fear—with reason— that the excitement of elections will divert the attention of their leaders from the movement's original goals, and worst of all, to little practical effect" (1998, 159).[8]

Too often, human activities, especially those involving notably "gendered" characteristics, are forced into the categories of "public" and "private."[9] So it is that the "public sphere" is too frequently contrasted in a mechanical fashion with "home and family." And too often such typologizing does not get us very far. There is somewhat more purpose to noting a "formal/informal" dichotomy in popular politics, as when Kapur in a paper on women's contributions to Mexican politics, contrasted "women's informal participation in movements such as the neighborhood kitchens and public protests, and formal participation in the legislature, government, and in party posts." (1998, 386–87). This dichotomy is linked, in turn, to María Luisa Tarrés's observation that the participation of women "in social and political movements in the last twenty years shows not only an ability to define interests linked to their sex, but also a great talent for gathering resources and forming their own organizations and spaces" (1996, 8). Where this has left men, especially men from the popular sectors, is not clear. Certainly, many have been involved to one extent or another in activities sponsored by major political parties. Others have continued to express to me their frustration at being unable to find a viable venue for their political aspirations and energies.

One central question that remains is what impact has the participation of women in social and political movements had on men, and has this had any lasting effect on men's spasmodic enthusiasm for electoral politics in the period 1988–2000 in Mexico.

VOICE: ELECTIONS, LEGITIMACY, AND PUBLIC POLITICS

Leading up to the August 21, 1994 presidential election, Gabriel's long *abstencionista* policy with respect to voting became a target of periodic disparagement by his closest friends like Marcos and Marcelo. Even if these friends did not particularly support the PRD candidate, for example, they often insisted that their political action, voting for Cárdenas anyway, would at least be a vote against the ruling PRI, whereas abstaining from voting would be indistinguishable from voting for the PRI. Gabriel might think that his politics were different than most people's, they argued, but really he was as bad as, or worse than, the PRI supporter Toño because he was fooling himself in the process.

My companions were actively grappling with an old and today frequently neglected topic in politics: What, after all, is suffrage worth to the dispossessed? In the minds of many in Colonia Santo Domingo, the question revolved around the extent to which elections could provide an opportunity to determine the course of Mexican history. These men and women are Mexican citizens, intently concerned with issues like justice, equality, and social well-being, and the value of voting in relation to accomplishing these objectives—where voting was conceived of as both a right and a duty—was an unresolved problem for most. Indeed, as Héctor Tejera has noted, increasingly there is a sentiment among many in the Mexican capital that "the means to improving the very conditions of life may be realized through the vote" (1998, 55), and that only insofar as Mexicans participate in elections will they be entitled to consider themselves agents of change.[10] It is in this sense that we can understand Renato Rosaldo's delicate evaluation of the issue of elections: "The vote is the citizen's most sacred right/rite" (1997, 33).

At the same time, for others, elections may represent a "displacement of the democratic formation of political will" onto routinized, innocuous, well-worn paths that lead to no substantial political change for the masses of people in Mexico.[11] It may seem unreasonable to expect more of democracy in Mexico than the existence of one, two, or more viable electoral parties—often regarded as the cornerstone for claims to democratization. This is especially true since, in Mexico, and especially in countries like Chile, Argentina, Panama, Brazil, and Peru, the mere existence of such formal elements of political life are routinely considered reason enough to support claims of *re*democratization, which in many of these countries means, in effect, the return to civilian rule. Yet, the smooth functioning of multiparty forms of liberal democracy in the relative absence of severe economic and social crises seems hardly tantamount to declarations of the emergence of truly participatory forms of governing.

In modern Mexico voting is promoted by the state, the schools, and the media as the highest civic duty and the one true mark of citizenship. Abstainers are, almost by definition, not fully Mexican. So in our street debate in May 1994, Toño chided the abstainers and opposition-voters in the crowd: "Unlike you, I am *proud* to be a Mexican!" Toño talked about his support for the PRI as squarely grounded in the understanding that unknown alternatives are far worse a prospect than even known tyrants. His reasoning illustrates how successful the efforts of Mexico's technocratic leaders have been to promote "fear of an alternative" among the citizenry, and thereby make democracy safe for Mexican neoliberalism (see Centeno 1997, 255).

Michael Higgins and Tanya Coen captured key aspects of the popular allegiance to the PRI prior to its defeat in the presidential election of 2000 when they quoted the political views of María Elena de Sosa, a resident of Oaxaca:

> No one tells me who to vote for; I vote for whoever I want, though, in fact, I have never voted in my life. Why? Because whether you vote or do not vote, you still have to work. And no matter what, the PRI wins. . . . If you do not vote, you get a lot of shit when trying to get something from the government. . . . I need to maintain this government even if it is run by the PRI because it maintains my sons. (2000, 45)

Actual abstention and other indicators of participation (or lack thereof) in the formal political process, like voter registration—for example, that most registered voters are women—reveal facts that most definitely do not speak for themselves. Rather, abstentionism and registration, to cite just these two phenomena, must be examined so as to learn the significance of their gendered and other political characteristics.

In response to the ruinous effects of neoliberalism on wide sectors of the populace in Mexico, it nonetheless remains the case that apparent quiescence is more characteristic of popular political culture than outright protest and rebellion.[12] Yet it would be wrong to dismiss inactivity, including abstentionism, as representative of nothing more than the benign frustrations of the lower and marginalized classes in Mexico City. Just as there is an important distinction between apathy and alienation, so too, when considering abstentionism, one must use extreme caution when interpreting the results of survey research on questions pertaining to political views. Oppenheimer is perhaps a bit too eager to report on the results of a poll that showed Mexico City residents in 1994 more preoccupied with traffic jams than with the Zapatistas (1998, 152–54, 348). Analysts consign popular concerns to trivial pursuits at their peril. This is corroborated clearly in the contradictory comment of Doña de Sosa: "I vote for whoever I want, though, in fact, I have never voted in my life."

In reference to certain of her neighbors who vote for the PRI, Doña Fili, who has been a community leader and Christian Base Community activist in Colonia Santo Domingo since the first days of the land invasion in the early 1970s, told me:

"Look, we want a change but . . . but not demagoguery. It's as we've always said, 'We want a change, we want a change,' and things just get worse. Because, really, that's just what's happened. For me what is important is *educación*.[13] I think that this is the base upon which there will be a change in the country. Because the people [*el pueblo*] are very ignorant. How many years has the PRI governed, and the truth is that they've been corrupt! It's not for nothing that we oppose them, but because it's *palpante* [palpable]. You can feel the corruption!

"And, sure, because there's no *educación*, we vote for the PRI. There are *vecindades* and alleys where people never read a newspaper or a book, and they go altogether and vote for the PRI. And if you say to them, 'Don't vote for the PRI,' they say, 'No, well, it's because they're going to throw my children out of school.' They're scared. Fear is what's going on. And they vote for the PRI and the PRI wins because . . . because the PRI wins!"

To what degree such sentiments represent new feelings of disillusion and disappointment, and to what degree they should simply be understood as the voice of invariably marginalized men and women in

Mexico City, are significant issues. What *is* changing in popular political moods and judgments? Or, to restate Alan Knight's query: Is there anything new under the Mexican sun? (1990, 87). Surely among the populace in Mexico City there is a widespread disenchantment with the alleged benefits of modernity and the national myth of institutionalized revolution. Equally as certain, there is broad concern, often more apparent in words than deeds, regarding the difference between democracy as an idealized goal and as an everyday reality (see Jaquette 1998, 226).

When he owned and ran a corner *tienda* on Huehuetzin Street in Santo Domingo, Marcelo was often privy to disputes and discussions among his customers regarding formal and informal politics. In addition, Marcelo regularly acted on election days as a poll watcher [*vigilante del partido*] for the PRD, to help ensure that vote fraud in the *colonia* was kept to a minimum. When asked about his participation with the PRD, Marcelo responded:

"I've participated with them because I feel they [the PRD] are better at keeping a finger on our pulse. More than anything today I want citizens' votes to be respected. In order for there to be a real democracy I think the vote needs to be respected. Because if the PRI continues in office, it's no longer by popular will but now only because of an elite, because of powerful figures who protect certain interests. Even if [then President] Zedillo said the elections are clean, it's a lie, because anyone can see the manipulation they're involved in."

I asked Marcelo if a majority of people in Colonia Santo Domingo vote for the PRI or for the PRD.

"How should I put this. There's a little bit of everything. There are *PRIistas,* there are *PANistas,* there are *ecologistas, PRDistas.* And, maybe in five or six of the polling stations we [*PRDistas*] get the vote. In another, there's a tie between the PAN and the PRI. In another, the PAN wins. In one or two, the PRI wins. Anyway, the majority vote for the opposition, one way or another. They don't want the PRI to win."

As Marcelo and I had talked previously about guerrilla movements in his home state of Guerrero, I asked him to compare the efficacy of these two ways of attempting political change.

"Well, look. . . . I think people take up arms in desperation. I think that maybe arms don't solve a thing, but this is the product of desperation. I'm not really sure but I think that's what's going on when those fellows [*cuates*] grab a rifle or a machine gun to fight. That's what happened in the Revolution, isn't it? Who knows? News here is so manipulated, so all you hear is that these are liars, rebels, causing the country so much harm. Well, maybe they're struggling for a just cause even if violence isn't right, but, well, they're pushed to the side by the government."

NATIONAL AND REGIONAL *LUGAREÑOS*

This is how people in Colonia Santo Domingo like Fili and Marcelo describe some of the changes in their popular political temperament and their patience for official politics-as-usual in Mexico since 1994. They are among the unruly *lugareños,* the local denizens of Mexico City who would have it other than the status quo. Yet, in their defiance of politics-as-usual, they are also notably compliant, still far more prone to verbal than to physical protests.[14]

After 1994 my male friends in Colonia Santo Domingo seemed more prone than in past years to joke about politicians. In 1996, for example, I talked to a number of men as we shared some peach wine coolers one sunny Sunday afternoon outside Marcelo's *tienda.* My young friend Timo Junior, still in his *futbol* garb from a game earlier that morning, asked me, "You know why they call Zedillo 'the Pigeon'? Because every three steps he craps, every three steps he craps!" Marcelo also remembered his delight in 1994 upon hearing the news that students at the National University had thrown garbage at Zedillo when he was running for president. Someone added that it had been the first time that had happened in thirty years. Times were changing, the men told me; there would be no more blind acquiescence to political leaders; even the president was now open to ridicule in the press, they noted.

Still, I think, not all changes are equivalent, and 1994 had brought an unusually profound perception of the *possibilities* for more basic changes in Mexico. As the community activist Bernardino Ramos once told me in a conversation prior to the 1994 elections:

"Look, Mateo, there are four possibilities. One, [electoral] fraud by the PRI, which then leads to uprisings . . . in maybe fifteen states. Two, opting for the lesser evil, where PAN wins and the electoral process is legitimated. Three, a draw, where no one wins, runoff elections are called, and you have a peaceful situation. Four, Cárdenas wins and you have a draw by force."

For Bernardino, as for few others of my acquaintance in Colonia Santo Domingo, it was critical to gain clarity about the "national picture" and to have a clear sense of how local activities in the *colonia* might impact larger events in the country as a whole. In this way, as Bernardino might have put it, being an unruly *lugareño* can carry significance on regional and national stages.

As it turned out, the August 21, 1994, presidential, congressional, and gubernatorial elections were quite "popular," in the sense that 78 percent of eligible voters turned out to cast their ballots, and they were, by all accounts, relatively clean and free of electoral fraud. The PRI won the presidency by a landslide, which was quite different from events in 1988. Further, Bernardino's comments to me had been uttered in 1994, three years before he would be appointed to the locally influential government position of Subdelegado de los Pedregales, which put him in charge of everything from water leaks under the streets to getting out the vote for the PRI on election days.

Berna had grown up in Colonia Ajusco, and for several years he had even been *colonia* president there; his reputation for reform and service to the community was unimpeachable. Yet, when we talked in 1999, he was clearly a bit uneasy in his new role as government politician and peddler of electoral promises.

In 1999, Doña Fili also voiced her intense concerns regarding voting and elections, giving even more emphasis to what she saw as a fundamental issue, the need for *educación,* to change people's political awareness and behavior. Fili has often been able to articulate better than other neighbors in Santo Domingo her misgivings, and at times opposition, to the strategy of elections as a route to solving Mexico's social ills. In her recollection of the very different popular politics of citizens throughout the capital following the devastating earthquake in September 1985, Fili echoes Carlos Monsiváis's impassioned assessment: "The solidarity of the population was really a power takeover" (1987, 17).[15] After the government had utterly failed in its response to the crisis, tens of thousands of Mexico City residents had assumed responsibility for rescue and relief efforts by spontaneously forming squads throughout the capital.

All this came tumbling out one chilly morning in early 1997, as Doña Fili and I sat around her kitchen table trying to keep warm with some Taster's Choice coffee that I had brought as a gift from the United States:

"In 1979 we organized the Unión de Colonias Populares (UCP), and initially we were very strong because we struggled, around education, transportation needs, health issues. We saw that, once organized, it was harder for them to manipulate us, for some guy in a suit to sweep us along behind him.

"The UCP was made up of workers, housewives, and also students."

"Were the students the leaders of the UCP?" I asked.

"Sure, for us, the students are the best [*lo máximo*], because they convey what they know to us. They tell us what books to read, because our culture in Mexico is very great, but we don't know it because all we're doing is watching television. That we had to read Juan Rulfo and other books. That's why we say, 'We older women love the students as if they were our own children because they tell us to learn.' Sometimes they recommend, for example, that we read a book by Elena Poniatowska, only that."

When their youngest son was born in 1986, Fili had once told me, she and her husband thought about giving him the middle name Mao, but in the end they had opted for Ernesto (for Che Guevara). Fili said they had decided against Mao because that name was too unfamiliar in Mexico City, whereas Ernesto was a more common name in Spanish. In our conversation about the UCP that day, I asked Fili to explain in more detail their reasons for and against giving their son the name Mao.[16]

"Because Mao has a lot of good things to say. I especially like what he says about self-criticism, because sometimes you think what you are doing is fine and that's that. 'That's what I say, so there!' Self-criticism is what I like in Mao, together with some other things."

"Like what?"

"Like his quote about paper tigers, and the fact that he wasn't just concerned with his community. We don't want there to be so much injustice, not just in Mexico but in other countries, too."

Fili continued by recounting to me her experiences in fomenting what she called "*educación popular*" in Santo Domingo, which she illustrated by telling me that she had put up "wall newspapers" [17] outside Junior High School #42 on October 2 one year to commemorate "the massacre of our students" in 1968.[18] For Fili, the term *community* carries with it as much the weight of class as it does place. For this reason, for her, the truly Mexican unruly *lugareños* are those who never forget watershed events, like October 1968, in Mexico.

Women who are involved in the upsurge of popular social movements—for example, independent public-health workers who offer classes on childbirth training and sexuality, or the single mothers who are portrayed on a popular television documentary series (with feminist slant) on Saturday nights, *Aquí nos tocó vivir*—such women are part of a grassroots feminist movement that has emerged in Mexico City and has had a substantial impact on how both women and men see themselves and one another, and, to a degree, on how they relate to one another.

Though Fili would *never* use such a coarse expression, such women are sometimes referred to by those for whom profanity is not offensive as *las viejas chingonas*—the brazen, presumptuous, and pushy women of Mexico City. *Las viejas chingonas* is a phrase which may be loosely glossed as "the women who don't take any crap." Carlos Vélez-Ibáñez calls them the "fucking strong women" (1983, 121). The expression *vieja chingona* is, in this sense, at root an oppositional identity internal to Mexican cultural citizenship.

What might account for such a wellspring of political activism on the part of women in Santo Domingo? I think the question itself is revealing, because it may show certain preconceptions within which such *militancia* on the part of women does not easily fit. Among other things, such queries speak to a common fallacious image of Mexican women (and Latinas in general), that they have been self-sacrificing *abnegadas* and submissive *sumisas* for centuries—if not millennia—and that they have only come to political life in the twentieth century. Just as it seems unusual to some to talk about fathers carrying children (see Gutmann 1996, 54–57), so, too, women are "known" to inhabit eminently domestic worlds. Yet even the commonly known phenomenon of women's higher attendance in churches of various kinds has been far too casually accepted (and facilely explained). Such trends must be seen as part of ongoing *and* emerging conflicts within households over gender identities and relations, and not simply as illustrations of classic struggles between tradition and modernity. Just as women's participation in popular organizations, for instance, is plainly associated with broader sociodemographic trends, such as the growing participation of women in work outside the home and the greater educational accomplishments of women in 2000 compared to past generations, so too responses by men to these activities on the part of women are grounded in their own changing roles in the cultural economy of modernity.

As researchers like Mercedes González de la Rocha (1994) and Sylvia Chant (1991) have carefully shown, socioeconomic and demographic transformations in the previous thirty years have indeed been changing family structures and social relations in urban areas of Mexico and throughout the Republic as a whole (see also González de la Rocha 1999b). Changes in production relations and fertility rates, for example, have deeply impinged on the loyalties felt and the company kept by men and women, both at the intimate level of households and families and in the broader social context of public political life and struggle.

For example, although development pundits internationally have bewailed what Chant sardonically has called the "problem" of single mothers, in real ways this problem is more apparent for governments, international agencies, and for men. In the view of development agency specialists, the problem of women-headed households frequently is discussed by using statistics, stereotypes, and sterile conceptual frameworks. Yet, as Chant explains, single motherhood is something that must be evaluated contextually (1999; see also Chant 1997). That is, the status of women as single and as mothers tells us little in itself as to the lives of these women and their families. Among other things, some analysts would today argue that even poverty must be related to subjective issues of power and control in households and not simply calibrated according to official tabulations of remunerated income. By no means am I arguing that poverty is all in one's head. Rather, once again, numbers, like facts, do not speak for themselves.

To pursue this point, in a general sense when discussing domestic divisions of labor, including with respect to decision making, we need to understand better the connection between changing social structures and gender relations based on inequalities. Why do women in some studies report that they were much happier after their husbands deserted them, even though they rarely initiate such separations, and why in certain historical situations women want to and are able to cause the dissolution of their marriages, and how does all of this relate to real and perceived economic (or physical?) constraints on women and households.

CHOICE: DEPENDENCY AND AUTONOMY

The men and women who transformed an igneous wilderness on Mexico City's south side into what is today Colonia Santo Domingo have constantly had to juggle, on the one hand, self-reliance to construct their neighborhood—dynamiting the rocks for roads, tapping illegally into power lines for electricity—and, on the other, dependency on "the outside" for jobs, food, consumer goods, entertainment, and the like.

In reference to self-reliance, one of my most perceptive colleagues in the *colonia*, Héctor Jiménez, told me that in the early days, "it was dangerous, because ownership of the lots wasn't legally clear. Anyone could try to take possession of a lot by force." In 1974 Héctor secured a

Figure 13. Héctor Jiménez nursing bad ankles in 1997.

double parcel, facing two streets and measuring around 410 square me-
ters, which in Santo Domingo is very substantial.

"I got it for 35,000 pesos," Héctor continued, "the whole thing! But
there was no electricity, no water, no sewage system, no nothing. . . . In
two weeks I had blocked off the whole area and begun to build here. It
was just my mother and me. We got here around 1974, and by our good
luck, neighbors in the area had put in a water pipe right to the door.
They had put in a public hydrant."

Such experiences continued through the ensuing twenty-five years,
most recently in 1992–93, when residents in Santo Domingo negotiated
with city authorities and among themselves for deep trenches to be dug
in the streets for sewer pipes. Similar to Mexicans in most rural areas of
the country, and in marked contrast to residents of middle- and upper-

class neighborhoods in the capital, people in Colonia Santo Domingo are accustomed to the regular exercise of limited self-government with respect to matters like building roads and ensuring citizens' safety in the *colonia*. Among other things, and unlike most wealthier neighborhoods in the capital, people know each other better and participate in common community projects in Santo Domingo.

How residents of the *colonia* would respond today were a politician to come along and pronounce, as did President Avila Camacho some sixty years ago, "*Yo voy a gobernar para todos*" (I am going to govern for all), is not an easy question to answer. Certainly, at the dawn of the twenty-first century, when Larissa Lomnitz's (1977) *marginados* have become anything but demographically marginal, many in the *colonias populares* of Mexico City would view this as a threat as much as a promise. They might greet such an announcement with as much skepticism as they would a repeat of President Miguel Alemán's promise, "*Un Cadilac para cada mexicano*" (A Cadillac for every Mexican).

Lessons learned by friends in Santo Domingo include those drawn from the *sexenio* (six-year presidency) of López Portillo (1976–82). My friend Alejandro reminded me that when López Portillo handed over the reins of power to his successor, Miguel de la Madrid, he had tears in his eyes as he explained that he was leaving office with no personal wealth and that the catastrophic financial crisis of 1982 in Mexico had not been his fault. Angela joined in the conversation, adding that shortly after he left office López Portillo was said to have bought a petrochemical complex in Spain, made possible in part (Angela's husband Juan quickly added) through the efforts of labor boss Fidel Velásquez, who called upon all members of the CTM union in Mexico to give up a day of their wages to help out poor López Portillo.

"And the idiots did it!" shouted Angela in true disgust.

Perhaps if every Mexican simply had access to safe and reliable transportation, then promises of luxury automobiles, to say nothing of governance and decision making, would matter less. As it is, what choices men and women in Santo Domingo and elsewhere have in their political lives is often linked in their minds to common concerns regarding democracy in Mexico as a whole. This is far from surprising, for even with the vagueness that is characteristic of how my friends in Santo Domingo use the term *democracy*, their definitions would generally include the central thrust of David Held's argument about democracy and modern states:

> The idea of democracy derives its power and significance . . . from the idea of self-determination; that is, from the notion that members of a political community—citizens—should be able to choose freely the conditions of their own association, and that their choices should constitute the ultimate legitimation of the form and direction of their polity. (1995, 145)[19]

If the heart and soul of democracy is concentrated in the viability of political choices, the fact that these seem quite limited to so many people in Santo Domingo should be cause for real distress. Increasingly over the decade of the 1990s, and especially in the last years of the Zedillo administration in Mexico, skepticism grew throughout the country, and in Colonia Santo Domingo, concerning the lack of genuine options for political change. My neighbors had reached conclusions similar to those of some Brazilians who had been interviewed by researchers in the 1970s. In that earlier study, the authors found: "What predominates is a profound skepticism about the efficacy of the vote" (Martínez-Alier and Boito Júnior 1977, 156; see also Stolcke 1988, 196–200). This is undoubtedly a sentiment that would ring true in any part of Latin America at virtually any point in the modern period.

By the late 1990s, there was a sense in certain parts of Mexico that coincided with another conclusion in Stolcke's work on elections and popular politics; that is, at most, one may effect change in local environments. In their immediate surroundings, neighbors have told me, they have a better chance of success in bringing about the changes they want. This view is similar to that described by Rubin (1997) regarding "regional democracy" in Juchitán, Oaxaca. There, he noted a widespread sense that political choices—exemplified but not limited to free elections—may exist on the local if not the national level. In Santo Domingo, too, the conviction that community mobilization around local demands can accomplish change has consistently been stronger than faith in bringing about change in Mexican society more broadly through whatever means.

To be sure, analysts must be careful not to make a fetish of autonomy, localism, or regional democracy, and thereby slip into a facile antifederal or anti-organizational bias (see Hellman 1992). As modern military theorists know, autonomous (or liberated) zones in urban areas can seldom simply enjoy any more than passing notoriety when besieged by vastly more powerful forces. Nonetheless, as I am repeatedly reminded by friends and neighbors in Colonia Santo Domingo, "Who is there we can rely on if not ourselves?"[20] This attitude serves, in a sense,

as an illustration of Roger Bartra's (1981) mordant account of the legit-
imizing functions of formal representative democracy in the networks of
political power in Mexico. As is equally true of formal civil liberties, universal suffrage is a surprisingly recent historical accomplishment in the
world. How these rights are exercised by diverse populations is related
to several factors, not the least of which concerns the relationship of
women, and grassroots feminism, to political dependency and autonomy. And the fact that in Santo Domingo men more than women express a great trust in elections as a means of social change should neither come as a surprise, nor should it be simplistically interpreted as
illustrative of greater politicization and political sophistication on the
part of men.[21] Judith Adler Hellman's (1994a) insistence that we not exaggerate the significance or the meaning of women's participation in social movements may surely be coupled with an equally strongly worded
caveat against exaggerating the significance of men's involvement in electoral politics (see Díaz Barriga 1998).

Even if sporadic, this more committed participation to voting as a
means of change by men certainly reflects more than the fact that
women were granted suffrage in Mexico only in 1953. It would nevertheless be a great mistake to attribute different degrees of interest and
faith in electoral politics between men and women to this date for suffrage. For one thing, only elderly grandmothers have personally experienced *not* having the legal right to vote. Rather, the question remains: Is
voting in Mexico "engendered," even if not generally regarded as such,
and if so, why? It is decidedly not a simple reflection of less interest in
political life, national or local, among women than men.

Indeed, as Elizabeth Jelin (1990) has demonstrated, in Latin America
generally, women are often more engaged than men in public survival issues regarding family consumption, and through these efforts they also
frequently become more knowledgeable than men about public political
affairs in general.[22] In certain respects, the open secret that many women
participate in political activism throughout the continent is evocative of
what Michael Herzfeld has called "social poetics." For Herzfeld, social
poetics may be discerned by studying how stereotypes (in this case, those
relating to women's political activities) are themselves used to multiple
purposes in diverse social interactions (1997, 15).

With specific reference to the case at hand, this means that women in
Santo Domingo do not simply go about the business of rectifying horrible living conditions, despite stereotypes that posit submissive and passive Mexican women. They often do so by openly flaunting such stereo-

types, and in this manner they cast larger shadows on the overall politics of democracy and self-rule in Mexico. Clearly, not all the women in Santo Domingo are *militantes* all of the time. But a large enough number are, at any given time, so that they consistently represent a serious political (and politicizing) force in the community as a whole.

This may be seen in the streets of the *colonia,* in terms of who is organizing whom for weekend *faenas* (collective work days) to repave streets, rebuild altars, or circulate whistles for monitoring suspicious outsiders who may be prowling the neighborhoods of Santo Domingo. As Alejandra Massolo has shown regarding women's collective actions in Mexico City in recent decades, "women constitute the main force propelling community participation programs" (1992, 73–74).

Women's playful twisting of stereotypes about their national qualities is evident inside homes as well. Before she died in November 1996, Angela used to delight in regaling visitors with a particularly unflattering portrayal of the *colonia*'s sporadically resident anthropologist: "Before Mateo came to Mexico, he thought all Mexican women were *abnegadas* [self-sacrificing]. So he asked me to introduce him to more of these women, since he was having a harder time meeting them than he thought he would." When I was present at the recounting of this apocryphal story, Angela would invariably turn to me and goad, "Isn't that right, Mateo?" For her exposé of Gringo gullibility—a lesson in how to apply the Latin American feminist slogan "Democracy in the city and the home"—without fail, Angela would get a round of guffaws from her friends.

My point is certainly not that in Colonia Santo Domingo men universally opt for expressing themselves politically through the ballot box, while women uniformly seek other means of ameliorating social inequalities and problems. With respect to the EZLN, for instance, Angela never had anything good to say.[23]

Nonetheless, for Angela and countless other women in Santo Domingo, democracy came to mean things in the 1970s, 1980s, and 1990s besides voting. Popular political choices were not, for them, reducible to elections. Deeply apprehensive about armed uprisings, like the one in Chiapas, Angela was even more contemptuous of governmental authority, if more than a little ambivalent as to whether there was anything else one could do to change the situation. "The Zapatistas don't play by the rules," she told Gabriel in an argument in her home. Gabi countered, "Well, the rules are designed to benefit the wealthy alone." Angela had to agree; she understood too well that the rules were thoroughly rigged against *la gente humilde* (the common folks) to contradict Gabriel on this point.

In response to a question I asked as to how much "real" support the Zapatistas had in Santo Domingo, Blanca told me around the same time of a cartoon she liked. In the cartoon are two people: one is Ramona, a well-known Zapatista leader, and the other is a person representing the PRI. Ramona's figure is tiny; the PRI figure is large. Nonetheless, the shadows they each cast are just the opposite: Ramona's extends far and wide, while the PRI's is tiny. In the same way, support for the PRI in the countryside—the so-called *voto verde* (green vote)—is said by some to be deceptively broad but shallow.

How and when people in Mexico City, and Mexico overall, have gone outside government channels to accomplish major and minor change has long been a point of heated debate in the streets and homes of Colonia Santo Domingo. Many women draw on their experiences in the economic sphere to guide their understanding of emerging political opportunities, or the lack thereof. In characterizing the response of poor women in urban Mexico to a series of never-ending crises, Mercedes González de la Rocha has written,

> The urban poor create and manipulate resources which the state and capital do not, and possibly could not, appropriate. The resources of poverty are . . . by no means measurable and cannot appear in national statistics. They belong to the world of private issues and events which take place at the domestic dimension. (1994, 263)

Viewing the domestic sphere, households, and families themselves not as inevitably the locus of conservatism and depoliticization but instead as sites of constant conflict and transformation regarding gender relations and much more, González de la Rocha (1999a) and other scholars have compelled us to rethink three related issues: (1) that what happens in the domestic dimension is not necessarily narrow and apolitical; (2) that the significance of what takes place domestically may in turn impact larger political transformations in society and may not merely be a reaction to more macro-social events; and (3) that we need to explore much more the assertion on the part of some that the poor are so preoccupied, by necessity, with matters of survival that they have no time or interest in the bigger questions of democracy and citizenship (see further discussion of these issues in Molyneux 2001).

Many scholars have written about the interests and ambitions of the poor, some emphasizing issues of mere survival, some the broader utopian aspirations of "even the poor," and others a mix of survival and utopian strategies. Nikki Craske, for example, talks of the issues and demands raised by residents of the *colonias populares* of Guadalajara, especially women. She says these issues center on basic infrastructure (water, sewers, roads, electricity, and street lighting); community services (public transport, schools, and health facilities); and, finally, what Craske has termed "citizenship demands" for genuine representation and accountability (1993, 116).

This reevaluation of perspectives on women has profound implications for how we are to discern changing gender relations in *colonias populares* like Santo Domingo, because it suggests that events in households and families may play more transformative roles in social relations than is generally acknowledged. Further, and of great consequence as well, such a revision leads to a reexamination of the impact of women's political involvement throughout Latin America, on women themselves *and* on men and masculinity across the region (see Viveros 2001).

In fact, much feminist research has recently challenged narrowly construed approaches to understanding women's place and work in Latin America, particularly the developmentalist paradigms that reduce women to "local" (a) reproducers, (b) social agents in community development, and (c) domestic crisis managers.[24]

This descriptive framework for understanding "women's place" in Mexico (and Latin America) has only certain features in common with the everyday experiences of women and men in Santo Domingo in the last two decades. In Santo Domingo and many other communities and regions in Mexico since the 1970s, women have often been the first to be touched by political, economic, and sociocultural changes in gender identities and relations. As often as not, men have been drawn into the maelstrom of transforming gender beliefs and practices by the women in their lives.

So it is that, in the *colonia,* wife beating is no longer (if it ever was) always a purely "domestic" (meaning private, hidden) affair. This shift is largely at the instigation of women's individual and collective efforts. In rumors and in open denunciations, domestic violence and abuse are regularly discussed among neighbors and raised as issues of broad concern by local groups of women, for instance, those affiliated with public-health teams active in the area. Surely, there are battered women who endure their suffering in secret and in silence. Just as surely, there are men in the *colonia* who routinely mock the more widespread community censure of wife beating. The point is not that Santo Domingo is

wholly unlike other communities in the capital city or the country overall. The point is, rather, that such "domestic" conflicts are not confined to the domicile any more than people in the neighborhood rely on
those whom Nancy Fraser (1989) calls "specialized publics" (e.g., social
workers, police) to resolve these kinds of "family" disputes.

My neighbor in Santo Domingo, Lourdes, gave me an object lesson
in her "public-community approach" to denouncing the confinement of
wives in their houses when she shouted to a neighbor watching a street
celebration from behind her gate: "Come on Rosa, come with us. You
can come out. Did he tell you you couldn't? So, then, come on." But
Rosa did not budge, and Lourdes concluded scornfully that after so
many years, Rosa had no desire to end her virtual domestic imprison-
ment (see Gutmann 1996, 214).

Nor is it the case that women and men divide into two neatly distin-
guishable categories vis-à-vis their positive or negative roles in social
change. My intent is precisely not to present such a static "two armies"
approach. Rather, in terms of social influence, I wish to highlight the
salient, if often unheralded, transformative positions that women—in
social movements and in family settings—have assumed in Santo Domingo in recent years.[25]

NOISE: MARCHES, STREET JUNTAS, AND CHANGE

Given a reconfigured understanding of domesticity's new meanings—
related as much to participation and struggle as it is to obedience and
passivity—we need to further explore the question of civil rights and
self-rule in working-class squatter settlements like Colonia Santo Domingo. For example, in contrast to many earlier analysts, Francisca
Lima (1992) has shown quite effectively the problems inherent in posit-
ing a ubiquitous and primordial dichotomy in Mexican studies between
casa and calle. Time of day has everything to do with who "controls"
the streets, just as "control of the house" is a concept whose imprecision
has regrettably not impeded overgeneralizations and oversimplifica-
tions about domestic patriarchy in Mexico generally. In many regions of
Mexico, for much of the day, women more than men are those most
commonly encountered in the street, and, to varying degrees, they are
the ones who can, for a time, anyway, legitimately claim the streets as
"their" space.

Or take another example involving "the street" and popular politics.
When I returned to Santo Domingo again in December 1996, friends

and neighbors were bitterly discussing a different kind of street controversy. For months that year, it seemed, there had been demonstrations
in the city center that had regularly brought traffic to a standstill. Television coverage carried the unsubtle message that these demonstrations
by union workers, campesinos, students, and indigenous groups accomplished nothing but making pollution worse and traffic jams more frequent. Many of my acquaintances in the *colonia* concurred. Others insisted that these demonstrations were signs of desperation, and thus, no
matter how counterproductive in terms of efficiency, they were helpful
and justified in their own way.

As Marcelo told me at the time, "Look, I know there's a lot of folks
who aren't happy about the marches. But the protesters . . . something
is hurting them. They're being ignored. So, they've got no choice but to
demonstrate in such a noisy way, because the government isn't listening
to the people's demands."

You cannot always determine the value of people's actions in terms of
efficiency, Gabriel had admonished me on another occasion. After all,
had he not spent most of a week's "extra" income on buying film for
an old Olympus camera he had bought at a flea market? Supporters of
the Zapatistas had carried out a *plantón* demonstration on the Zócalo
downtown and, he told me, that had been more important than anything else that week.

If he didn't take photographs, how would news of the demonstration
be spread, Gabi asked me? I replied that in the United States there had
been more news about Mexico that year (1994) than usual: Chiapas,
Colosio, and the presidential election. "Well, there's been *none* here,"
Gabi quickly asserted. Thus, in a vivid critique of rational choice, Gabriel and his companions had the sense that it was up to them to invent
a "popular" form of news through photos they shot and propaganda
they helped distribute in Santo Domingo. Men whose income was
barely two to three minimum wages would thus spend what little dis-
cretionary income they had on such displays of certain trends of popular political cultures in practice.

In the Huayamilpas Park near the *colonia,* others gathered on Sundays, and occasionally on Saturdays, to clean up the *laguna* of weeds
and debris. Former Maoist activists in the area had chosen this project
to facilitate continuing efforts to mobilize residents around social issues
and to maintain a presence there. A janitor at the nearby National University brought her dog on a leash to the clean-ups.[26] When I asked the
dog's name, she answered with a smile, "Tovarich! Do you know what

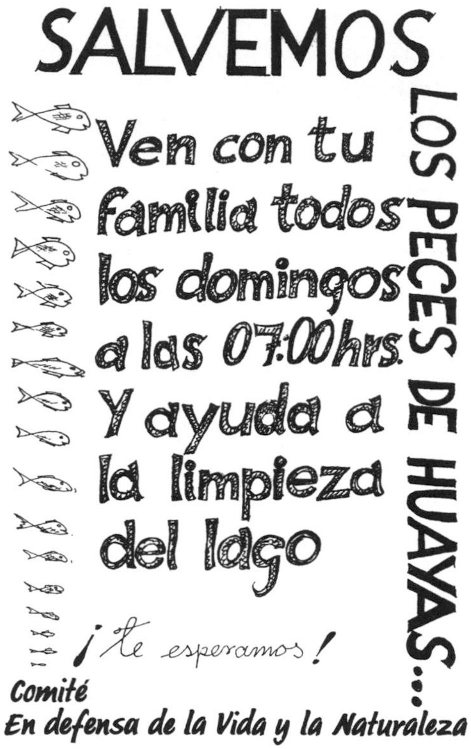

Figure 14. Leaflet calling on residents of Santo
Domingo and surrounding neighborhoods to
help clean up the Huayamilpas Lagoon, 1993.
Courtesy of Bernardino Ramos.

that means, Mateo?" She assumed that no Gringo would recognize the
Russian word for "comrade." She and her fellow compatriots were
eagerly looking for ways, here, through ecology, to fortify what often
proved to be fickle popular support for their mobilizing efforts.

Street *juntas* occurred throughout May 1994 on Huehuetzin in Colonia Santo Domingo. The city government was offering help in street
paving. My neighbor Amelia explained to all who would listen that
this overture represented no more than an election-year promise designed to keep the people satisfied and less oppositional. Others disputed this conclusion, arguing that as poor people, they had to take
whatever they could get. Someone else added that she was impressed at
what she knew of organizations like El Barzón and the Alianza Cívica,
primarily middle-class groups engaged in protests against government

financial and political policies. There was a lot that people in Santo Domingo could learn from the tactics employed by El Barzón and Alianza Cívica, she insisted; these organizations were also important because they showed "Now we're all poor." This last opinion was shared by a number of others present. No one was pleased by the miseries of others, but there was a sense of common hardship and purpose, as if cross-class connections might augur less isolation for the residents of Colonia Santo Domingo in the present crisis.

My friends and neighbors were grappling with problems that had long confounded leading social theorists in Mexico. As in the old debate between Carlos Monsiváis and Roger Bartra, men and women in the *colonia* were unclear whether the problem was that they lacked a program sufficient to take advantage of the conjunctural crisis, or whether, on the contrary, there were plenty of programs and the problem was that there was no consensus as to which one should be utilized, and therefore no one really knew what to do during periods of crisis. Some thought these were ultimately different ways of looking at the same problem: how, when, and why change occurs in Mexico.

Mexican popular political culture is tautologically understood as primordial *mexicanidad* (à la Bonfil Batalla [1987]) by some commentators in Colonia Santo Domingo, although they do not tend to be those who hold sway in the *colonia*. By the same token, defining oneself as "Mexican" is repeatedly linked in the popular imagination to stereotypes of *mexicanidad:* when I commented to a mother that the 150 tamales she was making for her grandson's birthday seemed like a lot of work, she responded, "*No tanto para una mexicana*" (Not much for a Mexican woman) Whereupon the boy's mother contradicted the grandmother: "Then I must not be a *mexicana!*"

Monsiváis, in particular, talks about a shared "national culture" in Mexico from the 1920s through the 1950s (see, e.g., 1976). Beginning in the 1960s, however, political currents at national, regional, and local levels transformed signs and practices associated with *mexicanidad*. Later, Monsiváis wrote that a sense of shared Mexicanness, and common nationalism in general, "depends on common and individual memories *and on a minimum confidence in progress*" (1992b, 71; emphasis added).[27] Lacking confidence in progress, of course, identification with nation and much else can come loose. One consequence of this coming loose can be the development of various forms of nationalism—for instance, one more elite and the other more popular.

This leads, or has led, not so much to a stance of anti-Mexicanism on the part of people in Santo Domingo as to a real challenge to the implicit faith that many placed in the leadership of the nation as represented by national politicians. As confidence in progress (cultural as well as economic) has been shaken, clarity about what it means to be a Mexican has been shaken as well. If Toño worried in 1994 about what might happen if the PRI did not win the presidency, about what kind of chaos might be unleashed that some other party would not be able to contain, he was echoing a point made by Roger Bartra:

> If in some way a large part of the [Mexican] population has become convinced that their Mexicanness is confirmed by and corresponds to the peculiarities of their system of government, it should come as no surprise that for many Mexicans the political crisis means that the national reality is collapsing. (1999, 20)

CONCLUSIONS: ¡VIVA MÉXICO, HIJOS DEL CAOS!

In discussing the meaning of "popular political culture" in Mexico, Guillermo de la Peña has said that the concept refers to the manner in which the poor adjust and resist, negate and seek out solutions to their political problems; it denotes not merely the inertia carried over from a traditional past or the distorted imitation of the hegemonic culture (1990, 87). Unquestionably, aspects of such adjustment and resistance, negation and seeking, are evident when older men and women in Colonia Santo Domingo declared in the 1990s that, despite the hardships of lugging water from distant faucets or building their homes cinderblock by cinderblock, they had been in some ways happier in the past, before things became "settled" in the *colonia*. Héctor made this point when he talked admiringly about neighbors having united to put in a pipe and public spigot in 1974. Doña Fili liked to remind me of how much she missed the solidarity of the early days in the *colonia,* in the early 1970s, when, notwithstanding the hardships of the time, she and her neighbors watched out for one another. In contrast to the early, heady days of the land invasion, in 1998 often one did not even know the families living nearby. "As if this were a middle-class neighborhood," Doña Fili added somewhat disdainfully, well illustrating de la Peña's point that "we must not fail to appreciate the *communitarian* euphoria of squatters seeking social services, or even families and relatives collectively seeking survival" (1990, 105).

When I could get him to talk about his childhood in Guerrero, Mar-

celo not infrequently mentioned that although he was one of ten children, "even as poor as we were, we never went without food." By 2000
he was far less optimistic about his ability to consistently provide for his
own five children. The lack of economic progress of the last generation
of men and women in Mexico City is staggering and startling to many.
So it was that Marcelo—a former *abanderado* whose stellar academic
performance in fifth grade had allowed him to proudly carry the Mexican flag and even meet then President Echeverría—was far from being
a champion of Mexican politics and Mexico's political prospects in the
year 2000.

The perception that democracy may be re-visioned through lenses of
ethnicity and gender is crucial. Nonetheless, in tracing the trajectory of
popular political aspirations and movements in Santo Domingo in
1994—from a street debate in May to the subsequent cynicism and despair later in the year—we must understand that hopes cannot be forever raised if men and women are not able to effect some of the changes
they dream of accomplishing.[28] In 1999 Gabriel was no longer quot-
ing Subcomandante Marcos much; instead, with a disingenuously stoic
smirk, he reminded me, "*En México nunca falta una mosca en la sopa*"
(In Mexico, there's always a fly in the ointment).

In the spring of 1994, when discussions in Colonia Santo Domingo
turned to the presidential election, men and women were debating what
role they might play in determining the future of their country. Some
in the community were mainly concerned with general *educación* of
the poor and dispossessed, and cared less for the outcomes of particular
electoral contests. Others were especially worried lest electoral outcomes upset preordained power allotments. Many seemed anxious at
possible connections between political instability and news reports that
the Mexican military was purchasing increasing numbers of "anti-riot
vehicles" from the United States.[29]

A sense of opportunities to be seized was present in political debates
among men in the *colonia* in 1994, just as the threat of *international*
reprisal for stepping out of line was always lurking in the background
as well. In the midst of lively dialogue regarding prospects for political change in Mexico in 1994—through elections, the Zapatistas, or
other means—the danger of U.S. intervention was a curiously recurrent
theme, often linked directly with the new Free Trade Agreement (see
chapter 4). "Know how you scare kids around here?" a favorite joke
that year began. "You shout, 'Buuuushhhhh.'" The sound imitated a

rocket whistling through the air and recalled U.S. President George Bush ordering bombing raids on Iraq.[30]

Since that time, and particularly as a result of ever more economic desperation in the wake of the financial collapse of 1995, the political mood among my friends in Colonia Santo Domingo is increasingly one of disenchantment, a feeling of being cut off from mainstream political maneuvering and from hope for a brighter future. As such, the course of popular political culture among many men in the *colonia* is akin to the more general process common in Mexico that Claudio Lomnitz has described: "Political ritual is substituting for arenas of discussion and argumentation, creating hegemonic idioms of agreement between various and diverse points of view (cultural and political)" (1995, 42; see also Lomnitz 1998).

Susceptibility to disillusionment—and for more than a few, conventional indifference—as to the possibility of political change in Mexico is stronger than ever today in the *colonia*, coincidentally or not, developing simultaneously with a tremendous rise in reported street robberies and other crimes in Mexico City after 1995. Such sentiments are disproportionately stronger among my male than my female friends, as if the men more than the women had pinned their political hopes on voting and electoral change.

In a community founded and long reliant for its very survival upon the independent political will and activities of large numbers of women, this should come as no surprise. As in other communities in Mexico in which women have been leaders and *militantes* in popular struggles since the 1970s, the standard definition of politics and doing politics has often slighted women's "informal" efforts to broaden and diversify the public sphere (see Massolo 1994, 35).

In a similar vein, Aida Hernández has written recently that accounts of the struggles of indigenous peoples in Chiapas cannot continue to ignore indigenous women, "these new political actors who are changing not only the cultural dynamic of their own communities but also the political arena of the state and the nation" (1998a, 116).

The temporarily converging histories represented by both the upsurge in interest and activism around elections in 1994 as well as the more enduring participation of women in social movements in the past decades in Mexico rather quickly diverged with the dissipation of the former by early 1995. Nonetheless, the impact on popular political culture of unruly *viejas chingonas* in diverse activities in the streets and homes of the capital will be vital to engendering democracy in Mexico.

POSTSCRIPT TO THE 2000 PRESIDENTIAL ELECTION

As for the implications of the defeat of the PRI and victory for Vicente Fox of the PAN in July 2000, most members of the press and political elites in Mexico and internationally hailed the event as a wonderful and peaceful transition of power. The opposition was now in office, the marginal political officials were now at the fulcrum of power. Middle-class professionals seemed only slightly guarded in their optimistic predictions for dramatic economic, political, and social change throughout the Republic. Regardless of the policies promoted by Fox and his PAN coalition, and perhaps even despite their particular plans for Mexico's future, the political arena had been irrevocably transformed and free electoral choice had been ushered in forevermore. Many individuals critical of Fox and of the PAN seemed convinced by a theory of stages: first, vote out the PRI and their elected dictatorship, then worry about the specifics of who and what would replace them.

In Santo Domingo the election was viewed more circumspectly by most people with whom I spoke in August 2000 and subsequently. Some were hopeful that indeed Mexico's Rubicon had been crossed. They wished to maintain a wait-and-see posture. In this, their outlook reflected one that is widespread throughout Latin America most of the time: because one cannot hope to change governments in any significant way, and because such transitions sometimes bring partial and temporary attention to glaring social ills, one might as well hope for the best.

With the election of Vicente Fox in 2000, dramatic change was indeed promised for people at all social levels of Mexican society, and "especially" for the poor of that country. The first step—ousting the PRI—had been achieved, but the assumption of more than a few residents of the *colonia* was that the outcome might do little more than replace the erstwhile dinosaurs with more disinterested tecnócratas.

CHAPTER 9

UNAM Strike

You have to be willing to be a victim of history along with everybody else, because nobody is spared that.

Tony Kushner

On April 20, 1999, a student strike was launched to protest announced tuition hikes at the Universidad Nacional Autónoma de México (UNAM), Mexico's National University. With nearly 300,000 students, UNAM is one of the largest universities in the world and has been essentially a tuition-free public institution. The nominal payment required of students has amounted to pennies a year and had been in effect since the 1940s. Generations of political, scientific, and intellectual leaders from Mexico and Latin America more broadly have been trained at the UNAM; indeed, four of the last six Mexican presidents and, apparently, Subcomandante Marcos attended UNAM.[1]

Despite the apparent acquiescence of University administrators, who quickly declared the tuition hikes "voluntary," the students voted to continue the strike and to demand more control in University affairs and a permanent moratorium on all proposals to impose tuition. As might be guessed, safeguarding the autonomy of the National Autonomous University of Mexico was a major goal of the strikers in 1999 and has been a focal point of student and teacher political struggles throughout the twentieth century. Like other major public universities throughout Latin America, UNAM has long laid claim to an intellectual sovereignty from any form of government control. Undoubtedly, such academic independence has often been more asserted than realized. Nonetheless, the claim continues to carry undeniable moral weight in Mexico into the twenty-first century.[2]

In particular, the UNAM student strikers saw their actions as a way to protest neoliberal policies in the arena of higher education, and in fact they were at times most effective in painting the strike as a frontline struggle against what they alleged were secret proposals by the World Bank to privatize Mexico's national oil company PEMEX, the electric industry, and UNAM. During the summer of 1999, numerous neighbors and acquaintances in Santo Domingo asked me if I understood that this and not simply a tuition hike was the real significance behind the students' closing of the UNAM campus.

Initially, support for the strike could be found within the ranks of the professorate, many of whom were veterans of the generation of '68. This support on the part of the teachers was short lived, however, and during the summer I heard often of the *"ultras"* who, my University colleagues told me, shared nothing in common with the radicals of the 1960s. Few of these friends cared to see irony in the fact that some of them had been labeled in a similar fashion as wild-eyed extremists in the 1960s and 1970s. During spring 1999, the media reported that nearly 70 percent of the students were meeting with professors for classes off campus. In the fall that year, according to official figures, although the *paristas,* as the strikers were called, continued to occupy nearly all classroom and administration buildings on campus, around 85 percent of students nevertheless registered for classes.

Ultimately, in the early hours of Sunday, February 6, 2000, some nine months after the strike had begun, 2,500 Mexican Army troops from the newly formed Federal Preventive Police entered the campus, arrested more than 600 strikers, and reclaimed the University in the name of the federal authorities. The press portrayed those arrested as representing an assortment of anarchists, ex-cons, drug dealers, and radicals connected to the same protesters who had disrupted a World Trade Organization convention in Seattle, Washington, in December 1999. Even as they condemned the entry of Army troops onto the UNAM campus— in the final analysis, memories of 1968 overshadowed all other considerations—many of my professor friends, at least in private, heaved a collective sigh of relief.

Not so in Colonia Santo Domingo. To my great surprise, many of my friends in Santo Domingo supported the strike and the youthful strikers, albeit in words more than deeds. Never before had I witnessed such different views regarding a political question as occurred between my friends who were professors and my friends who lived in Santo Domingo. To be sure, there was not uniformity in either group; but the gen-

eral consensus in each group was unmistakable. Some of this may have
had to do with the proximity of the *colonia* to UNAM—right across the
Metro tracks—and the fact that many residents in Santo Domingo
work or have family members who work as janitors at UNAM.[3] Because
of one or another particularity, I encountered more skepticism with respect to media coverage of the strike than I had around other issues like
Chiapas, when often my neighbors and friends would repeat the analysis expressed by television commentators with remarkable accuracy.

   Although some of my friends were prone to blame the maintenance
workers' *sindicato* (union), STUNAM, as being the real cause of all the
disturbances at UNAM because they were always demanding too much
money—a reflection of jealousy, perhaps, as these workers were relatively well paid compared to average salaries in the *colonia*—there was
remarkably little criticism of either the students or the professors. As
to the students, many identified them as coming from *familias humildes*
(poor families) too, and therefore just trying to keep their foot in the
door of higher education, for themselves and future generations. Even
more unexpectedly for me, few people I spoke with in Santo Domingo
during the strike voiced anything but admiration and respect for the
UNAM professors, calling them professionals dedicated to the education of Mexican youth.

EDUCATION AS A RIGHT OR PRIVILEGE

In addition to the fact that the strike and occupation of UNAM was occurring so close to the neighborhood, it quickly became apparent that
the main reason for such widespread, if diffuse, support in Colonia
Santo Domingo for the UNAM strike was because, for many people
there, the strike represented part of their social claim to a stake in the
future. Education was widely viewed as essential to upward class mobility, and in the idealized representation to which many in the *colonia*
subscribed, it was the responsibility of the government to provide a free
education to all who wished to pursue their studies. The popular sentiment was that during the presidential regimes of Carlos Salinas (1988–
94) and Ernesto Zedillo (1994–2000) the national assets had been sold
off at a rapid clip, and now the UNAM students were striking a blow
both for their potential upward class mobility and against neoliberalist
chicanery.

   I discussed the strike with Bernardino, the community-activist-turned-*delegación*-official, and asked him, "What do you think about the strike at UNAM?"

"I think that what's at the bottom of all this is the idea that the government should take responsibility for education. That is, if we want an educated people, a people capable of building a more just society, an equal society, a society in which the protagonists are the people. I think that the notion of privatizing education is related to a mercantilist vision of the system. That's the bottom-line problem, not so much if the *cuotas* are justified or not.[4] Because in the end education is costly, and it's important that all of us in society contribute [*cooperáramos*], no? The problem is what vision we have to bring about changes. If we make society more aware of the importance of its contribution, if mechanisms are generated so that society participates, undoubtedly society will participate. With backing, support. It's not a problem of sharing on a national scale but a problem of excluding broad sectors from education, especially keeping out the most unprotected, just to put education into the marketplace."

Like many others in the area around Santo Domingo, Bernardino strongly insisted on the right of all to a public education up to and through university. He was emphatic in his assertion that the poor must not be excluded from higher learning. He noted that in the 1970s and 1980s, UNAM had actually succeeded in bringing youth from many different class backgrounds together, and he clearly felt that this was something to celebrate and expand upon.

Such support for the students and their demands for no tuition could not, however, resolve the issue because of what had really caused the crisis in the first place. Norma commented to me that she thought "the solution would be for [the government] to stop paying the maintenance workers at UNAM, because they are on strike but they continue receiving their checks every two weeks."

"So, they are still working?" I asked Norma.

"No, they're not working. Some are, but not all. Administrators, for example, aren't working, because they're not allowed to enter. Security and I think maintenance, yes, they are allowed to enter."

"Professors are getting paid but not teaching classes," I commented—obviously this was before I realized that some professors were holding classes off campus.

"That is why more and more problems have been arising. There's no solution. There's never been anything like it at UNAM. Never!"

I had heard many rumors and accusations as to the composition of the strikers, so I asked Norma, "Who are the students involved in this movement?"

"They're *fósiles* [fossils].[5] Like the one who supposedly damaged the murals, I think he's fifty years old, but all he's done with his life is to make trouble and abuse others.[6] This helped to gather the malcontents who don't have anything to do with UNAM, who dedicate themselves simply to robbing, assaulting, commandeering buses. I have talked with students at UNAM. Mateo, what do you think? The pretext is the *cuota,* but in truth that is the least of their concerns."

"Based on what I've heard," I interjected, "the *cuota* may be just the beginning of a much larger increase. So the students are saying the increases must be stopped now."

"They say the same thing. They say that in the Articles [of the Mexican Constitution] . . . I don't remember, something about 'education must be free.' So they want to defend this Article. Many students are just desperately trying to finish out the semester. Many are saying, 'We've already lost the semester.' And there's not another one."

"How is this situation going to be resolved?" I asked.

"I see it as difficult, very difficult. I think the solution lies with the maintenance workers. If they don't get paid, they won't support the students anymore."

"So STUNAM is supporting the strikers?"

"Yes. Well, they say they are supporting them at any rate. Let the government stop paying the workers, then they would have to figure out how to eat! I think there must be a solution, but they can't find one, or they don't want to. I don't know. The situation is very difficult because the students won't take it anymore. They're showing us an example, showing all us Mexican assholes that we shouldn't let the government run our lives [*mangonear*] anymore either."

"It seems that on the one hand you disagree with the students and on the other you agree with them?" I chided Norma, who then admitted that she held contradictory opinions about the strikers, if not about the stated goals of the strike.

"On the other hand, yes! Let them struggle! Let them defend their rights! But they're also getting a lot of other people in trouble, and that's not good at all."

In short, Norma, like so many others, felt deeply moved by the strike and more or less impelled to take sides in the dispute. Yet she could not, because ultimately she could not reconcile her opposing desires both for the strike to be peacefully resolved and for the students to realize their most basic demands.

UNIVERSITY AUTONOMY

The core ideological principle of Latin American public universities throughout the twentieth century has been that of intellectual autonomy from the mundane and pernicious affairs of state. Promoted as a means to achieve academic rigor and objectivity by minimizing the influence of purely political concerns, autonomy has also been depicted by more conservative elements of Latin American societies as the ultimate refuge of leftist scoundrels. And, to be sure, the concept of autonomy in itself has never meant that scholarship in Latin America should be necessarily divorced from practical, political issues and policies. If anything, in anthropology and many other academic disciplines there has been a far closer connection between scholarly research projects and pressing questions of social inequality and injustice than is true in many countries including the United States.

Nonetheless, only by understanding the dogma of autonomy can a reader from the United States begin to fathom why and how the authorities in Mexico allowed a ragtag group of youths and others to occupy the most prestigious university in the country for nine months. Frankly put, it is inconceivable that a strike that shut down an entire campus could have lasted that long at a major university in the United States, much less at the preeminent institution of higher learning. In Mexico, it would appear, students, professors, and the public at large expect more from their universities, are less cynical about the rights and opportunities of a university education, and can be more outspoken in voicing their beliefs.[7]

My friends and neighbors were fed up with authorities and with believing the excuses and justifications proffered by the government. Any opposition to authority was to be supported on principle, it seemed. Early one evening in July 1999, Doña Fili walked me from her house in the southwest corner of Colonia Santo Domingo toward Las Rosas, the main thoroughfare, where I was going to catch the *pesero* (jitney) back to the house where I was staying on the other side of the *colonia*. She told me she was headed over to the Iglesia de la Resurrección on Avenida Aztecas. There, she and other members of the church that housed the Christian Base Communities were going to meet with some electricians and strikers about the situation at UNAM. It seemed that the students

¡En billetes como éste quisieran verse retratados los que han ofrecido nuestro país al capital extranjero, y que ahora amenazan con reprimir a los estudiantes por oponerse a sus planes!

Están furiosos contra nuestra huelga, porque *ya se habían comprometido* con los organismos financieros internacionales a *privatizar* las Universidades públicas del país, y le brincamos miles de estudiantes para impedirlo.

También se comprometieron a vender la industria eléctrica y los hospitales públicos, es lo que sigue. Van por la educación, la salud, los servicios indispensables para vivir. Se trata de los derechos de todos, que entre todos debemos defender, o los perderemos uno a uno.

Ellos controlan la radio, la prensa y la televisión. ¡Ya vimos la campaña de linchamiento que han lanzado en contra de nosotros los estudiantes! Que si ya estaba resuelto el problema, que si sólo éramos unos cuantos,, llegando al extremo de decir que "tenemos armas". Igual que decían en 1968 para justificar la represión al movimiento. *Mentira tras mentira.*

Pero no nos asustan. *No nos rendiremos.* Si cedemos, miles y miles de jóvenes que podrían haber estudiado una carrera universitaria acabarán en las banquetas de la ciudad o deambulando por los campos y suburbios de Estados Unidos. Esto es algo que nomás no podemos aceptar. *Una Universidad en donde quepamos todos*, particularmente *los de abajo*: ése es el centro de nuestra lucha.

Consejo General de Huelga. UNAM. *Julio de 99*

Figure 15. Leaflets in the form of U.S. one-dollar bills and Mexican two-hundred-peso notes, 1999. They were part of the propaganda efforts of students on strike at UNAM. The headline on the back of the U.S. bill protests efforts to sell Mexican assets to foreigners and the repression of students who oppose such plans. Courtesy of Marcos Ruvalcaba.

needed some of the special skills of electricians, and Fili and other Base Community activists were bringing them all together.

Just before we left her house, Fili called me into her kitchen. She went into a drawer and pulled out a manila envelope she said she had been saving for me. Inside were numerous flyers that student strikers had distributed in Santo Domingo, some newspaper clippings, and some mock paper money (one bill in dollars, the other in pesos) with the faces of Mexican President Zedillo and of different UNAM administrators printed on one side. On the reverse side of another bill that displayed the portrait of the famous Carmelite nun and poet Sor Juana de la Cruz (1651–1695) appeared the words: "Even more fake than this bill is what they are saying on the radio and television and in the newspapers in their brutal campaign of intimidation against the University students' strike!" Several friends like Fili gave me copies of these bills, which they had saved to show me.

Two years earlier, in the winter of 1997, Doña Fili had told me something about what UNAM had meant for her personally, and not just symbolically: "I read a little book of Mao's one time. It was when we went to a meeting of campesinos at the School of Economics at UNAM. And they were reading Marx—well, they used to read him, but not anymore. And there were little books by Lenin, though not anymore. That's why we learned, over there in that department, about Lenin and Carlos Marx. And with that little that we learned, well. . . . To be at zero and not know anything, and then to learn a little, a little. . . . We could learn a lot that way! We only learned a little. But that little we learned helped us a lot to organize ourselves. And, well, we don't want so much injustice, and that's why they struggled, too. Mao, Lenin, Marx, and all of them. Not just in Mexico, but in other countries."

THE *PARISTAS*

In 1999, when the strike was raising questions regarding formal book learning and university degrees, in conversations with neighbors in Santo Domingo, Fili had found herself defending these same students who were now on strike. One of the chief concerns her neighbors had raised was that the students were really just hooligan anarchists bent on destruction and not truly interested in getting an education and helping to solve social problems.

"Clearly, we are not going to say that the strikers are *la miel en la penca* [all sweetness and sunshine], right? They also have their faults because, well, they are youths and we know that youths are restless and it's hard to control everyone. But it's not like they accuse them of being. We can also accuse the government. Look how much harm they have done to us. And why don't they talk about that? They talk about the students being pseudo-students. That they're this, that they're that. But what are they! How dare they use these words when they themselves have made many errors, have robbed a whole people. For example, a student died, Martha Alejandra, because the driver of a bus they wanted to take over dragged them off and five youths were run over and Martha Alejandra died. And the government says nothing about this. They kidnapped one young man, and they took a switchblade to his chest. Another young woman was raped. Because they'd already been threatened. They'd received phone calls to their homes. And yet the media says nothing about all this."

When Gabriel and I discussed the strike in July 1999, he voiced many of the same concerns and opinions about media coverage and the social makeup of the *paristas* (the strikers):

"What do you want to know about UNAM, Mateo? I can't know much because I didn't study there. But what do you want to know about UNAM?"

"What's going to happen in the strike at UNAM?"

"If the people don't support the student movement, they are going to be left without education. Look, I don't go to all the marches [of the students] because I have to work. But when I can, I go. And when I have a little extra money and I can buy them some food, well, I do that, too. It's not just a matter of talking about problems; you have to be there for them and be accountable. There are a lot of people who talk bad about the students without having spoken to them, without having attended a march. *Falta mucha preparación* [essentially, 'there's a lot of ignorance'].

"A *compañero* who's a singer and musician and who devotes a lot of time to the student movement was telling me that at the beginning of the strike some students had a camera and some people went into the Veterinary Institute and they found University personnel already inside and they were killing animals—to discredit the students! The students took some photographs and left quickly, heading for Metro Copilco to develop the film. The thugs followed them and knocked the crap out of the students and took off with their camera and the roll of film. This strikes me as a fantasy, something laughable. If you're going to get involved in the movement, you better do it with *pies de plomo* ['feet of lead,' i.e., with your feet really on the ground] and really think things through. That's where there's a lot of ignorance!"

"The strikers are very young, right? Are they especially naive, with little experience? Or are they puppets for others?"

Ricardo, an older neighbor who'd joined us in the middle of the conversation, chimed in, "Most of them are manipulated by other people."

"I don't think so," responded Gabriel.

To which Ricardo retorted, "Yes, most of them are. I'm sure of this. I've talked to my daughter and with one of them [the students] and they aren't doing what they should be doing. How else do you explain it, given that most of them are not in agreement with the strike?"

"If most of the students weren't in agreement, the strike would long since have stalled," Gabriel told his friend.

"There are divisions among them now," Ricardo insisted.

At which point Gabi smiled and shook his head: "No. No. No, I don't think there are divisions because if there were it would have stalled already. What happens is that a lot of folks, even the ones who work there, everyone is trying to *satinizar* [Satan-ize] this movement. Everyone! The goddamned University [service] workers, the goddamned [STUNAM janitors'] union." He spoke directly to Ricardo, "You can't know anything if you don't talk to them. Go to UNAM, find the schools. Talk with them."

"I was already there," Ricardo claimed. "I talked with them and I realized some things. My daughter and my wife told me it wasn't good for them to participate."

"No, why not?" Gabriel taunted Ricardo. "There are women who are in the thick of the struggle. It's not like before. There's a really pretty song that Nacha Guevara sings: 'In the street, elbow to elbow, we're a lot more than two.' I don't speak badly of them, because it's good what they're doing. As to whether they're manipulated, well, that's hard. You know why this movement doesn't go away? Because they want an open dialogue and the government hasn't given this to them."

At which point, Ricardo turned to me and asked rhetorically, "Why an open dialogue? They want cameras to film the whole thing. Because they don't lend themselves to being manipulated by the government."

Gabi, in his best schoolteacher imitation patiently explained, "You know why? Because an open dialogue does not lend itself to the manipulation of the movement. Manipulation is easier when the leaders are closed off in negotiations. Are they right or not? What do you think Mateo?"

I begged off, stating, "There's been very little news about the strike in the United States. I've been talking to a lot of people in the past few days here, trying to understand what's going on. I am still trying to figure it all out."

"But what do you think?" Gabi persisted, unwilling to accept my excuses and evasive responses.

"I've heard a lot of completely opposing opinions," I said, still trying to weasel out of committing myself at this point in the conversation.

Gabi then broadened his attack: "Because of people who live in front of the television and learn everything they know from there. What goddamned media! A complete manipulation of the people."

GLOBALIZATION AND THE WORLD BANK

In 1968, despite Mexico's sponsorship of the Olympics, there remained a widespread sense then that events such as the October 2 massacre at Tlatelolco could occur in relative isolation and with impunity from the court of international public opinion. In contrast, in 1999 there was a profound sense that international forces underlay the crisis at UNAM and that the resolution of the conflict would be watched by millions worldwide. As I was repeatedly informed, the World Bank and the International Monetary Fund had demanded the privatization of the National University, and the Mexican government had, once again, capitulated. The tuition hike was merely the first step off the neoliberal cliff of privatization.

I spoke with Marcos about these issues, and about his own job as a janitor at UNAM and a fairly active member of STUNAM. First I wanted to get clarification as to whether the janitors were indeed getting paid and whether they were working.

"The University is paying our salaries. People have to check in in the morning."

"Six days a week, like before?" I asked him.

"Like before," he answered. "And if there's not work to do, you stay a while and then go home."

"What do you think is going to happen?"

"If it doesn't drag on, we're okay. But if it does drag on, maybe even the future of the union will begin to get shaky. Because now the executive committee of the *sindicato* (union) has withdrawn the economic assistance it was giving the students."

"They're not giving more money?"

Figure 16. Poster from the 1999 UNAM strike calling
for "Freedom for UNAM political prisoners!" Courtesy
of Fili Fernandez.

"The University [administration] made a pact with the union so that
we would not get involved in the conflict. So if we continue giving support, well, they are going to cut off our pay. And if they cut off our pay,
we would have to launch a strike, and then the future of the union would
indeed be uncertain, because the [University] authorities would say,
'We're not paying you! So you can do what you want, and maybe we'll
even sack you!'"

"Will the University possibly be shut forever?" I asked only half face-
tiously because some had expressed concern about this possibility.

"There's no way they are going to shut the University forever. But
there will be a transformation, and they are going to split us up in the

union. There will no longer be one union, but, like, twenty-seven unions."

"With less power, right?"

"With less power. It's the same thing that is happening in the SEP [Secretaría de Educación Pública (Department of Education)].[8] The same thing could happen in the University. So UNAM will have the power to say, 'You, you're useful and you can stay. And if not, you're gone.'"

"What do you think about the student strike?" I continued.

"It's become more political than student, because the goals of the strike are now more political than educational. A lot of politicians have stuck their fingers in."

"Groups on the left?"

"Like the PRD. Cuauhtémoc Cárdenas has intervened a lot."

"But Cárdenas is not supporting them, right?"

"No, because the students are so over the edge, so he said, 'If you want to do this, well go ahead and do it. It's your mess, no?' There's going to come a time when maybe they will even send troops into UNAM."

"Is that possible? As in '68?"

"Not so much like '68. I don't remember if it was 1980 or 1981 when we went on strike and they sent in troops. Same thing can happen. The authorities are already thinking about it, but because things have gotten so big, it's not so easy for the government. Because other, larger questions enter into play. The people might have to get involved in the conflict, and then it wouldn't be a student issue but a movement of workers, campesinos. This conflict would become much greater. Such a problem would be most inconvenient for the government because of the presidential election in 2000.

"As the students say, 'It doesn't matter to me personally if they raise the *cuotas,* but for those who follow after me it does. Because there are people without any money.' The ones who have money pay. But they don't say that all will pay. There are people who don't even have money to eat who are studying. People from different parts of the country who come here to study, whose parents give them some money to come here to study who don't even have enough to eat. They have to scrounge! As a janitor at UNAM I notice that a lot of students don't have enough change to even buy candy. So the students say, 'We don't want them to charge those who come after us.' And the economic situation is getting worse."

"For you, personally, is the situation more difficult?" I asked Marcos.

"Well, yes. You get used to a salary. A way of living. And prices keep going up on you, so your style of living has to go down. You have to suffer more. You have to look for other means of income. An example: In Tepozotlán[9] a peon earns ten pesos a day. From eight in the morning until five in the afternoon. You think he's going to live on ten pesos? Have you been in the Metro lately?"[10]

"Even less than minimum wage," I responded.

"Much less. Minimum wage is around thirty-four pesos [at the time, around $3.40 U.S. a day]. Now here come some campesinos from the north, from the Sierra de Puebla, asking for help because they also earn ten pesos a day. So we say, 'What's going on? What's happening with people? With the government?' Many *caciques*, people with money take it away from those who don't have it. For what? So they can build their big complexes, their nice haciendas, villas. People are realizing what kind of country we're becoming. Imagine what's going on with people! The government is trying to squeeze money out of us all over the place. They're all over, trying to privatize the electricity, petroleum, education."

"UNAM?" I asked rhetorically.

"Privatize UNAM and the rest is gravy, because UNAM is the embodiment of the people, of the whole country."

"Not only in Mexico. In Latin America. UNAM has been a source of leaders all over the continent."

"If they privatize UNAM, what is going to happen? The government is going to say, 'You will pay two thousand pesos monthly for tuition [approximately $200 U.S.]. Do you want to? If not, you know what, get out of here!' Imagine paying two thousand pesos each month. That's a lot! The government wants to squeeze money out of everywhere. Why? So when they retire, they have some money for themselves and their families, even their grandchildren. How wonderful there's so much justice! For example, there's the case of Raul Salinas, the brother of the ex-president. They put him in the slammer. Like it or not, he's not having fun. He's not going to return the money he stole, but he's in jail. At least he has suffered for four years. You can say, 'It's something, at least.' But it's something between them, not because the people asked for it, but because it's coming apart among them, within the very government."

"Are you worried about your own future at UNAM?"

"Well, yes. Because if they say to me, 'You know what? You don't work here anymore,' what am I going to do?"

"Set up your own little *tienda* here?" I pointed to the spot where our friend Marcelo had worked until recently, before he had abandoned Mexico City for the chance at better fortunes in Cuernavaca.

"Actually, we do want to put up a little business here, selling food. You already see people doing it all over. Here in Mexico we sell everything."

"Yes, but you never know if you will break even. It's hard work."

"You can make a living. Selling food you never lose, because what you don't sell you can eat!"

Short-term and personal solutions—like opening a food stand—to counter the effects of globalization and World Bank demands on Mexico are seen as realistic by my friends in Santo Domingo. Six months after troops regained control of UNAM, several acquaintances in the *colonia* had come to the conclusion that the federal and University authorities *allowed* the strike to continue as long as it did in the belief that an internally fractured institution would be that much easier to dismantle in the aftermath. The best they could do in such a climate of pervasive neoliberalism was hunker down and pray that their families would be spared the worst. The anti-authoritarianism of the students had been inspiring to many for a while, but the resolution of the strike probably came as less of a surprise to residents of Santo Domingo than it did to intellectuals who believed that experiences from 1968 would preclude a military intervention to end the strike.

CHAPTER 10

Political Fantasies

What possibilities today lie beyond reality?

Carlos Monsiváis

INTIMATIONS OF COMPLIANCE, SIGNS OF DEFIANCE

A few weeks after the presidential election in July 2000, when I mentioned to Gabriel that I was headed to a bookstore to buy a new edition of a book titled *La democracia ausente* (*Absent Democracy*), he shot back, "*Bueno, ahora está presente, !pero vale madres;*" (Good, now it's present, but it's worth shit!).[1] His was just one voice, of course, but when the PRI lost the presidency in the summer of 2000, Gabriel was hardly alone in feeling more worried than elated about the future for poor people in Mexico. In marked contrast to the jubilant perspective offered by the media in the wake of the July 2 presidential election, in Santo Domingo reactions to the election of the PAN candidate were more muted. In the *colonia* the election did not usher in a wave of optimistic expectations about the possibility much less the probability of positive social change under the aegis of PAN leadership.

Far more palpable was the sentiment that political passivity was the surest route to not being disappointed. The lower one's political expectations were, the less traumatic the results of political events like the election would be. Without pretending that those who abstained from voting had all developed a complete and consistent political agenda, still, *abstencionismo* should not be cavalierly dismissed merely as the consequence of apolitical apathy. In our more philosophical moments before and after the 2000 presidential election, Marcos, Marcelo, Gabi,

Toño, and I talked about feeling *atrapados* (trapped) by forces outside out control, while at the same time wondering why we spent so much time fantasizing about things being otherwise. Were we foolish to romanticize changing the societies into which we were born? We knew we had no control over the world of our birth, yet it was far from clear if and when we ever gain the ability to transform parts of our social worlds.

Like other reasonable social critics, my friends have stressed to me the influence that sociocultural factors have had, not only on their views but also on their actions. Cultures, societies, and institutions help to frame ideological and practical understandings of our world, they have told me innumerable times. On one occasion, when I mentioned Antonio Gramsci and his notion of contradictory consciousness—that is, the contradiction between the consciousness-understanding we have inherited from past generations, and the consciousness-understanding that can only develop in the course of practical activities aimed at actually transforming the world—Marcelo commented that the first part of Gramsci's equation seemed more straightforward than the last part. The late 1990s did not instill in my friends much cause for celebration that the world was being altered in significant ways and that they were a motive part of this process.

Times change and it is risky to make too many generalizations about popular politics in Mexico, or even popular politics in urban Mexico. In an essay about the experiences and social relations of men and women from the *sectores populares* in Guadalajara in the 1980s, and particularly about their attitudes toward society and politics, Guillermo de la Peña has shown clearly the broad importance for many of the people he interviewed of participation in voluntary organizations and social mobilizations. Yet, in Guadalajara, de la Peña also points out, "to speak of popular culture is to speak of religion" (1990, 84). Therefore, in addition to expressed political concerns regarding civic participation, de la Peña's informants in the popular sectors of the Guadalajara population told him that their political concerns also included issues involving family and religious life.

When I compare the issues that attracted the political attention of people from the *sectores populares* in Guadalajara in the 1980s with those on the minds of residents of Colonia Santo Domingo in the Mexican capital in the 1990s, there are significant similarities and differences. Chief among the dissimilarities is that few of the people de la Peña interviewed in his research on political culture in Guadalajara expressed outright hostility toward *los ricos*. In Santo Domingo in the 1990s, on the other hand, enmity toward *los ricos* was indeed common, and in this respect at least, the Mexico City neighborhood may be more representative of communities in contemporary Mexico, in which popular movements for land, social services, and to varying degrees demands for local political autonomy have prevailed in recent years.

There are clear, significant differences in the political concerns of different urban populations in different periods in Mexico. Still, de la Peña demonstrates that even the *sectores populares* of Guadalajara in the 1980s couched their political complaints and yearning in the language of *injusticia* (injustice). Whether residents are preoccupied with immediate concerns of income, health, and housing, or whether they are able to dwell on the more abstract issues of family and religion, in both Guadalajara in the 1980s and Santo Domingo in the 1990s, there is a sense that larger social forces are at play in determining the fortunes of people's lives, of the interconnected *injusticias* of daily life and social life generally. In Guadalajara, where, as de la Peña says, conservatism and official Catholicism have ideologically prevailed, it has not been as common for citizens to seek independent ways of resolving problems of *injusticia* as has been true in areas like Colonia Santo Domingo, where self-reliance has developed into a widespread culture of community identity. In Santo Domingo at least, despite the fact that most people's daily political actions are in general circumscribed by the horizons of individual, familial, and very limited forms of neighborhood collective activities, dreams of more fundamental, radical challenge to daily and lifelong injustices have surfaced from time to time. Especially in the 1970s and 1980s, community activists recall, one could even hear talk of socialism from unexpected quarters.

If in Santo Domingo the prospect of radical change was given electoral credibility as a result of the 1988 presidential election, when many believe the center-left candidate had actually won and then was denied office through PRI vote fraud, in subsequent years the course of electoral politics and especially the fall of the Soviet Union did much to rattle dreams of meaningful social change in contemporary Mexico.

More generally in the world, the 1990s were also a time when, to one extent or another, many people were

> haunted too by failed experiments in socialism in which the "rational" ordering of economy and society became a nightmare of bureaucratic dehumanization and soullessness, [when] bereft of the notion that history "pro-

gresses," or even that humans learn from history's most nightmarish epi-
sodes, we suffer[ed] a contemporary "disenchantment of the world" more
vivid than Weber let alone Marx ever imagined. (Brown 1995, 24, 26)

Nor were notions of history's progress, or even of socialism, of concern to leftists alone. In an essay on millenarianisms, Carlos Monsiváis
has discussed the ideological particularities of twentieth-century Mexican history:

> Revolution and migration have been the most important factors that have de-
> stroyed the spiritual resources of the people over the last century, while the
> failures of the *Cristeros* and *Sinarquistas* demonstrate how impossible islands
> of purity are in a world trampled underfoot by the cult of Progress. . . . With
> the fall of the Berlin Wall and the official end of the Cold War, an attempt is
> made to infuse the term "free market" with the properties of a totem presid-
> ing over an eternal social system. (1997, 134–35)[2]

For many people, in Mexico City as elsewhere, in *colonias populares*
like Santo Domingo as well as in the citadels of higher learning, in the
1990s socialism ceased to be discussed or even contemplated as a term
designating a dramatically different way of organizing society. At the
same time, although democracy as a watchword of liberalism was obviously no stranger to the politics of politics in Mexico, with the virtual
erasure of socialism from the realm of acceptable discourse on the world
stage, democracy even more became *the* ethical endpoint and *the* aim
of social struggle. The term *democracy* continues to be overused and
underdefined in contemporary Mexico whenever discussions of politics
occur.

IMPOVERISHED CULTURES OF AUTHENTICITY

After the first few months, the strike that began in early 1999 at the
National University derived more support from people in Santo Domingo than it did from professors long identified with the left. Indeed,
according to several friends in the *colonia*, toward the end of the strike,
in late 1999, the *rector* (president) of UNAM publicly denounced Santo
Domingo as home to ignorant rabble rousers. Doña Fili and others no
doubt constituted the ranks of such rebels, which was one reason why
she told me in August 1999, "Here in the *colonia*, the student strikers
have our support. There's a lesson they are teaching us, because they
are defending education." She continued, speaking bitterly about the

broader framework in which she and others viewed the strike and recent economic events in Mexico:

"That's how we should have defended ourselves against [the privatization of] the banks [in 1982], the railways, telephone. They told us they were going to privatize the banks to improve things, which was a lie. They privatized them and they told us over and over how it was going to improve things. And after the privatization we go to pay our light bill and they say, 'You have to pay five more pesos.' So we said, '¡Ay, chihuahua! This wasn't to improve things. Just the opposite; we're the ones hurt.'

"Later, if we saved 100 or 200 pesos (this was when they still hadn't removed the zeros),[3] okay, even if it wasn't too much, it was something. But when we returned we had 90, 80 pesos because they charged us for having this little money. And now the students are saying, 'We should defend ourselves!' Because we think those who can pay, well, they should go where they charge, to the [Universidad de] Lasalle, to the [Universidad] Ibero[americana], to the [Universidad] del Valle. Because people who have money go to that kind of place. But not everyone can. Some kids wander around with only a small sandwich in their stomach. And if you have to pay transportation to and from school, these families have to make a lot of sacrifices. We're talking about the children of workers. That's why we support the student strikers: it's the quotas they want to charge, but it's also the whole structure of education. And the government never tells us the truth about their plans for restructuring all that."

Changes to the whole structure of formal education and popular responses to this and other aspects of neoliberal restructuring is of evident concern to Doña Fili and her colleagues in Colonia Santo Domingo. One unfortunate consequence of Oscar Lewis's infamous formulation about the culture of poverty, many critics of Lewis claim, is that it implies that all poor people automatically share the same culture by virtue of their impoverished status and experiences, and that what it means to be poor is the same for all who suffer this status. This is a regrettable inference, especially because Lewis seems to have been concerned with precisely the opposite problem, taking the opinions and activities of men and women like Doña Fili from the popular sectors and confirming the importance of *not* denying them the ability (the agency) to define and transform meanings, ideals, and dreams—in short, changing their ethos as part of changing their world. And for Lewis, as for my friends in Colonia Santo Domingo, change was not always for the better. If one of

Lewis's foundational theses was that governments in general cannot be trusted to solve the problems of poverty—or at least that governments are unreliable in this respect—then the ethnography of Lewis should continue to hold interest and utility. In particular, the relationship between political economy and what Lewis and others of his generation termed culture and personality studies is relevant today.

Comparing his own studies with those of Robert Redfield, and defending himself against accusations of a prurient interest in the salacious aspects of his informants' lives, Lewis pointed to, "my greater interest in economics (not sex!)" (1967, 499). In fact, Lewis emphasized that he saw his work on poverty as "part of the larger culture of capitalism whose social and economic system channels wealth into the hands of a relatively small group and thereby makes for the growth of sharp class distinctions." The challenge for Lewis and for us today is to combine a rigorous political economy framework with a sensitive account of subjective perspectives and actions.

We cannot blame people like Doña Fili for their predicament when they find themselves caught in webs not of their own spinning. When larger socioeconomic and demographic shifts are recognized as ultimately global in proportion and seem ever more in control of their daily lives, is it any wonder that few hopes for change remained for her and other community residents of Santo Domingo? It certainly seems reasonable to argue that social problems are products of global restructuring such as through the North American Free Trade Agreement. It is in some respects easier to attribute causality to forces beyond one's control, and undoubtedly more difficult to identify willful complicity among broad sectors of the populace mixed with defiant resentment and simmering hostility to the impact of neoliberal globalization.

One way to understand what media analysts would call the "reception" of global restructuring, is to remember that in Colonia Santo Domingo opinions about NAFTA, Chiapas, the UNAM strike, and border crossings are far from uniform. Fili would be the first to admit that her claim, "Here in the *colonia,* the student strikers have our support," is more than a slight exaggeration. In Santo Domingo, class does not rigidly determine politics. In fact, and especially around large social issues, experiences and judgments are so varied in the community that it often seems that politics is more determinative of self-proclaimed working-class identity than such identity is determinative of politics.

Different experiences guide linguistic proclivities, as when the term *mayate* is variously employed to refer to men who have sex with other men or to African Americans. Partially, such differences stem from trans-nationalized divisions within the working class in Mexico, for instance, from the significant cultural trials faced by millions of Mexican women and men who spend time living and working in the United States, and from the equally complicated challenges of feminism and the more open presence of gays in Mexico.

It is perhaps because even after many years of living and talking with the people in Santo Domingo I am still for some people more than anything else "the Gringo on Huehuetzin Street," that over the years several neighbors and acquaintances have directed racist comments to me about African Americans. There could hardly be a better illustration of the salience of political divisions within the *colonia*. When I climbed into a Ruta 45 jitney one afternoon in the mid-1990s, I saw that Poncho was driving. For three years, Poncho had worked in construction around the Los Angeles area. We only knew each other in passing, so as we skidded to avoid a dog lumbering across the street, I asked Poncho how he had fared during his time in Los Angeles.

First, Poncho told me about the cars he bought there, sneaked into Mexico, and sold for a nice profit. He had done the same with some shipments of hot stereo equipment and made himself a tidy sum after delivery back home. At one point in his account of the part he had played in correcting Mexico's trade imbalance with the Gringos, Poncho shouted over his shoulder that the one thing he really hated about Los Angeles was the black people there: "Eight of ten who showed up for work didn't even last a day," he told me and the other passengers in the jitney. "What's more, they are all a bunch of thieves," he added, as if we could not have guessed his views by that point. Then he sought confirmation from me for his opinions. Expecting this solicitation, I told Poncho I thought he sounded a lot like white racists I had known. To his credit, Poncho backed off, quickly noting, "Well, there's good and bad of all kinds [*hay de todo*]." He was on the defensive, not comfortable being branded a white racist. Clearly he did not see himself in this way, and he had not anticipated that I, a Gringo, would make this insinuation. Poncho was not expecting a white guy from the United States to speak anything but nastiness about African Americans.

Cultures of authenticity, such as those which posit a neatly bifurcated world in which *los ricos* are pitted against *los pobres,* are part of the romantic conceptual arsenals of many men and women like Poncho in Santo Domingo. And while racist currents, for example, provide clear evidence of ideas that are patently antithetical to heartfelt notions of

Figure 17. Blackface piñata from a 1992 Christmas-
time *posada* on Huehuetzin Street in Santo Domingo.

undiscriminating unity, such a realization should certainly not persuade
us to altogether abandon the framework of class. Yet men like Poncho
are less obnoxious in their naively racist assertions than people who
knowingly use the misery of others to advance their own fortunes.

   Authenticity, as in claims to be the genuinely entitled working poor,
is a critical element in defiant posturing for many of my friends and acquaintances in Colonia Santo Domingo. Who wants to be known as a
lazy freeloader? At the intersection of class, ethnic, and gender categorizing, most people in the *colonia*, especially most men, represent themselves to others as, if nothing else, diligent and responsible about doing
work and earning money, just as, in a seemingly very different manner,

both men and women sometimes portray themselves as more authentic than their neighbors by claiming "original invader" status. Without a doubt, those known (or believed) to have participated in the original invasions of the area that later became Santo Domingo carry a certain political eminence unavailable to others who arrived only after the hard work of establishing the *colonia* was already largely accomplished.

In the course of chatting with a man who held an elected office in Santo Domingo one evening after a meeting of the block captains, this gentleman confessed to me that, contrary to what he told his neighbors and those who elected him to office, he had not actually lived in the *colonia* since 1971. The elected official, who for obvious reasons shall remain nameless here, had not endured the hardships of the early years— of staking a claim to land, defending the claim, and building a dwelling cement block by cement block. Even worse for his prestige and political authority, the official and his family had bought the property of others who had invaded and constructed a rudimentary home. He was no better than a carpetbagger and Johnny-come-lately to the *colonia*. The only reason I discovered this personal history was that I questioned certain discrepancies in the man's story. He confessed and begged me not to share this revelation with his constituency.

Authenticity, in this respect, derives much of its political potency from its claim to be an oppositional and defiant stance against authority. One's presence and participation in events such as the invasions of Santo Domingo were certainly matters of importance to the official's neighbors. Nor was his a parochial concern. The reputation of cultural anthropology generally rests in good measure on a similar premise: the ethnographer was *there* and (in some way) *lived* through the experiences described and discussed. I was *in* Colonia Santo Domingo when the national politician Ruiz Massieu was shot and killed on a Mexico City street in September 1994. I was part of conversations that day in Santo Domingo as people wondered over the significance of two major assassinations in the space of a few months, and what this might mean for Mexico's political state and future, and what it might indicate about the stability of the PRI regime, and whether it demonstrated the influence of the notoriously violent political scene in the United States, and what might happen next.

True enough, in my years living and working in Santo Domingo, I have obviously missed more than I have witnessed. In part, this is because I was not there in the *colonia* all the time. More significantly, it is because no study of popular politics in Santo Domingo can claim a complete portrait of political life. So my attempt has instead been to describe and explore the twists and turns experienced by my friends and neighbors in their engagements with "politics." Their political views and activities are seldom remarked upon in detail in academic studies or the media. Yet they are anything but unremarkable. In a book on contemporary Mexico it would be fair to ask how representative are the views and activities of a group of men and women in one part of one *colonia* in Mexico City. No one community in Mexico is illustrative of every political trend and change in any meaningful sense. Because they are Mexican citizens and their political lives are just as important as those of any other group of people chosen from a statistically representative sample, my Santo Domingo neighbors' views about, participation in, and abstention from a host of political activities—from voting to protest to debate—are of intrinsic interest for the study of compliant defiance in contemporary Mexico.

This study is part of charting defiance and compliance in contemporary Mexico, distinguishing between times when defiance is more modifying compliance, and when compliance is more an attribute of an underlying defiance. As such it is part of describing some of the most recent moments in the evolution of what Monsiváis (2000) refers to as "versions of the popular," in the sense of the changing histories of the underdog subaltern.

As an example of an influential "version of the popular," feminist critics have succeeded in giving a voice to working-class women as political militants in their own communities, as they testify to the *doble jornada* (second shift) suffered by many women who work outside the home for money and continue doing most of the housework and childcare in their homes as well. Aside from the pleasure many women derive from mocking antiquated (and, not infrequently, Gringo) notions of Mexican women as uniformly submissive and self-sacrificing, another more recent version of the popular among women in Santo Domingo concerns their determination to distinguish between remarks about men as a social category and those pertaining to their own husbands, fathers, brothers, and sons. In contrast to men in general, women in Santo Domingo have often spoken to me very positively about the men in their families, both with respect to men's willingness to help with housework, and in relation to the attitudes and activities of men toward women's militant activism.

More than one grandmother has told me that she is *"muy moderna,"* and has illustrated her claim by describing how ideas, manners, and beliefs have changed dramatically from her generation to her daughter's, and even more to her granddaughter's. At the same time, several of these women have also mentioned that in each generation one might also note changes in the thinking and behavior of men. Said one neighbor with a placid smile on her lips, "Mateo, you see how these women changed their men?"

Who changes whom and how is indeed a question. *How*, exactly, is democracy to be realized? If the impulse for democracy is to originate outside the legislative chambers, we must examine how the stimulus for popular sovereignty can continue to promote change. These are often regarded as questions to which only politicians and policy wonks have the answers, but people in Santo Domingo are routinely disrespectful and distrustful of political authorities and so continue to seek their own ways to understand and promote change. The fact that they customarily do so as individuals and as members of small family, neighborhood, or workplace groups is an ongoing source of frustration for them because, they feel, it does not augur well for their chances of success. Democracy, in its more romantic versions at any rate, is supposed to be grounded by plain, ordinary people like the residents of Santo Domingo. But other than waiting until the next election, the problem remains, how democracy is to be realized *by* them and not just *for* them in the name of one more condescending savior.

GOODBYE TO DINOSAUR POLITICS?

"Hey, Mateo!" Pedro greeted me in early August 2000, a month or so after the presidential elections. "Guess what? Now we have democracy in Mexico, too! We got to choose between a whole bunch of *imbéciles!*" The fruits of neoliberal politics were evidently spoiling on the vine. For the achievement of "real democracy" in Mexico, everyone had been told for many years, and especially in the years following the 1988 presidential elections, it was critical that voters should have candidates from more than one party (the PRI) from which to choose. Yet, somehow, with three major candidates in 2000—or two-and-a-half, because Cárdenas was never really in the running and thus his votes mainly served as a form of electoral protest—my acquaintances in Santo Domingo were uniformly unenthusiastic.[4] It was dinosaur politics as usual, many commented to me in late summer 2000, with the main difference now being that some new species had gained entrance into the Jurassic Park that had long been Mexico's political arena.

The debates over what democracy was supposed to look like, feel like, and how it actually functioned, were largely reduced in the media to the question of the elections and the central issue of whether the PRI candidate could be defeated. If he were to go down in defeat, then democracy could be declared a success. At the same time, if the PRI won, then democracy had not necessarily been beaten, and at least one could argue that there had been a real electoral horserace. Buried inside these analyses and forecasts was the unexamined issue of whether the term *citizenship* should refer to an actual relationship between residents of a republic and their government, or whether it merely refers to the status of those who gain public office.

This is not to dispute the very reasonable goal of choice in elections; the point is more to give voice to questions raised by many people in Santo Domingo, as to whether the goal of choice is satisfied merely by appearances alone. Because, it turns out, everyone, from politicians to postal workers to prostitutes, has all along been far clearer about what constitutes fraud and unfair elections—that is, what is *not* democracy—than they have been about how a fully popular sovereignty would function. Yet, unlike politicians, postal workers, prostitutes, and other working people are under less compulsion to defend democratic pretense. The allegorical weight of contrasts between "Western democracy" and (variously) "banana republics," "Oriental despotism," and "Muslim fanaticism," represents an expository burden for state bureaucrats more than for residents of *colonias populares*.[5]

More women held elected office at the national level in Mexico in 2000 than at any time in that country's history. In Mexico's Chamber of Deputies and Senate, a higher percentage of members were women than was the case in the U.S. House of Representatives and Senate. To be sure, these numbers do not speak for themselves, and the significance of multiparty elections and of the rising number of women elected to office remains to be explained. As Jeff Rubin has commented on the process of democratization in Latin America more broadly, "In assessing the democratic character of power relations, it is thus necessary to examine not only electoral competition, but the relationships between elections and the ways in which people experience power in other spheres of their lives" (1997, 162). But these numbers should give us pause before we resort too quickly to facile comparisons between veteran democracies like the United States and southern hemispheric trainees.

Drawing on recent political struggles, in particular in contested areas of Chiapas, Xóchitl Leyva Solano has written:

It is misleading to describe Ocosingo and Las Cañadas as places where citizens quietly vote for one or another political party. They are arenas in which social and political organizations form fragile alliances with parties and other interest groups, party leaders seek to co-opt indigenous leaders, and factions of formerly solid political groupings question their old loyalties and, if need be, change their affiliation to the opposition party whose candidates offer a better deal. Democracy in Las Cañadas is synonymous neither with increasing citizenship nor with pluralism, but it certainly means more participation of popular organizations in processes of decision making in the public sphere. (2001, 39)

If democracy is to retain any usefulness, it must speak to the more general problem of participation. When discussing political culture, John Gledhill (2000) points out, it is necessary to distinguish between democracy conceived as direct rule by the people, and one or another form of liberal democracy that is grounded in questions of civil liberties and opportunities. In an era in which everyone seems to hold democracy as sacred, at a time when repressive regimes are redefined as rogue or lapsed democracies, it might be well to ask how far the pundits have come in their political typologizing from the seemingly more Byzantine days of authoritarian-totalitarian distinctions.

Just as ancient Greece is often conjured up as the wellspring of democracy, so too is the Latin language summoned upon occasion to provide special insight into problems of analysis. In the spirit of appropriating certain customs for novel purposes, I introduce here three facetious terms to assist us in understanding the distinction between democratic participation and democratic rights. The expressions I have in mind are *modus vivendi, quod erat demonstrandum* (Q.E.D.), and, to crown the lot, *cui bono.*

Modus vivendi: If democracy is to be a way of living, if democracy is to embody a vital popular pact stipulating how societies are to function and change, then presumably the conclusion that Mexico has merely moved from holding one-candidate elections to multi-*imbécil* elections is valid and significant. Regardless of the initial flush of excitement provided by the PRI's 2000 electoral defeat, the distinction between the right to participate and the reality of participation to change Mexico remains highly salient in the minds of many Mexicans.

Quod erat demonstrandum: Q.E.D., in this case, refers to the desire to read history backwards and declare that contemporary events confirm that which was to be proved. If democracy is loosely, even if only implicitly, considered as a cluster of rights and opportunities, then by definition those less enthralled with processes presented as democratic (e.g., elections as the pinnacle and even the sum-total of democratic citizenship) have themselves opted out of democracy and have thereby lost their right and opportunity to participate.

Cui bono: Finally, without a doubt the decisive question asked in kitchens and street corners where men and women argue over politics in Mexico is this: Who are the ones who stand to gain from recent changes in Mexico's political fortunes? When all is said and done, who benefits, who loses, and who will probably remain largely unaffected by any particular political event? Nor are such questions mainly a matter of the residents of Santo Domingo being good, practical, down-to-earth folks. They have far more to do with concerns voiced by certain women and men that the words used to disguise aims and motives that are employed by politicians, political pundits, and party patriarchs should be stripped away to reveal actual, lived experiences and interests.

GLOBALIZATION AND AMERICANIZATION

In the post–World War II period, U.S.-style modernity and capitalist development were heralded by government officials and scholars in the United States as the *economic* model best suited to alleviate poverty, misery, inequality, and underdevelopment in vast regions of the southern hemisphere. The defeat of the United States in Vietnam was only one reason for the sinking fortunes of this paradigm by the end of the 1960s. In a sense, too, development schemes were victims of implosion on their own tortured logic (see Escobar 1995; Kearney 1996; Gupta 1998). In a strikingly similar fashion, at the dawn of the twenty-first century, in the wake of the collapse of the Soviet Union, U.S.-style democracy is being ever more fervently presented as the *political* answer to poverty, misery, inequality, and underdevelopment in vast regions of the southern hemisphere (see Frank 1993). There is much that is not new in the promotion of U.S.-style democracy as the path to civic salvation, of course, especially the typically pragmatic punch line—"We won, so that proves we're correct." In the sterile climate of the post–Cold War world in which the United States is the single remaining superpower, the notion that citizens of countries like Mexico have only to learn from their northern neighbor has occupied the field largely unopposed.

The North American Free Trade Agreement went into effect on January 1, 1994, and with it, certain Mexican leaders claimed, Mexico would leap from the Third World to the First World. Undoubtedly, in the course of arrangements such as those codified by NAFTA, in little time the top tier of Mexico's managerial class became enriched beyond their wildest possible dreams. Whether as a result of promiscuous neoliberal policies whereby national industries were sold to the handful of government functionaries (and their brothers . . .) at bargain-basement prices, whether as a result of the implementation of NAFTA itself, or whether owing to the fact that, as some claim, the Free Trade Agreement is really little more than a neoliberal treaty between the managers of three countries, the fact remains that most Mexicans have continued to limp along rather than having leapt to new economic heights. In this respect, NAFTA is anything but a novel arrangement, as even a rudimentary history of U.S.–Latin American relations shows. In writing about Manifest Destiny, the mid-nineteenth-century doctrine that argued that the United States had the right and duty to intervene, occupy, and control land and peoples throughout North America, including territory that belonged to Mexico, Deborah Poole has shown the continuities that have guided economic and political policies in U.S.–Latin American relations from the nineteenth to the twenty-first century: "The ideological and political project of Manifest Destiny relied in obvious ways on just this ability to erase the property lines (and title deeds) of real space" (1998, 116). Even two hundred years ago, "borderless" geographies involved more than the ideological imperatives of expanding empire; doctrines such as the Manifest Destiny sought not so much the erasure of all borders as their redrafting along the ephemeral lines of empire.

In the salons of certain anthropologists and literati who specialize in mythologizing cultural resilience, the concepts of *mestizaje* and indigenous essence, and the question of how and even whether to include the United States in the history of Latin America, have long been sensitive issues. In response to notions of primordial, timeless cultures proliferating in the region, Roger Bartra has asked, "Is there an age-old continuity in Latin American culture?" He answers with an emphatic, "No! . . . All signs of life in pre-Hispanic societies were eradicated. Today Latin America is irrevocably an extension of the West" (1995, 147). For this reason among many others, references to the United States as a model for Mexican democracy are certainly no less arcane than allusions to the Greek origins of theories of social equality. Mexico and the rest of the world are in certain respects haunted by the presence of the one remaining superpower—yet only Mexico and Canada share thousands of miles of border with this would-be omnipotent nation. And the mere existence of such a power lends credence to the ambition of elites throughout Latin America to "Americanize" their regimes and state apparatuses.

Further, as Bill Roseberry has written, "An anthropologist interested in Latin America should have something to say about Americanization." Referring especially to questions of cultural patrimony and change, Roseberry continued, "He or she should be able to reject the homogenizing stereotype without retreating into the equally stereotypic comfort of distinctiveness of his or her 'own people'" (1989, 82; see also Roseberry 1998; and Stern 1993). On a more mundane level, for many in contemporary Mexico the concept of *americanización* conjures up images of shared teen idols like Britney Spears and Enrique Iglesias. And Americanization means economic change, rumors of privatization of the petroleum industry, and the spread of maquiladoras down from the Río Bravo border. Maquiladoras provide a vivid illustration of the ambiguities of Americanization, because they simultaneously represent the potential for higher wages than are generally available to factory assembly workers in Mexico and the unmistakable harnessing of the country's economic destiny to U.S. and other foreign business futures.

As resentful as many Mexicans resident in the United States may be about the fact that, as they see it, cheap immigrant labor is a critical ingredient providing relatively widespread wealth in the United States, the maquiladoras are, by definition, assembly plants on Mexican national territory whose products can be exported duty free. The connotations of being a Mexican and the activities associated with campaigns like "Buy Mexican!" are constrained by the fact that globalization does not entail exactly the same responsibilities in all parts of the globe. Still less is democracy experienced in identical fashion by people in diverse locations in the contemporary world. At the same time, as Fernando Coronil cautions, with particular reference to a stubborn fascination with uncertainty in recent postcolonial studies, "Fragmentation, ambiguity, and disjuncture are features of complex systems, rather than their opposite" (1998, xi). There is no need to celebrate uncertainty as the goal of social analysis; it may be the result and often is the beginning of good analysis, but it is always nested, as Coronil says, within a larger configuration.

As is true in other locations internationally famous as archaeological sites, while tens of thousands of tourists from around the world have treasured their pilgrimages to Monte Albán, many working-class residents of Oaxaca City have passed their entire lives without visiting these famous Zapotec ruins less than thirty minutes by car from the city center. In Mexico City, for years I had invited Gabriel to talks I was giving

Figure 18. Mexican flags for sale to celebrate Mexico's Independence Day, September 16, 1992.

at one or another university in the area. He would generally express interest in coming, but at the last minute some problem would invariably arise and it became impossible for him to accompany me. It actually took nearly seven years for Gabriel to attend an academic event with me. He and other friends from Colonia Santo Domingo would sooner cross the U.S.–Mexico border, with all the terrors and risks that might entail, than cross the class border represented by a university lecture.

Globalization has not annulled geopolitics any more than it has fundamentally homogenized the experiences of people across lines of class, region, ethnicity, gender, or sexuality. At most, international affairs, or facets of it, may have become more accessible to more people. As elsewhere, undoubtedly, globalization in Mexico has been modified by nationalism, yet this, too, is not unique in history: nationalism is no more a permanent feature of the ideological landscape than democracy. If the concept is to have any vital, fresh significance, globalization must be examined as a contemporary phenomenon integrating transnational and local actors. With the deterritorialization of particular cultural affinities, there continue to exist possibilities for autonomous self-government with respect to certain aspects of life. This is reflected in Colonia Santo Domingo by local efforts to develop the drainage and sewer lines.

Whereas in other nearby communities residents have had to pay for digging trenches and laying pipes, in Santo Domingo neighbors were able to collectively demand that the city pay for these improvements. Not that dreams of autonomy and self-government have been abandoned in Santo Domingo; in a certain sense, globalization makes such thinking easier, as people may attempt to "think locally and act globally" (see Varese 1991; and Vargas-Cetina and Ayora-Diaz 1998).

EDUCACIÓN AND AGENCY

The term *educación* remains for many in Colonia Santo Domingo simply a shorthand reference to the formal system of schooling in which they and their children have participated to one extent or another. For others, however, for people like Doña Fili and Gabriel, the term *educación* in its fullest sense pertains to a larger concept of how people understand the world, which necessarily implies preparation and training,[6] and not simply the formal learning available from state-run educational systems. Abstract debates about voluntarism and determinism are rehearsed and revamped in Doña Fili's kitchen, in her *comunidad de base* at the Iglesia de la Resurrección, and in her activities with the Unión de Colonias Populares, just as they are also explored in Gabi's streetside counsel to the owners of the cars, trucks, and jitneys he repairs.

Some women *animadores* (organizers/facilitators) in the Christian Base Communities do claim to understand their society and, on the basis of this understanding, change it. And some steady customers of Gabriel's, who have old, rundown cars and never enough money for repairs, do feel bound by the dictates of economic compulsion. People in Santo Domingo do describe themselves as stifled or propelled by events out of their control. Yet they all say they can make changes because of what they believe. Precisely disturbed by the failure of professed socialist countries and movements to realize democratic promises, much less eradicate social inequalities, those who once believed in the possibility of radically transforming their societies by the late 1990s often told me that they preferred not to think too hard anymore about the odds for social change.

When asked about changes in the last few decades in Mexico, activist women and men, as well as many others I have known in Santo Domingo, have often pointed to gender relations as among the most significant examples of what is different today than in the past. Women working outside the home for money, women (and men) having fewer children, and, in some cases, men participating more in the domestic labor of the housework are some of the examples women and men use to illustrate changing gender relations. And although only university-affiliated feminists have ever mentioned to me the fact that more women presently hold political office than was the case before, in Santo Domingo in the 1990s it was common to hear mention of the *militancia* (militant activism) that had existed among women in the *colonia* since its founding, and the perception that women's agency on this score was contrary to clichés about Mexican women being submissive in their homes and passive in public.

Regardless of the accuracy of such historical insights—and the fact remains that women have long been represented in the ranks of the politically active in Mexico—such sentiments, pride for some and incredulity for others, put the lie to facile notions of resistance that would champion, especially, the most hidden and covert of survival techniques because, it is said, these are simply the only realistic options available to the dispossessed at the dawn of the twenty-first century. When the wave of *criminalidad* swept through Mexico City following the disastrous devaluation of the peso in late 1994 and early 1995, whispers could be heard in some scholarly circles that the poor were thereby demonstrating their power to protest against the regime's draconian austerity measures: taxi drivers who robbed their customers were now seen as being at the vanguard of political resistance. Although certainly a product of the economic crisis suffered by the majority of the capital's population, the thieving *taxistas* now became emblematic, not of the randomness of the crisis and of those who had been most impacted by the devaluation, but rather they came to embody the inexorable certainty that the poor in general were the target of suffering brought about by wider controlling forces. The desperation of the taxi drivers was popularly contrasted, not to the supposedly random selection of their victims, but instead to the rather more random policing of a city that had grown even more out of control.

With the horizons of political theory increasingly bounded in the 1990s by superficial slogans about achieving democracy, in Santo Domingo and elsewhere in the Mexican Republic many men and women, frustrated by escalating crime, by elections whose outcomes seemed always to be preordained, and by the outright sale of Mexican industries to the highest foreign bidders, began to look to religion as an arena in which they might encounter qualitatively new ways of understanding the world and their purpose in life. While Chiapas is certainly the best-known example of the growing influence of evangelism in Mexico in recent years, the spread of Protestant ideas, practices, and prohibitions has been profound elsewhere as well. In more than one Catholic baptism I have attended in Mexico City in the 1990s, the priest has managed to toss in gratuitous remarks about the pernicious influence of the Jehovah's Witnesses. If formal politics ultimately seemed less promising as an arena where dramatic change might occur, then perhaps in formal religion a break with official Catholicism showed greater potential for fresh starts.

In certain respects the sphere of competing religious sects additionally provides an apposite instance of the broader point of how people in Santo Domingo make a direct connection between what they think and what they do. It is common among my friends and neighbors in the *colonia* to hold themselves and others responsible for actions that are, in turn, linked to various belief systems, and first and foremost for many, the religious creed to which they subscribe. Similarly, these same people have little compunction about blaming themselves and others for failures and inactivity with respect to a gamut of social and political activities. Though not exactly identical to what might be termed a unified popular political self-consciousness, such theological disputes are not without relevance to emerging developments on the political landscape in Mexico in the 1990s. Official Catholicism, long taken for granted as synonymous with Mexican society and culture, has been beyond doubt thrown into a spiritual and practical crisis in several regions of the country in the latter years of the twentieth century. In contemporary Mexico, too, traditions constantly change. To the extent that my friends and neighbors have seen themselves as skilled agents of "traditional" culture's continuity and renovation, they have displayed enthusiasm or reluctance to participate in contemporary Mexico's political culture.

NOSTRUMS OF DEMOCRACY

If the PRI defeat and PAN victory of 2000 and the ensuing euphoria in many middle-class sectors are not necessarily permanent features of Mexico's political landscape, we nonetheless may well ask what it will take to dramatically alter the political situation in Mexico. What would a dramatically more democratic Mexico look and feel like? Focusing on a more sweeping question, one posed by Renato Rosaldo (1993, 181), we might ask: How can human emancipation ever really become politically conceivable in Mexico?

Conceivably, some observers might argue, it is not fair to ask what suffrage is worth to the politically and economically dispossessed in Mexico, given the fact that Mexicans have had a real choice in selecting a president only since 1988. Owing to the theory of stages, after all, one cannot expect real alternatives before there is the semblance of choice between candidates of different parties.

Frustrated with the fact that democracy for many people seems to rest on these and similar platitudes, I spent a week in August 2000 inviting my Santo Domingo friends to an academic gathering at the Colegio de México. I wanted to fashion a socially mixed audience for the presentation of the Spanish-language edition of my book (2000), which was based on my earlier research of gender relations, parenting, and machismo in the *colonia*. The presentation also represented a personal political fantasy: to bridge two social fields of friends and colleagues in Mexico City. It was patently evident that questions relating to gender and machismo were of interest to both my neighbors in the *colonia* and to my university colleagues, but I was far less certain they could talk to each other about these matters.

Ten or fifteen people in Santo Domingo told me they wanted to and would come to the book presentation. On the afternoon of the twenty-fourth, in the hours before the event, a number of problems arose for my friends. One person told me that he unexpectedly had to work overtime at the job, another that a relative was visiting out of the blue, and another that a child suddenly took sick; regrettably, they would not be able to attend the event.

Gabriel insisted that he would come, and that he was bringing his teenage daughter, Gabriela. But Gabi had cars and vans lined up down the street awaiting his ministrations and I began to have my doubts about him, too. If he came, it would mean a real financial sacrifice and plenty of irate customers. Half an hour before we were to catch a jitney, Marcos returned from work early. He shouted down the street and said he just needed time to catch a bite to eat and he would come with us. He disappeared inside his house, then quickly reemerged and headed out into the street. I assumed we had lost him as well to his many other duties.

At five o'clock, Gabriel returned from his house, freshly showered and with clean clothes. He whistled to Gabriela, who was talking with friends halfway down the block. Then he knocked on Marcos's gate. Marcos stuck his head out the door (he had returned, unseen by me), shoving down a taco with one hand and taking a swig of Coca-Cola with the other. He disappeared into his house to grab a sweater. The four of us, Gabriel, Gabriela, Marcos, and I headed out for Las Rosas Avenue.

Feeling grateful that these friends had found a way to join me at Colegio de México, instead of us taking two jitney routes I offered to spring for a taxi. We needed a large one—the ubiquitous VW *vocho* (bug) taxis could not easily accommodate three adults and a teenager. As we walked down the avenue, scouting for a larger taxi, Javier swerved by us in his VW van (*combi*). "Gabriel, I've been looking for you all over," he shouted. I assumed Javier had an engine problem for Gabi to solve; he drove the Ruta 45 between the upscale neighborhood of San Angel and the *colonia popular* of Ajusco in this *combi*. Javier is invariably friendly but I always have a hard time understanding him when he speaks in his half-laugh, half-mumble drawl. Yet after he pulled to a stop, Javier opened the door and invited us to climb aboard. We did. Gabriel had told him about the book presentation and Javier, driving his *combi*-carriage, had arrived to deliver us in style.

We drove in silence to the Colegio de México, as close to an academic palace as one encounters in Mexico. As we approached the entrance, Marcos remarked that he had driven by many times, though he had never entered the heavily guarded gates of this University. I expected trouble at the parking lot because beat-up vans are not common at the Colegio, but the security guards let us pass when we presented our official invitations to the event. As we had left Santo Domingo with enough time planned for the two jitneys we thought we were going to take to get to the Colegio, we now found that we were early, so we decided to go to the cafeteria. Gabriela and Marcos ordered cappuccinos; Gabriel and Javier coffee.

Twenty minutes later, we walked to the auditorium and sat down. Two other people from Santo Domingo, Doña Fili and María Elena, showed up around six o'clock. They had taken the two jitneys—and they were carrying several bags.[7] I sat them near Gabi and Marcos, so as to form a Santo Domingo contingent in the midst of the other attendees who were all academics. In the row in front of my friends from Santo Domingo was a group of *exiliadas* (exiles) from Uruguay, Chile, and Brazil; they were discussing the new Mexican visa requirements for those who had fled various dictators in Latin America in the 1970s. The six people from Santo Domingo had already altered the ambience in the room a bit. People were discreetly looking over at them and wondering who they might be. No one was pointing, but there was an air of curiosity.

After two hours of commentaries on the book, I got my turn to speak. I began by saying, "First, my great thanks to several people from Colonia Santo Domingo who are here with us tonight. Gabriel, Marcos, Doña Fili, . . ." As soon as I mentioned her name, Doña Fili stood up rather quickly, looked around, and started talking. I was confused, and all I could do was surrender the floor to her and listen.

Fili began by thanking everyone for inviting her. She said she did not have so many fancy titles as the other speakers she had heard introduced—in fact, I knew, she had all of one year of formal education. I had no idea what my academic friends might be thinking about this unorthodox "audience participation." Fili's tone was a mix of earnest rebuke aimed at the intelligentsia in general and a sensitive reaching across the divides of class. She talked for several minutes, repeatedly emphasizing one main point: When we talk about machismo, it is a mistake to limit our discussion to only family and household contexts. What about the PRI? Fili wanted to know. Were not PRI policies and politicians a perfect example of machismo? Sure, the women of Santo Domingo had struggled long and hard, and they had had to overcome a lot of opposition from many men in the *colonia*. It wasn't as if she and others didn't appreciate scholars writing about these women. But, Fili insisted, at least as many men had supported their women and eagerly sought to change gender relations in the home and society more broadly. It just did not make sense, Fili told the audience, to narrowly talk about power between men and women as if they lived in a vacuum, apart from wider social forces and factors. She urged the speakers and others present to leave the confines of their universities and come down to the *colonias populares* like Santo Domingo, to sit on the *banquetas* (sidewalks) and share their knowledge with the people in these neighborhoods, where few have access to books about culture and history much less professors to teach them about such things.[8]

When Fili closed, with an apology for taking up so much time, there was generous and sustained applause. No one wanted her to stop.

The seven of us—Gabriel, Gabriela, Marcos, Javier, Fili, María Elena, and I—were among the last to leave the event. When we did, all of us piled into Javier's *combi* and headed back to Santo Domingo. It had been an adventure, but it was now behind us. Henceforth, I knew, I would still go over to the University, as before, alone, leaving one

world behind to enter another. I expressed my relief that the event was
over and said something about my new project, a book on democracy.
We arrived at Fili's home shortly thereafter, and before she got out, Fili
looked at me and said, "You know, Mateo, when we talk about democracy in Mexico, we're not just interested in elections." For Fili, as for
others in Santo Domingo, if democracy was to have any relevance to
their lives, it must not be limited to the act of voting that lasts for five
minutes every few years.

The rest of us headed back to Huehuetzin Street, dropping off Gabriela at her mother's on the way. We decided to end the night at Marcos's house. But first we stopped to buy eight bottles of Negra Modelo
beer; we would each have two. Once we arrived at the house, Delia,
Marcos's wife, began making tacos, several for each of us, with wild
mushrooms and cheese. Someone voiced the opinion that, for whatever
reason, tacos just seemed to taste better in Mexico than in the United
States. The fact that it was not I who had made the comment and that
no one else in the room had ever been to the United States did not seem
to matter. It was indisputable, and therefore no dissension was voiced.

Gabriel, for some reason, began talking about baroque architecture
and music. I made a face, complained that I did not know what he was
talking about, and indicated that I had heard the term *baroque* but did
not know what exactly it referred to. Marcos chimed in to help Gabriel
explain to this philistine professor what *baroque* meant, and why it was
important to them that I at least have a feeling for the significance of this
architectural style and period. I admitted I had a sense of its design —
"Isn't it something to do with very fancy, ornate stuff?" was the best I
could manage at the time. Neither Gabi nor Marcos appeared even
mildly surprised by the fact that they could teach me some art history.

From baroque artistry, we moved unaccountably to the subject of instincts and animal behavior. Maybe it was the hour, the tacos, or the
beer, though I think it more reflected some friends just talking about
whatever came to mind. Why do certain animals not adopt the young of
others? Marcos asked. Why do some eat the young of others? He continued: What is natural and what is rational, what must be accepted as
a given and what is more amenable to choice and will?

I am not sure what the larger significance of our brief discussion of
the baroque signified, other than that underestimating the genuine concerns of *los de abajo,* society's underdogs, and reducing them to a
bundle of survival instincts is rarely to be recommended. Our conversation about animal instinct, and in particular the relevance of instinct to

questions of parenting, adoption, and what is truly natural behavior, reminded me once again of the centrality of blame and consequence in the lives of my friends and neighbors in the *colonia*. Although couched in more general terms, Marcos and Gabriel were, once again, rehearsing arguments they had articulated many times before regarding what kinds of ideas and behavior are predestined to prevail and which are more amenable to human will and agency.

Before we dropped her off, Doña Fili, as she often had, reminded me once again that I must not be satisfied with simplistic definitions of democracy, nor accept the narrow conception of voting, which prevailed more broadly in contemporary Mexican society, as the totality of democratic life. After all, if everyone is a democrat, there may not be anything so great about democracy anymore. If democracy is going to mean something significant for Fili and others in Santo Domingo, it cannot be left at the level of platitude and injunction. In Fili's case, too, she now talked less about a fundamental reordering of Mexican society than she used to, when socialism had not become a banned subject of discussion and an idealistic vision of the future. Yet even in an age when quiescence got the better of rebelliousness, despite all the twists and turns of popular politics in contemporary Mexico, Fili remained at heart a political romantic in the very best sense.

Struggle as she might to gain whatever small victories she could, Fili has never succumbed to substituting piecemeal goals for her dream of radical change. Somehow Fili has continued to believe that she and others have a say in what happens and does not happen in society. Nor can the question of how much control Fili and others in Santo Domingo actually have over their lives be resolved through dreaming alone; ultimately, it will be a matter of their practical efforts to make a wholly better world come to life.

Notes

1. On the more general significance of the term *desmadre* for modern Mexican politics, see Bartra's now famous commentary on "dismodernity" (1987, 26), and also Lomnitz (1996, 55).

2. For a sample of recent meanings and implications of democracy, see Wendy Brown: "The dream of democracy—that humans might govern themselves by governing together" (1995, 5); and "Democracy's virtue—cultivation and toleration of individual values and ends—is also its vice—the absence of a principle or end by which democratic societies can be fabricated as unified and unifying culture, the absence of a set of ideas that form, cohere, stabilize, and direct a social body" (1998, 426); Jürgen Habermas: "The addressees of the law should be able to conceive of themselves at the same time as its authors" (1998, 403); David Held: "Throughout the nineteenth and twentieth centuries theorists of democracy have tended to assume a 'symmetrical' and 'congruent' relationship between political decision-makers and the recipients of political decisions" (1995, 16); Guillermo O'Donnell and Philippe Schmitter: "Democracy's guiding principle is that of citizenship. This involves both the right to be treated by fellow human beings as equal with respect to the making of collective choices and the obligation of those implementing such choices to be equally accountable and accessible to all members of the polity" (1986, 7); and finally, of course, Alexis de Tocqueville: "If the men of our time should be convinced . . . that the gradual and progressive of social equality is at once the past and the future of their history, this discovery alone would confer upon the change the sacred character of a divine decree. To attempt to check democracy would be in that case to resist the will of God" ([1835] 1945, 7).

3. On presidential successions in Mexico, see Jorge Castañeda's important *Perpetuating Power: How Mexican Presidents Were Chosen* (2000).

4. On the *acarreo,* see Lomnitz, Lomnitz, and Adler (1993, 379–81).

5. As is well known, 14 percent of adult Mexicans will spend some time living in the United States, a fact whose cultural and political import has yet to be fully appreciated in many still rather bifurcated studies of one side or the other of the Rio Grande/Río Bravo.

6. In Mexico the complexity of comparison often arises in the form of complaints that I have received from some Mexican intellectuals whenever I even mention Octavio Paz (especially Paz 1961). When I have discussed Octavio Paz while addressing academic audiences in Mexico, I have occasionally been informed, "Only you Gringos still pay attention to Paz." And, it is true, Gringos have for decades been excessively obsequious toward Paz. Nonetheless, the fact remains that all significant writing by Mexicans themselves about *mexicanidad* and *lo mexicano,* of culture and life in Mexico today and historically, refers obligatorily to Paz (see Bartra 1992; Bonfil Batalla 1987; Monsiváis 2000; Lomnitz 1992; Valenzuela Arce 1998). In addition, and equally if not more important from the perspective of ethnography of *los de abajo* (the classic underclass underdogs), both the United States and Paz continue to be sources of reference for poor Mexicans in urban and rural areas—for women and men, girls and boys, who are seeking answers to the question: What does it mean that I am a Mexican?

7. Again, in the context of presentations of the United States as some kind of model democracy: What does it mean that 12.3 percent of African American males aged twenty-five to twenty-nine years were in prison or jail in 1999, compared to 1.5 percent of whites in the same age group (see Beck 2000). What, indeed, does this say about democracy and democratic rights and opportunities in the putative model for global democracy? My thanks to Jim Frank for the citation for these data.

8. On the contemporary debate in intellectual circles in the United States regarding the participation of millions of ordinary Germans in the Nazi holocaust, see Mahoney and Ellsberg (1999), who, for example, discuss questions of motivation and obedience on the part of German soldiers not affiliated with the more infamous Nazi units. For another discussion on the Holocaust, see Wolf (1999). For a nuanced presentation on agency from two political scientists, see Mahoney and Snyder (1999).

9. By *educación* Gabriel was talking about formal schooling, but he was also more generally referring to an awareness of social relations, a social consciousness and conscience.

10. See García Canclini's classic *Las culturas populares en el capitalismo* (1982), and his article on "La crisis teórica en la investigación sobre cultura popular" (1988); and Bonfil Batalla's "Los conceptos de diferencia y subordinación en el estudio de las culturas populares" (1988), as well as his treatment of pluralism in the classic *México profundo* (1987). See also the seminal essays on these topics by Stavenhagen, Bonfil Batalla, Galeano, and others in Colombres, *La cultura popular* (1982).

11. These intellectual trends in Mexico are of course part of larger theoretical trends and debates internationally. On the utility or futility of class analysis in social history and cultural anthropology in the Anglophone world, see, e.g., Thompson 1993; Rouse 1995; Kearney 1996; Hale 1998; Ortner 1998; Smith 1999; and Gledhill 2000.

12. My translation of the word *chingada* as "damned" in this slogan is more figurative than literal; as many readers may already know, *chingar* and *chingadola* are terms notoriously rendered in English as "screwed" and "fucked." "Damned" is more appropriate here. I also note in passing that for all its apparent practical implications, the question of "who's to blame" is actually a rather academic one. This is not raised to demean the issue, but simply to contextualize it better. For those engaged daily in the battles over health, housing, education, parenting, and employment that occupy a good portion of the energies of the poor, trying to assign blame in an *intangible* sense can appear as a rather technical inquiry.

13. In this context, it is instructive to recall Stanley Brandes's point in his study of fiestas and social control in rural Mexico: it is important not only "to explain change, but also to show why it is so often interpreted as continuity by the people themselves" (1988, 39).

CHAPTER I

1. Among the exceptions are ethnographic studies of local elections in India by Mayer (1966); in Crete by Herzfeld (1985); recent work on presidential campaigns in France by Abélès (1988, 1991, 1997); in Brazil by Martinez-Alier and Boito Junior (1977) and Stolcke (1988); and in Mexico, studies by Royce (1975); Gómez-Tagle (1986); Krotz (1990); and Lomnitz, Lomnitz, and Adler (1993). More indicative of the relative disinterest in anthropology for electoral matters, none of the terms *elections, suffrage,* or *voting* appears in the indexes of Morton Fried's *Evolution of Political Society* (1967), or of Joan Vincent's encyclopedic *Anthropology and Politics* (1990).

2. Neoliberalism refers to the range of free-market economic models that came to prevail in the 1980s and 1990s in Latin America (see Gledhill 1995; Haber 1997).

3. *Futbol* is "soccer," *flojera* means "laziness," and *tomado* means (here) "drunk."

4. Roger Bartra writes, "I think it is necessary to open the doors of the parties in which leftists have been institutionalized so that the currents of the new civil culture may penetrate with refreshing airs able to throw out the decrepit programs" (1993, 163).

5. Why is there so much anguish expressed in social science writing about power? I think it relates to confusion and conflict over blame and innocence, and with how we may best view the relationship between oppressors and those oppressed. In particular, the issue in the human sciences has often revolved around how much room for maneuver and change individuals and groups may reason-

ably expect. Certain "hard" social theories of structure can appear, at times, to be not so terribly different from theological doctrines of divine will.

6. The ethnographic fieldwork in Mexico City upon which this study is based was conducted from 1990 to 2000. I lived in the Santo Domingo neighborhood from August 1992 to August 1993, and returned to live and work in the *colonia* on numerous occasions during subsequent years for a matter of days or weeks, totaling an additional six to eight months there.

CHAPTER 2

1. In this way, the reception of *Children of Sánchez* was similar to reactions to *Down These Mean Streets,* Piri Thomas's 1967 classic study of poor Puerto Ricans in New York City.

2. The father's name was Jesús, not Alberto Sánchez.

3. Although *agencia* is increasingly used in Latin America as the Spanish translation for the English term *agency,* Roger Bartra (personal communication) suggests that *mediación* is a more appropriate word in Spanish.

4. The progenitor of what we might call Second Wave Agency Theory is, of course, Max Weber. Through his appreciation of the role of religious movements in changing people's thinking as a way of promoting social change, Weber's emphasis on human creativity, albeit as understood within the context of political economy, is often contrasted with simplistic models of cultural and economic determinacy. There are key distinctions between first- and second-wave theories of agency. The former uses not only Weber's ideas about charismatic religious leadership ([1919] 1946), but also his concern regarding the "disenchantment of the world" through intellectualization and rationalization. Among recent, that is, second-wave advocates of agency, we often find a ready valorization of precisely the rational faculties of the lower stratum.

5. In Lewis we also find a remarkable, if untapped, point of reference for postcolonial scholarship—for instance, on questions about the degree to which it is helpful to focus on culture to the neglect of economics and political relations. See Williams and Chrisman (1994); Spivak (1999).

6. On the origins and contradictory aspects of Lewis's theoretical work, as well as for fascinating details about his ethnographic methods and his correspondence with colleagues, see Susan Rigdon's biography of Lewis, *The Culture Façade: Art, Science, and Politics in the Work of Oscar Lewis* (1988).

7. Because it is a widely acknowledged feature of Mexican society, machismo is in this sense illustrative of Herzfeld's notion of "cultural intimacy" (1997, 3, 16).

8. Angela's use of the term *papá* to refer to Juan's activities and identity in the past implies that he, she, and their children no longer saw him as a father in the same way.

9. Juan was nonetheless able to prevent Angela from obtaining outside work.

10. It could also be argued that because he had never married, he shopped often.

11. That this "muting" was experienced by some men, though by no means

all men, is a complicated matter. It seems related to several factors, among them the question of social space (the home, the street) and divergent notions of public and private; interpersonal relations and familial manifestations of privilege, ridicule, and stigma; and possibly the historical emergence of certain cultural challenges on the part of women against men in the home.

12. For some of the burgeoning literature on machismo, see Brusco (1995); Carrier (1995); Fuller (1998); Gutmann (1996); Lancaster (1992); Núñez Noriega (1994); and Ramírez (1999).

13. My thanks to Gilberto Anguiano and Luz Fernández Gordillo of the *DEM* for allowing me access to their files for the project.

14. The author is referring to the *Diccionario de la lengua española,* 19th ed., published by the Real Academia Española (Madrid, 1970).

15. With respect to the puerile influence of machismo among academic and political elites, Paredes writes about historian Walter Precott Webb, who held "an almost infantile admiration" for macho cowboys, and of Theodore Roosevelt, whose "admiration for cowboys was excessive, almost childish" (1967, 227, 231).

16. In a sense, too, the argument raised by Leacock was the famous question emphasized decades earlier by W. E. B. Du Bois ([1903] 1995): What are the implications of focusing social attention on the experience of problems instead of on the people actually suffering from the problems? See also Gordon (1997, 63–64).

17. Whether Lewis should be found guilty by association is not the point. Though it appears that he did little to publicly disassociate himself from certain U.S. government programs in the 1960s, in his writings reliance on the munificence of governments is entirely absent. The individual political party affiliations, if any, of Lewis, Leacock, Valentine, and Harrington may have influenced the debate. Harrington, for example, went on to become leader of the Democratic Socialists of America, an organization often critical of the Communist Party, USA, which in turn published Leacock's introduction to Engels's *Origin of the Family, Private Property, and the State* (1972). Thus, substantial underlying debates on the left in the United States were clearly involved regarding the poor, their role in social change, and questions of structure, consciousness, and political leadership. Whether driven into hiding because of McCarthyite fears or because of simple academic politesse, these were never publicly aired. See the paper by Harvey and Reed (1996) on the relationship between left political debates and criticisms of Lewis in the 1960s.

18. In a passage describing the role of women in social movements in Mexico, Vivienne Bennett writes: "Once women understand that their daily lives are structured by gendered inequality . . . then the focus of organizing changes or expands. At least part of the objective of women's actions becomes the transformation of gender relations" (1998:117). For some scholars, even to say "once" in this manner might represent too perilous a leap toward an appreciation of consciousness.

19. See, e.g., Barrett and McIntosh (1982); Thorne and Yalom (1992); Hansen and Garey (1998).

20. García and Oliveira (1994); González and Tuñón (1997); González de la

Rocha (1994); Massolo (1992); and Oliveira (1989) have all written on this subject. Among the most important anthropologically sensitive studies of urban households in Mexico in English, see especially Vélez-Ibáñez (1983); Selby, Murphy, and Lorenzen (1990); and Chant (1991).

21. Rarely in the United States does one travel so casually from poor to wealthy homes on a regular basis as an anthropologist may in Mexico City. Perhaps as a result of my privileged Gringo status, class divisions in Mexico, if less often class conflicts there, have always seemed to me shockingly blatant. For description and analysis of debates in households in Santo Domingo regarding the naturalization of mothering and mother–child bonding, see also Gutmann (1998).

CHAPTER 3

1. The joke circulated in 1999, notwithstanding the fact that Díaz Ordaz had died in 1979, and well before Bill Clinton entered the annals of oral infamy.

2. Although Tlatelolco is often called a public housing complex in English, this term can be misleading for readers in the United States, because it implies subsidized residential housing for the urban poor. In Mexico, on the contrary, housing complexes like the one at Tlatelolco were (and still are) occupied by middle-class families, usually those in which at least one household member is employed by a government-affiliated institution. In the case of Tlatelolco, the site was already of symbolic significance because of its proximity to the Plaza de las Tres Culturas, where in 1521 the Spanish conquistador Hernán Cortés formally defeated the Aztec leader Cuauhtémoc.

3. It is impossible to offer precise figures for the number of demonstrators, soldiers, and others killed in the Tlatelolco massacre. See Aguayo Quezada (1998) for a recent and comprehensive report on the differing numbers offered by government and press sources at the time.

4. In a similar manner, in the United States the shooting by National Guard troops of four white students at Kent State University in Ohio in May 1970 was treated as truly shocking. Yet, when later that same month two black students at Jackson State University in Mississippi were killed, the event was buried. The Jackson State murders are still less well known to people in the United States than the killings at Kent State. For those unfamiliar with this history, Phillip Lafayette Gibbs and James Earl Green were killed May 15, 1970, when seventy-five city and state police officers opened fire on Jackson State student protesters gathered on the campus of this historically black university.

5. In addition to Aguayo Quezada (1998), on the events and significance of October 2, 1968, see also Cazés (1993); Edmonds (2000); Poniatowska (1975); Scherer García and Monsiváis (1999); and Zolov (1999).

6. Whereas 1968 had a national and even international impact, the strike of 1999 proved traumatic for the capital more than elsewhere in Mexico.

7. More than a few rebels of 1968 also went on to assume important posts in the Mexican government.

CHAPTER 4

1. Thanks to Claudio Lomnitz, Lynn Stephen, and Thomas Wilson for comments on earlier versions of this chapter, one of which appeared in *Critique of Anthropology* 18, no. 3 (1998): 297–315, and another in *Alteridades* 19 (2000): 109–22.

2. In a letter from Taco Bell International dated January 14, 1998, I was informed that although nothing was available in Mexico, franchises were for sale elsewhere in Latin America, including in Chile, Costa Rica, the Dominican Republic, Ecuador, Guatemala, Honduras, Peru, and Puerto Rico.

3. Lest we be too tempted to overestimate the novelty of globalization and transnationalism, here is a commentary from 150 years ago:

> The bourgeoisie has through its exploitation of the world-market given a cosmopolitan character to production and consumption in every country. To the great chagrin of Reactionists, it has drawn from under the feet of industry the national ground on which it stood. All old national industries have been destroyed or are daily being destroyed. . . . In place of old wants, satisfied by the productions of the country, we find new wants, requiring for their satisfaction the products of distant lands and climes. In place of the old local and national seclusion and self-sufficiency, we have intercourse in every direction, universal inter-dependence of nations. (Marx and Engels [1847] 1992, 112)

4. This chapter is thus meant to contribute to the emerging study of national culture and modernity in Mexico. For other studies, see Claudio Lomnitz's (1996) work on contemporary Mexican nationalism, and Florencia Mallon's (1995) exploration of how popular political cultures at the level of villages in Mexico and Peru interacted with regional and national arenas to construct national politics in the nineteenth century. See also Knight (1997).

5. See Hellman (1993) and Loaeza (1994) for thoughtful exceptions to this generalization. For an interesting paper on the responsiveness of U.S. and Mexican regimes to perceptions of popular opposition to the Agreement, see Morris and Passé-Smith (2001).

6. Jaime Serra Puche was formerly Mexico's Secretario de Comercio y Fomento Industrial, which is roughly equivalent to the Secretary of Commerce in the United States. As indicated by his quest to engage with "the challenge of interdependence," Serra Puche was an outspoken proponent of NAFTA in Mexico in the early 1990s.

7. BANRURAL is the Banco Nacional de Crédito Rural (National Rural Credit Bank).

8. Guerrero's coast includes the resort areas of Acapulco, Ixtapa, and Zihuatenejo.

9. During a conference for U.S. scholars at the Chapultepec Castle in 1992, I was asked by then U.S. cultural attaché John Dwyer, "Do you know the history of this place?" I replied, "You mean the Niños Héroes?" I was referring to the Mexican military cadets who in 1847 died defending the Castle from an invading army led by U.S. General Winfield Scott. Dwyer slapped me lightly on the shoulder and said, "No, not *that* history." It turned out he was referring to

the peace accords that had been signed at the Castle by government and guerilla forces from El Salvador on New Year's Eve 1991. See de la Peña (1999, 13) for recent invocations of the Niños Héroes which link defense of ethnic citizenship with territory in Mexico.

10. For expositions of these various positions, see Aguilar Camín ([1976] 1989); Bartra (1989, 1992); Lomnitz (1992); Monsiváis (1981); Paz ([1947] 1961); Ramos ([1934] 1962).

11. My thanks to Simone Poliandri for confirming the Latin cited by Héctor.

12. On the hagiography of the Virgin of Guadalupe, see the major study by Lafaye (1976). On national character studies in anthropology, see the comments in Manson (1986).

13. The fact that the DEA is known in Mexico popularly by its acronym alone is an indication of the extent of its disrepute in Mexico.

14. Suspicions like this concerning North Americans are widespread among people in Latin America who are political *militantes*. Valfre once asked me, "Is there anything in your publications that the CIA can learn from?" Such concerns reflect an awareness of the extensive covert activities by U.S. agents throughout the continent as much as they may reflect unwarranted paranoia. For another typical CIA allegation, this one in Nicaragua in the late 1980s, see Lancaster (1992, 75–77).

15. On Solidaridad/PRONASOL's short-term infrastructure building without long-term jobs creation, see Cornelius, Craig, and Fox (1994); Lustig (1994); and Dresser (1994).

16. "*Muy pronto, sólo llevarán el sello 'Hecho en México' el tequila, la tardanza y los* Mexican curios." The last part of the sentence, "Mexican curios," was stated in English. For a fascinating analysis of state monopolies of natural resources in Venezuela, see Coronil (1997).

17. *Pulque* is an inexpensive alcoholic beverage made from the sap of the maguey, or century plant.

CHAPTER 5

1. Many of the ideas for this particular chapter were first sparked by my participation in a wonderful conference in Zamora, Michoacán, in October 1997. The proceedings of the conference have since been published (see Mummert 1999). My ideas on the border have benefited greatly as well from ongoing discussions with Miguel Díaz Barriga, who is always ready to deflate many of my stranger trial balloons. Thanks also to Joe Heyman and Michael Kearney for several good suggestions for improving this chapter.

2. In Santo Domingo I have heard people use the expression, "*Trabajar como negro, vivir como blanco*" (Work like a black, live like a white). When I asked one friend what she meant by this, she asked me, "Don't blacks have to work a lot more than whites in the United States?" I am unclear on the extent to which the expression reflects implicit knowledge of racism in the United States or stems from residual ideologies owing to historical slavery in Mexico itself.

3. On human rights abuses along the border, see Huspek, Martinez, and Jimenez (1998).

4. As mentioned earlier, one in seven adult *mexicanos* will spend some part of their lives working in the United States. The equivalent figure in reverse, that is, if 14 percent of U.S. citizens were to spend some time working in Mexico, would be around forty million. It is unlikely that 40 million people from the United States have even ever visited Mexico. The implications of so many people from one country working in another are curiously understudied. In part, perhaps owing to the nationalist ideology in Mexico, the implications of U.S. influence in every aspect of life for 100 million Mexicans has long been acknowledged yet shunned as a subject of scholarship. Some of the hybrid cultures studies have focused on these issues in the United States (see, e.g., Davis [1992]), whereas studies of hybridity in Mexico have generally dealt with "internal" matters of *mestizaje* and the like. More nuanced, well-grounded histories of U.S. cultural influence in Mexico would be welcome additions to the literature.

5. The *Diccionario del español usual en México* (El Colegio de México 1996, 596) has as a second definition of *mayate*: "*Hombre homosexual activo.*" The *Barrio Language Dictionary* (Fuentes and López 1974, 97) defines *mayate* as: "A black person (Derog.)." Jiménez (1976, 106) gives "*homosexual, sodomita*" as definitions of *mayate*. Although he does not give either "homosexual" or "negro" as definitions, Santamaría (1959, 707–8) also lists "fig. fam. *Borracho*" (drunk) as a third definition of *mayate*.

6. See Higgins and Coen (2000, 114), who write that *mayate* "often means an active gay male or one who penetrates. It can also refer to a very masculine male who is involved in some kind of street hustle, including sex, crime, and sometimes violence." See also Prieur for the more nuanced connotations of the term *mayate* as employed by some male prostitutes and transvestites in the Nezahualcóyotl area east of Mexico City. Among these men, the term *mayate* refers not to all men who have sex with other men, and still less to African Americans, but only to "a man who looks like a man and has sex with men who are regarded as *homosexuales,* and usually also with women" (1998, 26).

CHAPTER 6

1. The criticisms directed against Sagan for saying nothing new were echoed in the United States at the time, especially in certain quarters of academia where, it was alleged, Sagan dumbed down complex astronomy for the masses. No doubt there were editorial decisions involved in explaining the cosmos to a wide audience, most of whose members did not have postgraduate training in astrophysics. Still, I wonder how much rancor stemmed (in addition to puerile jealousy) from patronizing views that if millions of people appreciate astronomy, it must be bad or at least badly presented.

2. The direction of our conversation then shifted, as Gabriel asked me, "Did you already do your thesis? Do you have theses there?" I told him we did, and that I still had to do it after returning to Gringolandia. He wanted to know what I was going to call it, so we spent some time discussing various titles for the thesis.

3. I am indebted to Michael Kearney for his close reading of the earlier paper and this chapter and his suggestions for improving each.

4. On social movements in the region, see especially Alvarez, Dagnino, and Escobar (1998); Eckstein (1989b); Escobar and Alvarez (1992); Foweraker and Craig (1990); and Massolo (1992).

5. Certainly, those involved in the many-stranded feminist movement would not fall into this generally demoralized category; women's/feminist/gender studies, queer theory, and the political movements associated with feminism broadly conceived were exceptional in the United States, at least, in that their influence grew, albeit in spurts, rather than waned during this period.

6. See Herzfeld's (1997, 14) related discussion of binary models of elite and ordinary people, and ensuing claims and contestation over these attributions.

7. There is also a methodological issue at play here. In Mexico, as in the United States and many other countries of the world, when anthropologists conduct ethnographic fieldwork in their hometowns they usually continue living in their regular homes, typically in middle-class quarters. Yet their fieldwork is generally conducted in poorer areas. Thus, they often literally commute from the neighborhood of one class to another. Mexican colleagues have generally expressed delight that I was living and not just working in Santo Domingo; a few, perhaps defensively, have declared that the twenty-four-hour-a-day "immersion" method of ethnography is bankrupt and antiquated: "Only Gringos would be so pretentious," one young anthropologist chided me.

8. For recent commentary on Ramos, see Bartra (1992, 75–80); Gutmann (1996, 224–26); and Limón (1998, 76–80).

9. And in point of fact Bacardí Añejo is the rum of choice among most of my friends on Huehuetzin Street. Whether this reflects a minimally higher standard of living than in other working-class areas, whether the ads for Añejo on television that portray yuppie globe-trotters have reached their mark, or whether my middle-class informants were merely passing on misperceptions, I do not know.

10. At the time one U.S. dollar was equal to seven Mexican pesos.

11. For a discussion of *cooperación* in fiestas in Tzintzuntzan, Mexico, see Brandes (1988, 49). Rent parties in the United States are also a form of *cooperación,* as friends and neighbors pay a door fee to enter the party at the end of the month, thereby helping the party givers pay for the next month's rent.

12. George Foster might suggest another reason for the woman's nocturnal activity: the desire to avoid the envy of neighbors (see 1967, 153–66).

13. For classics in this genre, see Moore (1978); Touraine (1988); Skocpol (1994); Tarrow (1994); and Tilly (1998).

14. See the contrasting views of Cornelius (1975) and Vélez-Ibáñez (1983) on the structural humility or rebelliousness among various Mexico City residents.

15. For a selection of the responses to Stoll's critique of Menchú (in brief, that she misled millions of readers in presenting events that had commonly occurred to indigenous peoples in Guatemala as part of her own personal history), see Warren (2001), Rus (1999), and Lancaster (1999).

16. We see here a connection between personal and national survival politics. As shown in chapter 5 on NAFTA, by the mid- and late 1990s there was a widespread sentiment in Santo Domingo that regardless of whether Mexican

elites had in the past carried out a foreign policy independent of the United States, this was no longer the case. In the example here, with the investiture of the Nobel medal cynical commentary appeared in the press and in the streets to the effect that Salinas was affecting opposition to the U.S.-backed regime in Guatemala. Many who may have been fooled at the time by the President of Mexico's defense of Indian rights were disabused of the illusions in due course.

17. For additional opinions about campesinos in the provinces, see Gutmann (1996, 59–64).

18. Angela's urn was later moved to a crypt nearer Santo Domingo, which allowed for more frequent visits by family and friends.

19. For more on rites of rebellion, see Kertzer (1988) and Gluckman (1960).

20. For a related discussion of political resistance and the ritual use of elements from Gluckman's conceptualization of these issues, see Comaroff and Comaroff (1999).

21. See Chodorow (1999) for recent discussion on multiple parallels between psychoanalysis and anthropology, including with respect to methodological approaches and concerns.

22. Ongoing discussions regarding the rise of Nazism share some common features with debates in Mexico City over the ability of common people to change the course of history. Eric Wolf, for example, makes clear that his purpose in examining the origins of National Socialism was especially "to show how . . . ideas relate to particular social, political, and economic arrangements of the past, and how they were caught up in the transformations of those arrangements" (1999, 200).

23. On taxi rides in Mexico City, see also Hellman (2000).

24. Many of these issues are covered in more depth in Lomnitz (2000).

25. And increasing numbers of women were hired as traffic police in the late 1990s, ostensibly because they were (at least initially) less prone to demanding bribes from drivers.

26. For a rich ethnographic examination of rural violence in Oaxaca, see Greenberg (1989).

CHAPTER 7

1. The significance of Mexico's "other border" with Guatemala became a critical factor in developing a rebellious critical mass in Chiapas, and through the Zapatistas the war in Guatemala has influenced popular politics in general in Mexico. A number of studies have been published in English on the 1994 uprising and subsequent developments. Among the best are Collier and Quaratiello (1994); Collier and Stephen (1997); Harvey (1998); Womack (1999); and Stephen (2002). For briefer analysis by Mexicans, written in English, of Chiapas, see also Arizpe (1996); Monsiváis (1997); Bartra (1999).

2. On women and Chiapas, see Hernández Castillo (1998b).

3. The organizations I designate here as "campesino" are sometimes referred to in English as "peasant-based." Along with Kearney (1996), I wish to avoid the term *peasant* because in the anthropological literature it is freighted with erroneous implications of class homogeneity for all those who till the land.

CHAPTER 8

1. My appreciation to Gil Joseph, who commented on an earlier version of this chapter at a 1998 conference on "Mexican Popular Political Culture, 1800–2000" at the Center for U.S.–Mexican Studies. Thanks (and apologies) also to the reviewers of a very awkward earlier version of this chapter that I mistakenly submitted to a journal or two. I thought my ideas were lucidly presented; they clearly were not. The present version of that earlier essay has benefited from these reviewers' measured comments as well as those of Peter Kingstone, who made valuable suggestions for improving this chapter.

2. One PRI slogan in the 1994 presidential election campaign, "For the Well-Being of Your Family," was targeted to appeal to women in particular (see Bailey 1994, 8).

3. As mentioned in chapter 1, anthropologists have paid surprisingly little attention to elections.

4. On the role of ritual in presidential elections, especially in the campaign of 1988, see Lomnitz, Lomnitz, and Adler (1993). More particularly, on the transitions between "democratic dictators," see Castañeda (2000). More generally, on labyrinthine formal political power in Mexico, see Smith (1979).

5. Some political scientists may have problems with the data and methodology I have employed in parts of this book, and especially in this chapter, which treats a sacred cow of that sororal social science: elections. In part, these types of disagreements inevitably arise in cross-disciplinary discussions. Such disciplinary disputes involve questions of process and outcomes, of course, as emerging trends may not be well captured either in exit polls or strictly quantitative treatments of election results. See Kampwirth (1998) for a discussion of these very issues for elections in Nicaragua and El Salvador.

6. Following Lynn Stephen (1997a), my use of the term *grassroots feminism* emphasizes the integration of class and gender concerns in a manner similar to what is connoted by the Spanish term *feminismo popular*.

7. See Lomnitz (1995) for a brief history of the public sphere in Mexico. In addition to Lomnitz, on the numerous conceptual connections between public/private dichotomies and those pertaining to rural/urban spaces, see García Canclini (1989) and also the novel thesis of González (1987) on *"matriotismo"* in the putative Catholic, conservative, and apathetic hinterland of Mexico.

8. See Royce (1975) on the role of men in social movements and in running for formal political offices in Juchitán, Oaxaca, in the 1960s.

9. See Stephen (1997a, 268–69) on the merging of public and private in practice in Latin America.

10. For an elucidation of this concept, see the 1998 special issue of *Nueva Antropología* edited by Sylvia Gómez-Tagle, entitled "Participación ciudadana y procesos electorales."

11. The phrase "displacement of the democratic formation of political will" comes from Jürgen Habermas (1991, 36), who was commenting on a very different political and historical situation which I believe is nonetheless pertinent to the discussion of democracy and popular political culture in Mexico. Notwithstanding the very different contexts, Habermas's characterization of gov-

ernmental manipulation of electoral campaigns in unified Germany is relevant because of similarities in how state political parties in each country have sought to excite popular participation in elections.

12. See Gledhill's (1995) comments in this regard, and his more general examination of questions of rebellion and change (1997).

13. Like Gabriel, who was quoted talking about *educación* in the preface, by *educación* Fili means much more than formal schooling. Implicit in her comments is the view that *educación* involves questions of social awareness and consciousness as much as it does book learning.

14. Mallon has written of "the explosion of regional and local studies of historical experience, in Africa and Latin America, that multiplied and fragmented supposedly unified national or continental narratives" (1993, 372). She goes on, however, to call for a corrective redefinition of paradigms amid the fragments, and specifically "a recommitment, on redefined terms, to the importance of understanding broader narratives, structures, and power relations." These points are critical to understanding the relationship between regional and national identities, including in the multiple uses of the word *lugareño*. For my friends in Mexico City, the term *lugareño* refers mainly to one's national identity as a Mexican, though sometimes it can take on a narrower meaning. Regardless, it is always a positive, subject-position expression of solidarity of one kind or another. In this, it is different from other meanings of the term in other locales. See, for example, Radcliffe and Westwood (1996, xii, 108), in which *lugareno* carries rather exclusively rural connotations.

15. For interesting discussions of *"autoactividad"* and *"autorganización,"* albeit based on pre-1982 experiences of popular political culture, see both Monsiváis (1981) and Gilly (1981).

16. See Díaz Barriga (1998) for more on the UCP. See also Bruhn (1997) on the relation of the UCP and the PRD and electoral politics in general.

17. *Periódicos murales,* recalling the big-character posters (*dazibao*) of the Cultural Revolution in China.

18. See the discussion on 1968 in chapter 3.

19. On the history of gender and the state more generally in Latin America, see Dore (1996) and Dore and Molyneux (2000).

20. On the ethnographic reality and programmatic utility of the term *autonomy* in Chiapas in the late 1990s, see Collier and Stephen (1997) and Stephen (1997b).

21. Michael Herzfeld (1985, ch. 3) provides a fine-grained portrait of engendered popular political culture and municipal elections in Crete. From the coffeehouse to the ballot urn, elections are shown to be consummately male activities, in terms of male control of voting by household members and with respect to widespread electoral "passivity" on the part of wives, mothers, and daughters.

22. This analysis stands in contrast to the more customary account that women's primary mode of entry into social movements and popular politics in Latin America is through their claims as mothers.

23. Angela had been convinced by a newspaper account that quoted a renegade from the EZLN who said that Bishop Samuel Ruiz of Chiapas had been

hoodwinked by the Zapatistas, although her son Noé tried to convince her that in fact Ruiz was "one of them."

24. For critiques of these paradigms, see, for example, Radcliffe and Westwood (1996) and Stephen (1997a).

25. I use the term *unheralded* in the sense of political and political-economic analysis. Certainly, feminists have drawn attention to women, though even they have focused more on women's influence among women than on men and women in combination, that is, on society.

26. The fact that the dog was on a leash was in itself unusual for Mexico.

27. The notion that "popular [folk] culture" is the source of national culture is not unique to observers of Mexico, of course, as Eduardo Galeano pointed out when he noted that one of the ten most frequent errors or lies about national culture in Latin America as a whole is that "popular culture resides in typical traditions" (1982).

28. For an excellent postmortem on the 1994 presidential election in context, see Centeno (1997, 247–62).

29. See *La Jornada,* 6 June 1994. Such purchases have apparently continued (see *La Jornada,* 15 March 1998). See also Aguayo Quezada (1998) for archival documentation of longstanding U.S. interests (and intervention) in the electoral process in Mexico.

30. I was struck by the attention paid by neighbors in Santo Domingo to Bill Clinton's first State of the Union address in 1993. Friends asked me if I, too, would be watching it on television that night, and the day following the speech, I was asked about particular points Clinton had made. I simply could not imagine anyone other than academics or policy analysts in the United States paying this much attention to the yearly report of a foreign leader. Among other things, I was impressed by the felt need on the part of several neighbors to follow the politics of the United States so closely, with the tacit goal of better gauging their own political futures. In the era of globalization, clearly not everyone is a global citizen in the same sense: popular political culture in Mexico of necessity involves leaders of dominant foreign powers in ways that citizens of the United States are able to ignore.

CHAPTER 9

1. Several of these Mexican presidents then moved on to graduate programs at Harvard and Yale.

2. Most of the basic information on the UNAM strike has been gleaned from the World Wide Web pages of *La Jornada* (http://www.jornada.unam.mx) and *Proceso* (http://www.proceso.com.mx).

3. In trips to Oaxaca and Guadalajara during late summer 1999, I encountered far less interest in and knowledge of the strike, either in the major press or among friends.

4. The term *cuotas* (literally, "quotas") refers to the tuition system initially proposed by the UNAM administration, whereby those students who could pay would be charged tuition.

5. Known popularly as *fósiles*, these students are said to be people who have

spent many years studying at the University, repeating many classes and never completing the equivalent of a bachelor's degree.

6. Incorporated into a famous mural at the University was a list of important dates in the history of Mexico. The last entry in the list was originally a question mark ("?"). In summer 1999, one of the strikers painted in "1999" to replace the "?" Given that the mural was legally considered part of the cultural patrimony of the country, the media emphasized that any defacement of the initial design was a scurrilous attack on the nation. The protest painter was easily identified in a video that had been filmed as he altered the mural.

7. On the student movement in Mexico, see Mabry (1982).

8. The Sindicato Nacional de los Trabajadores de la Educación (SNTE) in the Secretaría de Educación Pública is known as one of the strongest unions in all Latin America. It has enrolled up to 250,000 members at any one time; members are grouped into *secciones* around areas like physical education, high-school education, and technical and administrative education. A dissident group called the Coordinadora Nacional de Trabajadores de la Educación was formed in the late 1990s.

9. Tepoztlán is a small town on the northern outskirts of Mexico City. Marcos has in-laws who live in Tepoztlán, and some years earlier, we had visited these relatives together.

10. The peso was worth approximately ten cents (U.S.) at the time of this interview in summer 1999. A single ticket on the Metro cost one-and-a-half pesos.

CHAPTER 10

1. See Bartra 2000.

2. Most of those participating in a series of Cristero rebellions (1926–29) were campesinos who opposed the anticlericalism of the Mexican government (see Purnell 1997). *Sinarquismo* (in contrast to *anarchismo*) was a social movement led by the Catholic Church that developed in the wake of the defeat of the Cristeros in 1929 (see Zermeño Padilla 1997).

3. In January 1993 the "nuevo peso" was introduced in Mexico. The value of the new peso was the same as that for the old pesos, except for "removing three zeros"—that is, the face value of the new peso was 1/1000th that of the old peso.

4. Among my university colleagues, on the contrary, there was far more widespread excitement. I wondered if some of their elation following the PRI's defeat stemmed from the fact that president-elect Vicente Fox quickly formed numerous commissions and committees around a host of social issues and named numerous prominent intellectuals with a wide range of political views to these posts. To my university friends, if not to many residents of Colonia Santo Domingo, Fox's early appointments seemed to indicate that his regime would be the most politically inclusive in Mexico's post–World War II history.

5. See Herzfeld (1992) for a related discussion of Western democracy's symbolic roots.

6. Paolo Freire, a Brazilian historian, coined the term *conscientização*, which he defined in this way: "The term *conscientização* refers to learning to perceive social, political, and economic contradictions, and to take action against the oppressive elements of reality" (Freire 1968, 19 n.1). In the same sense, the term *educación* can refer to how a child is brought up, similar to the connotation of the English phrase "a child's *formation*."

7. In one bag was a good-sized piece of lava from the volcano Xitle, which they gave me after the event. Xitle is an extinct volcano whose lava flowed more than two thousand years ago over what is now Colonia Santo Domingo and the surrounding Pedregal area. Those flows deposited the 20–30 feet of solid rock upon which the *colonia* of Santo Domingo now sits. The volcanic rock has become a symbol for the area, representing both the difficulties residents faced in establishing their neighborhoods and the actual rock they had to cut through to construct their houses there. The rock Fili and María Elena gave me that night sits proudly today in our front yard in Providence.

8. After the book presentation, Fili did make an arrangement with Daniel Cazés for him to bring books from UNAM to the residents of Santo Domingo.

Glossary

ABSTENCIONISTA Literally, "abstentionist." One who abstains from voting.

CACIQUE Mexicanism referring to neighborhood/village political boss. The term, sometimes translated as "political boss," is often associated with social organization in rural areas; nonetheless, *caciques* are far from unknown among the poor in urban centers. Originally referred to an Aztec village leader.

CAGUAMA Quart of beer.

CAMPESINO Rural worker.

CHILANGO Someone born in Mexico City.

CHRISTIAN BASE COMMUNITIES From Spanish *comunidades eclesiales de base*. A grassroots movement within the Catholic church in Latin America aimed at securing justice through direct efforts of clergy and lay people.

CLASES POPULARES A term employed by certain social analysts beginning in the 1980s to refer to what others used to call the working class.

COLONIA Neighborhood.

COLONIAS POPULARES Poor, working-class neighborhoods.

COOPERACIÓN Literally, "cooperation." Various forms of mutual assistance, for instance, between friends, family, and neighbors.

COYOTE Literally, "coyote." Mexicanism for someone who is paid to guide people across Mexico–U.S. border.

CUATE Mexicanism for (male) friend (originally from Náhuatl for twin).

CUBA (LIBRE) Rum and Coca-Cola drink.

CUOTAS Literally, "quotas." Refers to the tuition system initially proposed by the UNAM administration, whereby those students who could pay would be charged tuition.

DEDAZO The "fingering" of someone. Mexicanism referring to selection process whereby a sitting Mexican president chooses his successor.

DEFEÑO Pertaining to someone or something from "D.F.," the Distrito Federal, i.e., Mexico City.

DESMADRE Literally, "unmother." Mexicanism for something that is a mess, screwed up.

DINOSAURIO Literally, "dinosaur." Mexicanism for old-guard politician of the PRI.

ECOLOGISTA Literally, "ecologist." Used figuratively to denote supporters of the Ecology Party.

EJIDO Plot of land in the communal property system that has been practiced in Mexico since the Revolution.

EZLN Ejército Zapatista de Liberación Nacional.

FAENA Collective work day.

FLOJERA Laziness; popularly said to be trait of men in particular.

FÓSILES Literally, "fossils." Students who have spent many years studying at the University, repeating many classes and never completing their bachelor's degree.

FUTBOL Soccer.

LOS DE ABAJO Literally, "those on the bottom." The title of a famous novel by Manuel Azuela, translated into English as *The Underdogs*.

MALINCHISTA Mexicanism for traitor to nation; more loosely refers to someone who is disloyal. Reference to La Malinche, the indigenous translator and lover of Spanish conquistador Hernán Cortés.

MAQUILADORA Assembly plant whose products are not subject to export/import tariffs.

MARICÓN Queer, faggot; derogatory term whose ultimate referent is a man who has sex with other men, but as in English, a word also utilized in fairly complex ways to denigrate a man in Mexico, too.

MAYATE A man who has sex with other men, or a man who has sex with another man who is homosexual, or an African American; meaning depends largely on context.

MEXICANIDAD (LO MEXICANO) Mexicanness; cultural characteristics held to be typically Mexican.

MIGRA Mexicanism for agents of U.S. Immigration and Naturalization Service and U.S. Border Patrol.

MILITANTE Grassroots political activist.

NAFTA North American Free Trade Agreement (NAFTA; in Spanish, Tratado de Libre Comercio, or TLC). Treaty between Canada, Mexico, and the United States that went into effect January 1, 1994.

OTRO LADO Literally, "the other side." The United States.

PAISANO Someone also from Mexico.

PAN Partido Acción Nacional; right-leaning political party in Mexico.

PANISTA Supporter of the PAN.

PARACAIDISTA Literally, "parachutist." Mexicanism for land squatter, invader.

PARISTA (Student) striker in UNAM strike of 1999–2000.

PLANTÓN Mexicanism for protest occupation (e.g., a sit-in).

PRD Partido de la Revolución Democrática; left-leaning political party in Mexico.

PRDISTA Supporter of the PRD.

PRI Partido Revolucionario Institucional; ruling party in Mexico for most of the twentieth century.

PRIISTA Supporter of the PRI.

PRONASOL Programa Nacional de Solidaridad.

PROVINCIA Literally, "province." Any part of Mexico outside the capital.

PUEBLO Depending on context, village, neighborhood, or people.

PULQUE An inexpensive alcoholic beverage made from the sap of the maguey, or century plant.

RÍO BRAVO Name in Mexico for what people in United States generally refer to as the Rio Grande.

SOLIDARIDAD *See* PRONASOL.

STUNAM Maintenance workers' union at the Universidad Nacional Autónoma de México (UNAM).

TECNÓCRATA Mexicanism for technocratic politician or government administrator.

TIENDA Small sidewalk or corner store.

TLC Tratado de Libre Comercio (TLC; in English, North American Free Trade Agreement, or NAFTA). Treaty between Canada, Mexico, and the United States that went into effect January 1, 1994.

UNAM Universidad Nacional Autónoma de México (Mexican National Autonomous University).

VECINDAD Typically a block of one-room apartments with communal water spigots and baths.

ZAPATISTAS Members (and more loosely, supporters) of the EZLN.

Bibliography

Abélès, Marc

    1988 "Modern Political Ritual: Ethnography of an Inauguration and a Pilgrimage by President Mitterrand." *Current Anthropology* 29(3): 391–99.

    1991 *Quiet Days in Burgundy: A Study of Local Politics*. Translated by Annella McDermott. Cambridge: Cambridge University Press.

    1997 "Political Anthropology: New Challenges, New Aims." *International Social Science Journal* 49(3): 319–32.

Abu-Lughod, Lila

    1990 "The Romance of Resistance: Tracing Transformations of Power through Bedouin Women." *American Ethnologist* 17(1): 41–55.

Aguayo Quezada, Sergio

    1998 *1968: Archivos de la violencia*. Mexico City: Grijalbo/Reforma.

Aguilar Camín, Héctor, ed.

    [1976] 1989 *En torno a la cultura nacional*. Reprint, Mexico City: Consejo Nacional para la Cultura y las Artes/Instituto Nacional Indigenista.

Aguirre Beltrán, Gonzalo

    1986 *Antropología médica*. Mexico City: Centro de Investigaciones y Estudios Superiores en Antropología Social.

Alatorre, Javier, and Rafael Luna

    2000 "Significados y prácticas de la paternidad en la ciudad de México." In *Paternidades en América Latina*, edited by Norma Fuller, 241–75. Lima: Pontificia Universidad Católica del Perú.

Alvarez, Sonia E.

    1998 "Latin American Feminisms 'Go Global': Trends of the 1990s and Challenges for the New Millennium." In *Cultures of Politics/Politics of*

Cultures: Revisioning Latin American Social Movements, edited by Sonia E. Alvarez, Evelina Dagnino, and Arturo Escobar, 293–324. Boulder, Colo.: Westview.

Alvarez, Sonia E., Evelina Dagnino, and Arturo Escobar, eds.
1998 *Cultures of Politics/Politics of Cultures: Revisioning Latin American Social Movements.* Boulder, Colo.: Westview.

Amin, Samir
1993 "The Issue of Democracy in the Contemporary Third World." In *Low Intensity Democracy: Political Power in the New World Order,* edited by Barry Gills, Joel Rocamora, and Richard Wilson, 59–79. London: Pluto Press.

Amnesty International
1998 *United States of America: Human Rights Concerns in the Border Region with Mexico.* Translated by Amy Jacobs. New York: Amnesty International.

Andreas, Peter
1999 "Borderless Economy, Barricaded Border." *NACLA Report on the Americas* 33(3): 14–21.

Arizpe, Lourdes
1973 *Parentesco y economía en una sociedad nahua.* Mexico City: Instituto Nacional Indigenista/Secretaría de Educación Pública.

1989 *Cultura y desarrollo: Una etnografía de las creencias de una comunidad mexicana.* Mexico City: Universidad Nacional Autónoma de México/El Colegio de México/Porrúa.

1996 "Chiapas: The Basic Problems." *Identities* 3(1/2): 219–33.

Augé, Marc
1999 *An Anthropology for Contemporaneous Worlds.* Translated by Amy Jacobs. Stanford, Calif.: Stanford University Press.

Azuela, Manuel
1938 *Los de abajo: Novela de la revolución mexicana.* Mexico City: Pedro Robredo.

1939 *Los fracasados.* Mexico City: Ediciones Botas.

Bailey, John
1994 *The 1994 Mexican Presidential Election: Post-Election Report.* Washington, D.C.: Center for Strategic and International Studies.

Barbieri, Teresita de
1992 "Sobre la categoría género: Una introducción teórico-metodológica." In *Fin de siglo: Género y cambio civilizatorio* 17, 111-28. Santiago de Chile: Ediciones de las Mujeres, ISIS Internacional.

Barkin, David
1991 *Un desarrollo distorsionado: La integración de México a la economía mundial.* Mexico City: Siglo Veintiuno.

Barrett, Michèle, and Mary McIntosh
1982 *The Anti-Social Family.* London: Verso.

Bartra, Roger
1981 *Las redes imaginarias del poder político.* Mexico City: Era.

1987 *La jaula de la melancolía: Identidad y metamorfosis del mexicano.* Mexico City: Grijalbo.

1989 "Culture and Political Power in Mexico." *Latin American Perspectives* 16(2): 61–69.

1992 *The Cage of Melancholy: Identity and Metamorphosis in the Mexican Character.* Translated by Christopher J. Hall. New Brunswick, N.J.: Rutgers University Press.

1993 *Oficio mexicano.* Mexico City: Grijalbo.

1995 "South of the Border: Mexican Reflections on Distorted Images." *Telos* 103: 143–48.

1999 *La sangre y la tinta: Ensayos sobre la condición postmexicana.* Mexico City: Oceano.

2000 *La democracia ausente.* 2d ed. Mexico City: Grijalbo.

Beck, Allen J.
2000 "Prison and Jail Inmates at Midyear 1999." *U.S. Bureau of Justice Statistics Bulletin,* http://www.ojp.usdoj.gov/bjs/pub/pdf/pjim99.pdf.

Benería, Lourdes
1992 "The Mexican Debt Crisis: Restructuring the Economy and the Household." In *Unequal Burden: Economic Crises, Persistent Poverty, and Women's Work,* edited by Lourdes Benería and Shelley Feldman, 83–104. Boulder, Colo.: Westview.

Bennett, Vivienne
1992 "The Evolution of Urban Popular Movements in Mexico Between 1968 and 1988." In *The Making of Social Movements in Latin America: Identity, Strategy, and Democracy,* edited by Arturo Escobar and Sonia E. Alvarez, 240–59. Boulder, Colo.: Westview.

1998 "Everyday Struggles: Women in Urban Popular Movements and Territorially Based Protests in Mexico." In *Women's Participation in Mexican Political Life,* edited by Victoria E. Rodríguez, 116–30. Boulder, Colo.: Westview.

Besserer, Federico
2000 "Sentimientos (in)apropriados de las mujeres migrantes: Hacia una nueva ciudadanía." In *Migración y relaciones de género en México,* edited by Dalia Barrera Bassols and Cristina Oehmichen Bazán, 371–88. Mexico City: Gimtrap/IIA/UNAM.

Bilello, Suzanne
   1997 "Massacre of Tlatelolco." In *Encyclopedia of Mexico: History, Society, Culture,* edited by Michael S. Werner, 782–85. Chicago, Ill.: Fitzroy Dearborn.

Bliss, Katherine
   1999 "Paternity Tests: Fatherhood on Trial in Mexico's Revolution of the Family." *Journal of Family History* 24(3): 330–50.

Bonfil Batalla, Guillermo
   1987 *México profundo: Una civilización negada.* Mexico City: Grijalbo.

   1988 "Los conceptos de diferencia y subordinación en el estudio de las culturas populares." In *Teoría e investigación en la antropología social mexicana,* 97–108. Mexico City: Cuadernos de la Casa Chata, Centro de Investigaciones y Estudios Superiores en Antropología Social/Universidad Autónoma Metropolitana–Iztapalapa.

   1992 "Dimensiones culturales del Tratado de Libre Comercio." In *La educación y la cultura ante el Tratado de Libre Comercio,* edited by Gilberto Guevara Niebla and Néstor García Canclini, 157–78. Mexico City: Nexos/Nueva Imagen.

Brandes, Stanley
   1988 *Power and Persuasion: Fiestas and Social Control in Rural Mexico.* Philadelphia: University of Pennsylvania Press.

Brook, Peter
   1998 *Threads of Time: Recollections.* Washington, D.C.: Counterpoint.

Brown, Wendy
   1995 *States of Injury: Power and Freedom in Late Modernity.* Princeton, N.J.: Princeton University Press.

   1998 "Democracy's Lack." *Public Culture* 10(2): 425–29.

Bruhn, Kathleen
   1997 "The Seven-Month Itch? Neoliberal Politics, Popular Movements, and the Left in Mexico." In *The New Politics of Inequality in Latin America: Rethinking Participation and Representation,* edited by Douglas A. Chalmers et al., 144–69. Oxford: Oxford University Press.

Brusco, Elizabeth
   1995 *The Reformation of Machismo: Evangelical Conversion and Gender in Colombia.* Austin: University of Texas Press.

California Chamber of Commerce and California Trade and Commerce Agency
   1993 *North American Free Trade Guide: The Emerging Mexican Market and Opportunities in Canada under NAFTA: Creating Jobs Through Trade.* La Jolla: Center for U.S.–Mexico Studies, University of California at San Diego.

Capellán, Angel
1985 *Hemingway and the Hispanic World.* Ann Arbor, Mich.: UMI Research Press.

Carrier, James
1995 *De los otros: Intimacy and Homosexuality among Mexican Men.* New York: Columbia University Press.

Castañeda, Jorge G.
1993 *Utopia Unarmed: The Latin American Left after the Cold War.* New York: Vintage.

1995 *The Mexican Shock: Its Meaning for the U.S.* New York: The New Press.

2000 *Perpetuating Power: How Mexican Presidents Were Chosen.* New York: The New Press.

Castellanos, Rosario
1965 "Cultura y violencia." *Excelsior,* 20 February, pp. 6A, 8A.

Cazés, Daniel
1993 *Memorial del 68: Relato a muchas voces.* Mexico City: La Jornada Ediciones.

Centeno, Miguel
1997 *Democracy within Reason: Technocratic Revolution in Mexico.* 2d ed. University Park: Pennsylvania State University Press.

Chant, Sylvia
1991 *Women and Survival in Mexican Cities: Perspectives on Gender, Labour Markets and Low-Income Households.* Manchester, U.K.: Manchester University Press.

1997 *Women-Headed Households: Diversity and Dynamics in the Developing World.* Houndmills, Basingstoke, U.K.: Macmillan.

1999 "Las unidades domésticas encabezadas por mujeres en México y Costa Rica: Perspectivas populares y globales sobre las madres sin pareja." In *Divergencias del modelo tradicional: Hogares de jefatura femenina en América Latina,* edited by Mercedes González de la Rocha, 97–124. Mexico City: Centro de Investigaciones y Estudios Superiores en Antropología Social/Plaza y Valdés.

Chodorow, Nancy J.
1999 *The Power of Feelings.* New Haven, Conn.: Yale University Press.

(El) Colegio de México
1996 *Diccionario del español usual en México.* Mexico City: El Colegio de México.

Collier, George A., with Elizabeth L. Quaratiello
1994 *Basta! Land and the Zapatista Rebellion in Chiapas.* Oakland, Calif.: Food First.

Collier, George A., and Lynn Stephen, eds.
   1997 Special edition entitled "Ethnicity, Identity and Citizenship in the Wake
      of the Zapatista Rebellion." *Journal of Latin American Anthropology*
      3(1).

Collier, Ruth B.
   1999 *Paths toward Democracy: The Working Class and Elites in Western Eu-*
      rope and South America. Cambridge: Cambridge University Press.

Colombres, Adolfo, ed.
   1982 *La cultura popular.* Tlahuapan, Puebla, Mexico: Premia.

Comaroff, Jean, and John Comaroff
   1999 "Occult Economies and the Violence of Abstraction: Notes from the
      South African Postcolony." *American Ethnologist* 26(2): 279–303.

Cook, Maria Lorena
   1997 "Regional Integration and Transnational Politics: Popular Sector
      Strategies in the NAFTA Era." In *The New Politics of Inequality in Latin*
      America: Rethinking Participation and Representation, edited by Douglas
      A. Chalmers et al., 516–40. Oxford: Oxford University Press.

Cornelius, Wayne A.
   1975 *Politics and the Migrant Poor in Mexico City.* Stanford, Calif.: Stanford
      University Press.

Cornelius, Wayne A., Ann L. Craig, and Jonathan Fox
   1994 "Mexico's National Solidarity Program: An Overview." In *Transform-*
      ing State-Society Relations in Mexico: The National Solidarity Strategy,
      edited by Wayne A. Cornelius, Ann L. Craig, and Jonathan Fox, 3–26. La
      Jolla: Center for U.S.–Mexico Studies, University of California at San
      Diego.

Coronado Malagón, Marcela
   2000 "Los apodos de la resistencia: Estereotipos gentilicios zapotecas en el
      Istmo de Tehuantepec: Procesos de identidad, movimiento social y pro-
      ducción discursiva." *Alteridades* 19: 79–88.

Coronil, Fernando
   1997 *The Magical State: Nature, Money, and Modernity in Venezuela.* Chi-
      cago, Ill.: University of Chicago Press.

   1998 Foreword to *Close Encounters of Empire: Writing the Cultural History*
      of U.S.-Latin American Relations, edited by Gilbert M. Joseph, Catherine
      C. LeGrand, and Ricardo D. Salvatore, ix–xii. Durham, N.C.: Duke Uni-
      versity Press.

Craske, Nikki
   1993 "Women's Political Participation in *Colonias Populares* in Guadalajara,
      Mexico." In *'Viva': Women and Popular Protest in Latin America,* edited
      by Sarah A. Radcliffe and Sallie Westwood, 112–35. London: Routledge.

1998 "Mexican Women's Inclusion into Political Life: A Latin American Perspective." In *Women's Participation in Mexican Political Life,* edited by Victoria E. Rodríguez, 41–62. Boulder, Colo.: Westview.

1999 *Women and Politics in Latin America.* New Brunswick, N.J.: Rutgers University Press.

Crossette, Barbara
2000 "When Democracy Runs Off the Rails." "Week in Review," *New York Times,* 4 June, p. 1.

Davis, Charles L.
1998 "Mass Support for Regional Economic Integration: The Case of NAFTA and the Mexican Public." *Mexican Studies/Estudios Mexicanos* 14(1): 105–30.

Davis, Mike
1992 *City of Quartz: Excavating the Future in Los Angeles.* New York: Vintage.

1999 "Territorio y ciudadanía étnica en la nación globalizada." *Desacatos* 1: 13–27.

Dennis, Philip A.
1979 "The Role of the Drunk in a Oaxacan Village." In *Beliefs, Behaviors, and Alcoholic Beverages: A Cross-Cultural Survey,* edited by Mac Marshall, 54–64. Ann Arbor: University of Michigan Press.

Díaz Barriga, Miguel
1994 "El relajo de la cultura de la pobreza." *Alteridades* 4: 21–26.

1998 "Beyond the Domestic and the Public: *Colonas* Participation in Urban Movements in Mexico City." In *Cultures of Politics, Politics of Cultures: Re-Visioning Latin American Social Movements,* edited by Sonia E. Alvarez, Evelina Dagnino, and Arturo Escobar, 252–77. Boulder, Colo.: Westview.

Dietz, Mary
1992 "Context Is All: Feminism and Theories of Citizenship." In *Dimensions of Radical Democracy,* edited by Chantal Mouffe. London: Verso.

Di Leonardo, Micaela
1998 *Exotics at Home: Anthropologies, Others, American Modernity.* Chicago: University of Chicago Press.

Dillon, Sam
1996 "Free Trade? Don't Sell Us That." *New York Times,* 4 August, p. E-6.

Dore, Elizabeth, ed.
1996 *Gender Politics in Latin America: Debates in Theory and Practice.* New York: Monthly Review Press.

Dore, Elizabeth, and Maxine Molyneux, eds.
2000 *The Hidden History of Gender and the State in Latin America.* Durham, N.C.: Duke University Press.

Dresser, Denise
1994 "Bringing the Poor Back In: National Solidarity as a Strategy of Regime Legitimation." In *Transforming State-Society Relations in Mexico: The National Solidarity Strategy,* edited by Wayne A. Cornelius, Ann L. Craig, and Jonathan Fox, 143–65. La Jolla: Center for U.S.–Mexico Studies, University of California at San Diego.

Du Bois, W. E. B.
[1903] 1995 *The Souls of Black Folk.* Reprint, New York: Signet.

Dunn, Timothy J.
1996 *The Militarization of the U.S.–Mexico Border, 1978–1992: Low Intensity Conflict Doctrine Comes Home.* Austin: University of Texas Press.

Eckstein, Susan
1989a "Power and Popular Protest in Latin America." In *Power and Popular Protest: Latin American Social Movements,* edited by Susan Eckstein, 1–60. Berkeley: University of California Press.

Eckstein, Susan, ed.
1989b *Power and Popular Protest: Latin American Social Movements.* Berkeley: University of California Press.

Edmonds, Mira
2000 "Venceremos! The 1968 Mexican Student Movement: A Domestic Crisis in International Context." Senior Honor's Thesis, History Department, Brown University.

Eschbach, Karl, Jacqueline Hagan, and Nestor Rodriguez
2001 "Causes and Trends in Migrant Deaths along the U.S.–Mexico Border, 1985–1998." Center for Immigration Research, University of Houston, Houston, Texas. http://www.uh.Edu/cir/death/htm

Escobar, Arturo
1995 *Encountering Development: The Making and Unmaking of the Third World.* Princeton, N.J.: Princeton University Press.

Escobar, Arturo, and Sonia E. Alvarez, eds.
1992 *The Making of Social Movements in Latin America: Identity, Strategy, and Democracy.* Boulder, Colo.: Westview.

EZLN (Ejército Zapatista de Liberación Nacional)
1994 *EZLN documentos y comunicados.* Mexico City: Era.

Fanon, Frantz
1963 *The Wretched of the Earth.* Translated by Constance Farrington. New York: Grove.

1967 *Black Skin, White Masks.* Translated by Charles Lam Markmann. New York: Grove.

Fernández Poncela, Anna. M.
1996 "The Political Participation of Women in Mexico Today." In *The Changing Structure of Mexico: Political, Social, and Economic Prospects,* edited by Laura Randall, 307–14. Armonk, N.Y.: M. E. Sharpe.

Figueroa Perea, Juan Guillermo
1998 "La presencia de los varones en los procesos reproductivos: Algunas reflexiones." In *Varones, sexualidad y reproducción: Diversas perspectivas teórico-metodológicas y hallazgos de investigación,* edited by Susana Lerner, 163–89. Mexico City: El Colegio de México.

Foster, George
1967 *Tzintzuntzan: Mexican Peasants in a Changing World.* Boston, Mass.: Little, Brown.

Foweraker, Joe, and Ann Craig, eds.
1990 *Popular Movements and Political Change in Mexico.* Boulder, Colo.: Lynne Rienner.

Fox, Jonathan
1997 "The Difficult Transition from Clientelism to Citizenship: Lessons from Mexico." In *The New Politics of Inequality in Latin America: Rethinking Participation and Representation,* edited by Douglas A. Chalmers et al., 391–420. Oxford: Oxford University Press.

Franco, Jean
1992 "Going Public: Reinhabiting the Private." In *On Edge: The Crisis in Contemporary Latin American Culture,* edited by George Yúdice, Jean Franco, and Juan Flores, 65–83. Minneapolis: University of Minnesota Press.

Frank, Andre G.
1993 "Marketing Democracy in an Undemocratic Market." In *Low Intensity Democracy: Political Power in the New World Order,* edited by Barry Gills, Joel Rocamora, and Richard Wilson, 35–58. London: Pluto Press.

Fraser, Nancy
1989 *Unruly Practices: Power, Discourse, and Gender in Contemporary Social Theory.* Minneapolis: University of Minnesota Press.

1997 *Justice Interruptus: Critical Reflections on the "Postsocialist" Condition.* New York: Routledge.

Freire, Paulo
1968 *Pedagogy of the Oppressed.* Translated by Myra Bergman Ramos. New York: Seabury Press.

Fried, Morton
1967 *The Evolution of Political Society: An Essay in Political Anthropology.* New York: Random House.

Fuentes, Carlos
1996 *A New Time for Mexico.* Berkeley: University of California Press.

Fuentes, Dagoberto, and José A. López.
    1974 *Barrio Language Dictionary: First Dictionary of Caló.* La Puente,
    Calif.: Sunburst Enterprises.

Fuller, Norma
    1998 "Reflexiones sobre el machismo en América Latina." In *Masculini-
    dades y equidad de género en América Latina,* edited by Teresa Valdés and
    José Olavarría, 258–66. Santiago: FLACSO.

Fuson, Robert H.
    1961 "The Origin of the Word *Gringo.*" In *Singers and Storytellers,* edited
    by Mody C. Boatright, Wilson M. Hudson, and Allen Maxwell, 282–84.
    Dallas, Texas: Southern Methodist University Press.

Galeano, Eduardo
    1982 "Literatura y cultura popular en América Latina: Diez errores o men-
    tiras frecuentes." In *La cultura popular,* edited by Adolfo Colombres, 93–
    109. Tlahuapan, Puebla: Premia.

Gamio, Manuel
    [1916] 1982 "El metalismo yanqui y el mexicano". In *Forjando patria,* 3d
    ed. Mexico City: Porrúa.

García, Brígida, and Orlandina de Oliveira
    1994 *Trabajo feminino y vida familiar en México.* Mexico City: El Colegio
    de México.

García Canclini, Néstor
    1982 *Las culturas populares en el capitalismo.* Mexico City: Nueva Imagen.

    1988 "La crisis teórica en la investigación sobre cultura popular." In *Teoría
    e investigación en la antropología social mexicana,* 67–96. Mexico City:
    Cuadernos de la Casa Chata, Centro de Investigaciones y Estudios Supe-
    riores en Antropología Social/Universidad Autónoma Metropolitana–
    Iztapalapa.

    1989 *Culturas híbridas: Estrategias para entrar y salir de la modernidad.*
    Mexico City: Grijalbo.

    1992 "Prehistoria económica y cultural del Tratado de Libre Comercio." In
    La educación y la cultura ante el Tratado de Libre Comercio, edited by
    Gilberto Guevara Niebla and Néstor García Canclini, 3–14. Mexico
    City: Nexos/Nueva Imagen.

    1995 *Consumidores y ciudadanos: Conflictos multiculturales de la globali-
    zación.* Mexico City: Grijalbo.

    1999 *La globalización imaginada.* Mexico City: Paidós.

Gills, Barry, Joel Rocamora, and Richard Wilson
    1993 "Low Intensity Democracy." In *Low Intensity Democracy: Political
    Power in the New World Order,* edited by Barry Gills, Joel Rocamora, and
    Richard Wilson, 3–34. London: Pluto Press.

Gilly, Adolfo

1981 "La acre resistencia a la opresión: Cultura nacional, identidad de clase y cultura popular." *Cuadernos Políticos* 30: 45–52.

Gilmore, David D.

1990 *Manhood in the Making: Cultural Concepts of Masculinity.* New Haven, Conn.: Yale University Press.

Gledhill, John

1995 *Neoliberalism, Transnationalization, and Rural Poverty: A Case Study of Michoacán, Mexico.* Boulder, Colo.: Westview.

1997 "Liberalism, Socio-economic Rights, and the Politics of Identity: From Moral Economy to Indigenous Rights." In *Human Rights, Culture and Context: Anthropological Perspectives,* edited by Richard A. Wilson, 70–110. London: Pluto Press.

2000 *Power and Its Disguises: Anthropological Perspectives on Politics.* 2d ed. London: Pluto.

Gluckman, Max

1960 "Rituals of Rebellion in South-East Africa." In *Order and Rebellion in Tribal Africa: Collected Essays with an Autobiographical Introduction.* Glencoe, Ill: Free Press.

Gómez-Tagle, Sylvia

1986 "Democracia y poder en México: El significado de los fraudes electorales en 1979, 1982 y 1985." *Nueva Antropología* 9(3): 127–57.

Gómez-Tagle, Sylvia, ed.

1998 Special edition entitled "Participación ciudadana y procesos electorales." *Nueva Antropología* 54.

Gómez de Silva, Guido

1988 *Breve diccionario etimológico de la lengua española.* Mexico City: El Colegio de México/Fondo de Cultura Económica.

González, Luis

1987 "Suave matria: Patriotismo y matriotismo." *Nexos* 108: 51–59.

González Casanova, Pablo

[1965] 1970 *Democracy in Mexico.* Translated by Danielle Salti. Oxford: Oxford University Press.

González Montes, Soledad, and Julia Tuñón, eds.

1997 *Familias y mujeres en México.* Mexico City: El Colegio de México.

González de la Rocha, Mercedes

1991 "Family Well-Being, Food Consumption, and Survival Strategies during Mexico's Economic Crisis." In *Social Responses to Mexico's Economic Crisis of the 1980s,* edited by Mercedes González de la Rocha and Agustín Escobar Latapí, 115–27. La Jolla: Center for U.S.–Mexican Studies, University of California at San Diego.

1994 *The Resources of Poverty: Women and Survival in a Mexican City.* Oxford: Blackwell.

1999a "Hogares de jefatura femenina en México: Patrones y formas de vida." In *Divergencias del modelo tradicional: Hogares de jefatura femenina en América Latina,* edited by Mercedes González de la Rocha, 125–53. Mexico City: Centro de Investigaciones y Estudios Superiores en Antropología Social/Plaza y Valdés.

González de la Rocha, Mercedes, ed.
1999b *Divergencias del modelo tradicional: Hogares de jefatura femenina en América Latina.* Mexico City: Centro de Investigaciones y Estudios Superiores en Antropología Social/Plaza y Valdés.

Gordon, Lewis R.
1997 *Her Majesty's Other Children: Sketches of Racism from a Neocolonial Age.* Lantham, Md.: Rowman and Littlefield.

Gramsci, Antonio
[1929–35] 1971 *Selections from the Prison Notebooks of Antonio Gramsci.* Edited and translated by Quintin Hoare and Geoffrey Nowell Smith. New York: International.

Greenberg, James B.
1989 *Blood Ties: Life and Violence in Rural Mexico.* Tucson: University of Arizona Press.

Greene, Graham
[1940] 1962 *The Power and the Glory.* Reprint, New York: Viking.

Gupta, Akhil
1998 *Postcolonial Developments: Agriculture in the Making of Modern India.* Durham, N.C.: Duke University Press.

Gutmann, Matthew C.
1993 "Rituals of Resistance: A Critique of the Theory of Everyday Forms of Resistance." *Latin American Perspectives* 20(2): 74–92.

1994 "Los hijos de Lewis: La sensibilidad antropológica y el caso de los pobres machos." *Alteridades* 4(7): 9–19.

1996 *The Meanings of Macho: Being a Man in Mexico City.* Berkeley: University of California Press.

1997 "The Ethnographic (G)Ambit: Women and the Negotiation of Masculinity in Mexico City." *American Ethnologist* 24(4): 833–55.

1998 "*Mamitis* and the Traumas of Development in a *Colonia Popular* of Mexico City." In *Small Wars: The Cultural Politics of Childhood,* edited by Nancy Scheper-Hughes and Carolyn Sargent, 130–48. Berkeley: University of California Press.

1999 "Ethnicity, Alcohol, and Acculturation." *Social Science and Medicine* 48(2): 173–84.

2000 *Ser hombre de verdad en la ciudad de México: Ni macho ni mandilón.* Mexico City: El Colegio de México.

In press "Dystopian Travels in Gringolandia: Engendering Ethnicity among Mexican Migrants to the United States." *Ethnic and Racial Studies.*

Haber, Paul L.
1997 "Neoliberalism." In *Encyclopedia of Mexico: History, Society, Culture,* edited by Michael S. Werner, 1014–19. Chicago: Fitzroy Dearborn.

Habermas, Jürgen
1991 "What Does Socialism Mean Today? The Revolutions of Recuperation and the Need for New Thinking." In *After the Fall: The Failure of Communism and the Future of Socialism,* edited by Robin Blackburn, 25–46. London: Verso.

1998 "The European Nation-State: On the Past and Future of Sovereignty and Citizenship." *Public Culture* 10(2): 397–416.

Hale, Charles R.
1998 "Cultural Politics of Identity in Latin America." *Annual Review of Anthropology* 26: 567–90.

Halvorson, James, and Chris L. Moser
1965 *Mesoamerican Notes* (Mexico City), vol. 6.

Hannerz, Ulf
1969 *Soulside: Inquiries into Ghetto Culture and Community.* New York: Columbia University Press.

Hansen, Karen V., and Anita I. Garey, eds.
1998 *Families in the U.S.: Kinship and Domestic Politics.* Philadelphia: Temple University Press.

Harrington, Michael
1962 *The Other America: Poverty in the United States.* New York: Macmillan.

Harvey, David, and Michael H. Reed
1996 "The Culture of Poverty: An Ideological Analysis." *Sociological Perspectives* 39(4): 465–95.

Harvey, Neil
1998 *The Chiapas Rebellion: The Struggle for Land and Democracy.* Durham, N.C.: Duke University Press.

Held, David
1995 *Democracy and the Global Order: From the Modern State to Cosmopolitan Governance.* Stanford, Calif.: Stanford University Press.

Hellman, Judith Adler
1992 "The Study of New Social Movements in Latin America and the Question of Autonomy." In *The Making of Social Movements in Latin Amer-*

ica: Identity, Strategy, and Democracy, edited by Arturo Escobar and Sonia E. Alvarez, 52–61. Boulder, Colo.: Westview.

1993 "Mexican Perceptions of Free Trade: Support and Opposition to
NAFTA." In *The Political Economy of North American Free Trade,* ed-
ited by Ricardo Grinspun and Maxwell A. Cameron, 193–204. New
York: St. Martin's.

1994a "Mexican Popular Movements, Clientelism, and the Process of Democratization." *Latin American Perspectives* 21(2): 124–42.

1994b *Mexican Lives.* New York: New Press.

2000 "Opting for Fox." *NACLA Report on the Americas* 34(2): 6–10.

Hernández Castillo, Rosalva Aida
1998a "Between Hope and Adversity: The Struggle of Organized Women in
Chiapas since the Zapatista Rebellion." *Journal of Latin American Anthropology* 3(1):102–20.

Hernández Castillo, Rosalva Aida, ed.
1998b *La otra palabra: Mujeres y violencia en Chiapas, antes y después de
Acteal.* Mexico City: Centro de Investigaciones y Estudios Superiores en
Antropología Social.

Herzfeld, Michael
1985 *The Poetics of Manhood: Contest and Identity in a Cretan Mountain
Village.* Princeton, N.J.: Princeton University Press.

1992 *The Social Production of Indifference: Exploring the Symbolic Roots
of Western Bureaucracy.* Chicago: University of Chicago Press.

1997 *Cultural Intimacy: Social Poetics in the Nation State.* New York:
Routledge.

Heyman, Josiah McC.
1995 "Putting Power in the Anthropology of Bureaucracy: The Immigration
and Naturalization Service at the Mexico–United States Border." *Current
Anthropology* 36(2): 261–87.

2001 "Class and Classification at the U.S.-Mexico Border." *Human Organization* 60(2): 128–40.

Higgins, Michael J.
1974 "Somos Gente Humilde: An Ethnography of a Poor Urban Colonia." Ph.D. diss., Department of Anthropology, University of Illinois at
Champaign-Urbana.

Higgins, Michael, and Tanya Coen
2000 *Streets, Bedrooms, and Patios: The Ordinariness of Diversity in Urban
Oaxaca: Ethnographic Portraits of Street Kids, Urban Poor, Transvestites,
Discapacitados, and Other Popular Cultures.* Austin: University of Texas
Press.

Hodges, Donald C.
　1986 *Intellectual Foundations of the Nicaraguan Revolution*. Austin: University of Texas Press.

Huspek, Michael, Roberto Martinez, and Leticia Jimenez
　1998 "Violations of Human and Civil Rights on the U.S.–Mexican Border, 1995–1997: A Report." *Social Justice* 25(2): 110–21.

Jameson, Fredric
　1998 "Notes on Globalization as a Philosophical Issue." In *The Cultures of Globalization*, edited by Fredric Jameson and Masao Miyoshi, 54–77. Durham, N.C.: Duke University Press.

Jaquette, Jane S.
　1998 "Conclusion: *Haciendo Política*—The Mexican Case in Perspective." In *Women's Participation in Mexican Political Life*, edited by Victoria E Rodríguez, 219–27. Boulder, Colo.: Westview.

Jelin, Elizabeth
　1990 "Citizenship and Identity: Final Reflections." In *Women and Social Change in Latin America*, edited by Elizabeth Jelin, 184–207. London: Zed Books.

Jiménez, Armando
　1976 *Vocabulario prohibido de la picardía mexicana*. Mexico City: Editorial Posada.

Joseph, Gilbert M.
　1998 "Close Encounters: Toward a New Cultural History of U.S.–Latin American Relations." In *Close Encounters of Empire: Writing the Cultural History of U.S.–Latin American Relations*, edited by Gilbert M. Joseph, Catherine C. LeGrand, and Ricardo D. Salvatore, 3–46. Durham, N.C.: Duke University Press.

Kampwirth, Karen
　1998 "Feminism, Antifeminism, and Electoral Poltics in Postwar Nicaragua and El Salvador." *Political Science Quarterly* 113(2): 259–79.

Kaplan, Temma
　1982 "Female Consciousness and Collective Action: The Case of Barcelona, 1910–1918." *Signs* 7(3): 545–60.

Kapur, Vatsala
　1998 "Women's Contribution to the Democratization of Mexican Politics: An Exploration of their Formal Participation in the National Action Party and the Party of the Democratic Revolution." *Mexican Studies/Estudios Mexicanos* 14(2): 363–88.

Kearney, Michael
　1995 "The Local and the Global: The Anthropology of Globalization and Transnationalism." *Annual Review of Anthropology* 24: 547–65.

1996 *Reconceptualizing the Peasantry: Anthropology in Global Perspective.*
Boulder, Colo.: Westview.

Kertzer, David I.
1988 *Ritual, Politics, and Power.* New Haven, Conn.: Yale University Press.

Knight, Alan
1990 "Historical Continuities in Social Movements." In *Popular Movements and Political Change in Mexico,* edited by Joe Foweraker and Ann L. Craig, 78–102. Boulder, Colo.: Lynne Rienner.

1997 "Latin America." In *Companion to Historiography,* edited by Michael Bentley, 728–58. London: Routledge.

Krotz, Esteban
1990 "Antropología, elecciones y cultura política." *Nueva Antropología* 11(38): 9–19.

Kushner, Tony
1997 *Tony Kushner in Conversation,* edited by Robert Vorlicky. Ann Arbor: University of Michigan Press.

Lafaye, Jacques
1976 *Quetzalcóatl and Guadalupe: The Formation of Mexican National Consciousness, 1531–1813.* Translated by Benjamin Keen. Chicago: University of Chicago Press.

Lancaster, Roger N.
1988 *Thanks to God and the Revolution.* New York: Columbia University Press.

1992 *Life Is Hard: Machismo, Danger, and the Intimacy of Power in Nicaragua.* Berkeley: University of California Press.

1999 "Rigoberta's Testimonio." *NACLA Report on the Americas* 32(6): 4–7.

Leacock, Eleanor B., ed.
1971 Introduction to *The Culture of Poverty: A Critique,* edited by Eleanor B. Leacock, 9–37. New York: Simon and Schuster.

1972 Introduction to *The Origin of the Family, Private Property, and the State,* by Friedrich Engels, 7–67. New York: International.

Leon, Magdalena, ed.
1994 *Mujeres y participación política: Avances y desafíos en América Latina.* Bogotá: Tercer Mundo Editores.

Lerner, Susana, ed.
1998 *Varones, sexualidad y reproducción: Diversas perspectivas teórico-metodológicas y hallazgos de investigación.* Mexico City: El Colegio de México.

Lewis, Oscar

1949 "Husbands and Wives in a Mexican Village: A Study of Role Conflict."
    American Anthropologist 51: 602–10.

[1951] 1963 *Life in a Mexican Village: Tepoztlán Restudied.* Reprint, Ur-
    bana: University of Illinois Press.

1959 *Five Families: Mexican Case Studies in the Culture of Poverty.* New
    York: Basic Books.

1960 *Tepotzlán: Village in Mexico.* New York: Holt, Rinehart and Winston.

1961 *The Children of Sánchez: Autobiography of a Mexican Family.* New
    York: Viking.

1964a *Los hijos de Sánchez.* Mexico City: Joaquín Mortiz.

1964b *Pedro Martínez: A Mexican Peasant and His Family.* New York:
    Vintage.

1965 *La Vida: A Puerto Rican Family in the Culture of Poverty—San Juan
    and New York.* New York: Vintage.

1966 "A Thursday with Manuel." *New Left Review* 38: 3–21.

1967 "The Children of Sánchez, Pedro Martínez, and La Vida" and "Reply."
    Current Anthropology 8(5): 480–500.

1969 "A Puerto Rican Boy." In *Culture Change, Mental Health, and Poverty,*
    edited by Joseph C. Finney, 149–54. Lexington: University of Kentucky
    Press.

Leyva Solano, Xóchitl

2001 "Regional, Communal, and Organizational Transformations in Las
    Cañadas." *Latin American Perspectives* 28(2): 20–44.

Lima, Francisca

1992 *Familia popular, sus prácticas y la conformación de una cultura.* Mex-
    ico City: Instituto Nacional de Antropología e Historia.

Limón, José

1998 *American Encounters: Greater Mexico, the United States, and the
    Erotics of Culture.* Boston: Beacon.

Loaeza, Soledad

1994 "The Changing Face of Mexican Nationalism." In *The NAFTA De-
    bate: Grappling with Unconventional Trade Issues,* edited by M. Delal
    Baer and Sidney Weintraub, 145–57. Boulder, Colo.: Lynne Rienner.

Lomnitz, Claudio

1992 *Exits from the Labyrinth: Culture and Ideology in the Mexican Na-
    tional Space.* Berkeley: University of California Press.

1995 "Ritual, Rumor, and Corruption in the Constitution of Polity in Mod-
    ern Mexico." *Journal of Latin American Anthropology* 1(1): 20–47.

1996 "Fissures in Contemporary Mexican Nationalism." *Public Culture* 9: 55–68.

1998 *Modernidad indiana: Nueve ensayos sobre nación y mediación en México.* Mexico City: Planeta.

Lomnitz, Claudio, ed.
2000 *Vicios públicos, virtudes privadas: La corrupción en México.* Mexico City: CIESAS/Porrúa.

Lomnitz, Larissa
1977 *Networks and Marginality: Life in a Mexican Shantytown.* Translated by Cinna Lomnitz. New York: Academic Press.

Lomnitz, Larissa, Claudio Lomnitz, and Ilya Adler
1993 "The Function of the Form: Power Play and Ritual in the 1988 Mexican Presidential Campaign." In *Constructing Culture and Power in Latin America,* edited by Daniel H. Levine, 357–401. Ann Arbor: University of Michigan Press.

Lustig, Nora
1994 "Solidarity as a Strategy of Poverty Alleviation." In *Transforming State-Society Relations in Mexico: The National Solidarity Strategy,* edited by Wayne A. Cornelius, Ann L. Craig, and Jonathan Fox, 79–96. La Jolla: Center for U.S.–Mexico Studies, University of California at San Diego.

Mabry, Donald J.
1982 *The Mexican University and the State: Student Conflicts, 1910–1971.* University Station: Texas A & M University Press.

Mahoney, James, and Michael Ellsberg
1999 "Goldhagen's *Hitler's Willing Executioners:* A Clarification and Methodological Critique." *Journal of Historical Sociology* 12(4): 422–36.

Mahoney, James, and Richard Snyder
1999 "Rethinking Agency and Structure in the Study of Regime Change." *Studies in Comparative International Development* 34(2): 3–32.

Malkin, Victoria
1999 "La reproducción de relaciones de género en la comunidad de migrantes mexicanos en New Rochelle, Nueva York." In *Fronteras fragmentadas,* edited by Gail Mummert, 475–96. Zamora: El Colegio de Michoacán.

Mallon, Florencia E.
1993 "Dialogues Among the Fragments: Retrospect and Prospect." In *Confronting Historical Paradigms: Peasants, Labor, and the Capitalist World System in Africa and Latin America,* edited by Frederick Cooper, Allen F. Isaacman, Florencia E. Mallon, William Roseberry, and Steve J. Stern, 371–401. Madison: University of Wisconsin Press.

1995 *Peasant and Nation: The Meaning of Postcolonial Mexico and Peru.* Berkeley: University of California Press.

Manson, William C.
1986 "Abram Kardiner and the Neo-Freudian Alternative in Culture and Personality." In *Malinowski, Rivers, Benedict, and Others: Essays on Culture and Personality,* edited by George W. Stocking Jr., 72–94. Madison: University of Wisconsin Press.

Markoff, John
1997 "Really Existing Democracy: Learning from Latin America in the Late 1990s." *New Left Review* 223: 48–68.

Martinez-Alier, Verena, and Armando Boito Júnior
1977 "The Hoe and the Vote: Rural Labourers and the National Election in Brazil in 1974." *Journal of Peasant Studies* 4(3): 147–70.

Marx, Karl
[1852] 1969 "The Eighteenth Brumaire of Louis Bonaparte." In *Selected Works,* 398–529. Moscow: Progress Publishers.

[1871] 1970 *The Civil War in France.* Reprint, Peking: Foreign Languages Press.

Marx, Karl, and Fredrich Engels
[1847] 1992 "The Communist Manifesto." Reprint, Oxford: Oxford University Press.

Massolo, Alejandra
1992 *Por amor y coraje: Mujeres en movimientos urbanos de la ciudad de México.* Mexico City: El Colegio de México.

1994 "Política y mujeres: Una peculiar relación." In *Los medios y los modos: Participación política y acción colectiva de las mujeres,* edited by Alejandra Massolo, 13–44. Mexico City: El Colegio de México.

1998 "Women in the Local Arena and Municipal Power." In *Women's Participation in Mexican Political Life,* edited by Victoria E. Rodríguez, 193–203. Boulder, Colo.: Westview.

Mayer, Adrian C.
1966 "The Significance of Quasi-Groups in the Study of Complex Societies." In *The Social Anthropology of Complex Societies,* edited by Michael Banton, 97–122. London: Tavistock.

McDonald, James H.
1997 "A Fading Aztec Sun: The Mexican Opposition and the Politics of Everyday Fear in 1994." *Critique of Anthropology* 17(3): 263–92.

Mejía Prieto, Jorge
1987 *Así habla el mexicano: Diccionario básico de mexicanismos.* Mexico City: Panorama.

Melhuus, Marit
  1997 "Exploring the Work of a Compassionate Ethnographer: The Case of
  Oscar Lewis." *Social Anthropology* 5(1): 35–54.

Menchú, Rigoberta
  1984 *I . . . Rigoberta Menchú: An Indian Woman in Guatemala,* edited by
  Elizabeth Burgos, translated by Ann Wright. New York: Verso.

Mendoza, Vicente T.
  1962 "El machismo en México." *Cuadernos del Instituto Nacional de Investigaciones Folklóricas* (Buenos Aires) 3: 75–86.

Mitchell, Timothy
  1998 "Nationalism, Imperialism, Economism: A Comment on Habermas."
  Public Culture 10(2): 417–24.

Moliner, María
  1991 *Diccionario de uso del español.* 2 vols. Madrid: Gredos.

Molyneux, Maxine
  1985 "Mobilisation without Emancipation? Women's Interests, the State and
  Revolution in Nicaragua." *Feminist Studies* 11(2): 227–54.

  2001 *Women's Movements in International Perspective: Latin America and
  Beyond.* Houndmills, Basingstoke, Hampshire, U.K.: Palgrave.

Monsiváis, Carlos
  [1976] 1989 "La nación de unos cuantos y las esperanzas románticas (Notas sobre la historia del término 'Cultura Nacional' en México)." In *En
  torno a la cultura nacional,* edited by Héctor Aguilar Camín, 159–221.
  Reprint, Mexico City: Instituto Nacional Indigenista.

  1981 "Notas sobre el estado, la cultura nacional y las culturas populares en
  México." *Cuadernos Políticos* 30: 33–43.

  1987 *Entrada libre: Crónicas de la sociedad que se organiza.* Mexico City:
  Era.

  1992a "De la cultura mexicana en vísperas del Tratado de Libre Comercio."
  In *La educación y la cultura ante el Tratado de Libre Comercio,* edited by
  Gilberto Guevara Niebla and Néstor García Canclini, 179–209. Mexico
  City: Nexos/Nueva Imagen.

  1992b "La identidad nacional ante el espejo." In *Decadencia y auge de las
  identidades: Cultura nacional, identidad cultural y modernización,* edited
  by José Manuel Valenzuela Arce, 67–72. Tijuana: El Colegio de la Fron-
  tera Norte.

  1995 *Los rituales del caos.* Mexico City: Era.

  1997 *Mexican Postcards.* Translated by John Kraniauskas. London: Verso.

  2000 *Aires de familia: Cultura y sociedad en América Latina.* Barcelona:
  Anagrama.

Moore, Barrington
1978 *Injustice: The Social Bases of Obedience and Revolt*. New York: M. E. Sharpe.

Morris, Stephen D., and John Passé-Smith
2001 "What a Difference a Crisis Makes: NAFTA, Mexico, and the United States." *Latin American Perspectives* 28(3): 124–49.

Mummert, Gail, ed.
1999 *Fronteras fragmentadas: Género, familia e identidades en la migración mexicana al norte*. Zamora: El Colegio de Michoacán.

New Left Review
1966 Special edition entitled "Themes." *New Left Review* 38: 1/2.

Nieto, Raúl
1998 "Experiencias y prácticas sociales: En la periferia de la ciudad." In *Cultura y comunicación en la ciudad de México*, edited by Néstor García Canclini, 234–77. Mexico City: Universidad Autónoma Metropolitana/ Grijalbo.

Nivón, Eduardo
1998 *Cultura urbana y movimientos sociales*. Mexico City: Universidad Autónoma Metropolitana–Iztapalapa/Consejo Nacional para la Cultura y las Artes.

Núñez Noriega, Guillermo
1994 *Sexo entre varones: Poder y resistencia en el campo sexual*. Mexico City: UNAM/Porrúa/El Colegio de Sonora.

O'Donnell, Guillermo, and Philippe Schmitter
1986 *Tentative Conclusions about Uncertain Democracies*. Baltimore, Md.: Johns Hopkins University Press.

Oliveira, Orlandina de, ed.
1989 *Trabajo, poder y sexualidad*. Mexico City: El Colegio de México.

Ong, Aihwa
1996 "Cultural Citizenship as Subject-Making: Immigrants Negotiate Racial and Cultural Boundaries in the United States." *Current Anthropology* 37(5): 737–62.

1999 *Flexible Citizenship: The Cultural Logic of Transnationality*. Durham, N.C.: Duke University Press.

Oppenheimer, Andres
1998 *Bordering on Chaos: Mexico's Roller-Coaster Journey Toward Prosperity*. Boston: Little, Brown.

Ortner, Sherry
1998 "Identities: The Hidden Life of Class." *Journal of Anthropological Research* 54(1): 1–17.

Pan American Health Organization (PAHO)
   1998 *Health in the Americas.* Vol. 2. Washington, D.C.: World Health
        Organization.

Paredes, Américo
   1961 "On *Gringo, Greaser,* and Other Neighborly Names." In *Singers and
        Storytellers,* edited by Mody C. Boatright, Wilson M. Hudson, and Allen
        Maxwell, 285–90. Dallas, Texas: Southern Methodist University Press.

   1967 "Estados Unidos, México y el machismo." *Journal of Inter-American
        Studies* 9(1): 65–84. Translated and reprinted in *Folklore and Culture on
        the Texas-Mexican Border,* 215–34 (Austin: University of Texas Press,
        1993).

   1977 "On Ethnographic Work among Minority Groups: A Folklorist's Per-
        spective." Reprinted in *Folklore and Culture on the Texas-Mexican Bor-
        der,* 73–110 (Austin: University of Texas Press, 1993).

   1978 "The Problem of Identity in a Changing Culture: Popular Expressions
        of Culture Conflict along the Lower Rio Grande Border." Reprinted in
        Folklore and Culture on the Texas-Mexican Border, 19–47 (Austin: Uni-
        versity of Texas Press, 1993).

Paz, Octavio
   [1947] 1961 *The Labyrinth of Solitude: Life and Thought in Mexico.* Trans-
        lated by Lysander Kemp. New York: Grove.

Peña, Guillermo de la
   1990 "La cultura política entre los sectores populares de Guadalajara."
        Nueva Antropología 11(38): 83–107.

Poniatowska, Elena
   1971 *La noche de Tlatelolco.* Mexico City: Era.

   1975 *Massacre in Mexico.* New York: Viking.

Poole, Deborah
   1998 "Landscape and the Imperial Subject: U.S. Images of the Andes, 1859–
        1930." In *Close Encounters of Empire: Writing the Cultural History of
        U.S.–Latin American Relations,* edited by Gilbert M. Joseph, Catherine
        C. LeGrand, and Ricardo D. Salvatore, 107–38. Durham, N.C.: Duke
        University Press.

Prieur, Annick
   1998 *Mema's House, Mexico City: On Transvestites, Queens, and Machos.*
        Chicago: University of Chicago Press.

Purnell, Jennie
   1997 "Cristero Rebellion." In *Encyclopedia of Mexico: History, Society,
        Culture,* edited by Michael S. Werner, 374–78. Chicago: Fitzroy Dear-
        born.

Radcliffe, Sarah, and Sallie Westwood
  1996 *Remaking the Nation: Place, Identity, and Politics in Latin America.*
  London: Routledge.

Ramírez, Rafael
  1999 *What It Means to Be a Man: Reflections on Puerto Rican Masculinity.*
  Translated by Rosa E. Casper. New Brunswick, N.J.: Rutgers University
  Press.

Ramos, Samuel
  [1934] 1962 *Profile of Man and Culture in Mexico.* Translated by Peter G.
  Earle. Austin: University of Texas Press.

Rigdon, Susan M.
  1988 *The Culture Façade: Art, Science, and Politics in the Work of Oscar
  Lewis.* Urbana: University of Illinois Press.

Robberson, Tod
  1995 "Recall Mexican Army, Chiapas Rebels Warn: Zedillo Amnesty Offer
  Apparently Rejected." *Washington Post,* 17 February, p. A28.

Rodríguez, Victoria E.
  1998 "The Emerging Role of Women in Mexican Political Life." In *Women's
  Participation in Mexican Political Life,* edited by Victoria E. Rodríguez,
  1–20. Boulder, Colo.: Westview.

Rodríguez Gómez, M. Guadalupe
  1998 "Making a Globalized Nation in the Countryside: El Barzón, a Popular Movement in Contemporary Mexico." *Urban Anthropology* 27(2):
  197–232.

Rosaldo, Renato
  1993 *Culture and Truth: The Remaking of Social Analysis.* Boston: Beacon.

  1997 "Cultural Citzenship, Inequality, and Multiculturalism." In *Latino
  Cultural Citizenship: Claiming Identity, Space, and Rights,* edited by
  William V. Flores and Rina Benmayor, 27–38. Boston: Beacon.

Roseberry, William
  1989 *Anthropologies and Histories: Essays in Culture, History, and Political
  Economy.* New Brunswick, N.J.: Rutgers University Press.

  1998 "Social Fields and Cultural Encounters." In *Close Encounters of Empire: Writing the Cultural History of U.S.–Latin American Relations,* edited by Gilbert M. Joseph, Catherine C. LeGrand, and Ricardo D. Salvatore, 515–24. Durham, N.C.: Duke University Press.

Rosenberg, Tina
  2000 "The Precarious Nature of Latin Democracies." "Week in Review,"
  New York Times, 27 February, p. 16.

Rouse, Roger
   1995 "Thinking through Transnationalism: Notes on the Cultural Politics of Class Relations in the Contemporary United States." *Public Culture* 7(2): 353–402.

Rovira Sancho, Guiomar
   2001 "*La ley Cocopa,* promotora del respeto a la mujer india." *La Jornada,* 22 February. http://www.jornada.unam.mx/2001/feb01/010222/019n1pol.html

Royce, Anya Peterson
   1975 *Prestigio y afiliación en una comunidad urbana, Juchitán, Oaxaca.* Translated by Carlos Guerrero. Mexico City: INI/SEP.

Rubin, Jeffrey W.
   1997 *Decentering the Regime: Ethnicity, Radicalism, and Democracy in Juchitán, Mexico.* Durham, N.C.: Duke University Press.

Rus, Jan, ed.
   1999 "If Truth Be Told: A Forum on David Stoll's *Rigoberta Menchú and the Story of All Poor Guatemalans.*" Special issue of *Latin American Perspectives* 26(6).

Rus, Jan, Rosalva Aída Hernández Castillo, and Shannan L. Mattiace
   2001 "Introduction: The Indigenous People of Chiapas and the State in the Time of Zapatismo: Remaking Culture, Renegotiating Power." *Latin American Perspectives* 28(2): 7–19.

Safa, Patricia
   1991 *¿Por qué se envia a los hijos a la escuela?* Mexico City: Grijalbo.

Sanabria, Harry
   2000 "Resistance and the Arts of Domination: Miners and the Bolivian State." *Latin American Perspectives* 27(1): 56–81.

Santamaría, Francisco J.
   1942 *Diccionario general de americanismos.* 2 vols. Mexico City: Pedro Robredo.
   1959 *Diccionario de mejicanismos.* Mexico City: Porrúa.

Sartre, Jean-Paul
   [1944] 1989 *No Exit.* Reprint, New York: Vintage International.

Scherer García, Julio, and Carlos Monsiváis
   1999 *Parte de guerra, Tlatelolco 1968: Documentos del general Marcelino García Barragán: Los hechos y la historia.* Mexico City: Nuevo Siglo.

Scott, James C.
   1985 *Weapons of the Weak: Everyday Forms of Peasant Resistance.* New Haven, Conn.: Yale University Press.

   1990 *Domination and the Arts of Resistance: Hidden Transcripts.* New Haven, Conn.: Yale University Press.

Selby, Henry A., Arthur D. Murphy, and Stephen A. Lorenzen
 1990 *The Mexican Urban Household: Organizing for Self-Defense.* Austin: University of Texas Press.

Senzek, Alva
 1997 "The Entrepreneurs Who Became Radicals." *NACLA Report on the Americas* 30(4): 28–29.

Skocpol, Theda
 1994 *Social Revolutions in the Modern World.* Cambridge: Cambridge University Press.

Smith, Gavin
 1999 *Confronting the Present: Towards a Politically Engaged Anthropology.* Oxford: Berg.

Smith, Peter H.
 1979 *Labyrinths of Power: Political Recruitment in Twentieth-Century Mexico.* Princeton, N.J.: Princeton University Press.

Spivak, Gayatri C.
 1999 *A Critique of Postcolonial Reason.* Cambridge, Mass.: Harvard University Press.

Stack, Carol
 1996 *Call to Home: African Americans Reclaim the Rural South.* New York: Basic Books.

Stephen, Lynn
 1997a *Women and Social Movements in Latin America: Power from Below.* Austin: University of Texas Press.

 1997b "The Zapatista Opening: The Movement for Indigenous Autonomy and State Discourses on Indigenous Rights in Mexico, 1970–1996." *Journal of Latin American Anthropology* 2(2): 2–39.

 1999 "The First Anniversary of the Acteal Massacre." *Cultural Survival Quarterly* 23(1): 27–29.

 2002 *Zapata Lives: Histories and Cultural Politics in Southern Mexico.* Berkeley: University of California Press.

Stephen, Lynn, and George A. Collier
 1997 "Reconfiguring Ethnicity, Identity, and Citizenship in the Wake of the Zapatista Rebellion." *Journal of Latin American Anthropology* 3(1): 2–13.

Stern, Steve J.
 1993 "Africa, Latin America, and the Splintering of Historical Knowledge: From Fragmentation to Reverberation." In *Confronting Historical Paradigms: Peasants, Labor, and the Capitalist World System in Africa and Latin America,* edited by Frederick Cooper, Allen F. Isaacman, Florencia

E. Mallon, William Roseberry, and Steve J. Stern, 3–20. Madison: University of Wisconsin Press.

1995 *The Secret History of Gender: Women, Men, and Power in Late Colonial Mexico.* Chapel Hill: University of North Carolina Press.

1998a "The Decentered Center and the Expansionist Periphery: The Paradoxes of Foreign-Local Encounter." In *Close Encounters of Empire: Writing the Cultural History of U.S.–Latin American Relations,* edited by Gilbert M. Joseph, Catherine C. LeGrand, and Ricardo D. Salvatore, 47–68. Durham, N.C.: Duke University Press.

1998b "What Comes After Patriarchy? Reflections from Mexico." *Radical History* 71: 54–62.

Stevens, Evelyn P.
1974 *Protest and Response in Mexico.* Cambridge, Mass.: MIT Press.

Stolcke, Verena
1988 *Coffee, Planters, Workers and Wives: Class Conflict and Gender Relations on São Paulo Plantations, 1850–1980.* New York: St. Martin's.

1995 "Talking Culture: New Boundaries, New Rhetorics of Exclusion in Europe." *Current Anthropology* 36(1): 1–24.

Stoll, David
1999 *Rigoberta Menchú and the Story of All Poor Guatemalans.* Boulder, Colo.: Westview.

Taggart, James M.
1992 "Fathering and the Cultural Construction of Brothers in Two Hispanic Societies." *Ethos* 20(4): 421–52.

Tarrés, María Luisa
1996 "Espacios privados para la participación pública: Algunos rasgos de las ONG dedicadas a la mujer." *Estudios Sociológicos* 14(40): 7–32.

Tarrow, Sidney G.
1994 *Power in Movement: Social Movements, Collective Action, and Politics.* Cambridge: Cambridge University Press.

Tejera Gaona, Héctor
1998 "Encuentro de expectativas: Las campañas electorales y la cultura política en el Distrito Federal." *Nueva Antropología* 54: 31–56.

Thomas, Piri
1967 *Down These Mean Streets.* New York: Alfred A. Knopf.

Thompson, E. P.
1993 *Customs in Common: Studies in Traditional Popular Culture.* New York: New Press.

Thorne, Barrie, and Marilyn Yalom, eds.
    1992 *Rethinking the Family: Some Feminist Questions.* 2d ed. Boston: Northeastern University Press.

Tilly, Charles
    1998 *Durable Inequality.* Berkeley: University of California Press.

Tocqueville, Alexis de
    [1835] 1945 *Democracy in America.* Vol. 1. Reprint, New York: Vintage.

Touraine, Alain
    1988 *Return of the Actor: Social Theory in Postindustrial Society.* Minneapolis: University of Minnisota Press.

Valentine, Charles A.
    1968 *Culture and Poverty: Critique and Counter-Proposals.* Chicago: University of Chicago Press.

Valenzuela Arce, José Manuel
    1998 *El color de las sombras: Chicanos, identidad y racismo.* Tijuana: El Colegio de la Frontera Norte.

Varese, Stefano
    1991 "Think Locally, Act Globally." *NACLA Report on the Americas* 25(3): 14–17

Vargas-Cetina, Gabriela, and Steffan Igor Ayora-Diaz
    1998 "Local Expressions of Global Culture: Four Case Studies from Mexico." *Urban Anthropology* 27(2): 123–33.

Vélez-Ibáñez, Carlos G.
    1983 *Rituals of Marginality: Politics, Process, and Culture Change in Central Urban Mexico, 1969–1974.* Berkeley: University of California Press.

Vincent, Joan
    1990 *Anthropology and Politics: Visions, Traditions, and Trends.* Tucson: University of Arizona Press.

Viveros Vigoya, Mara
    2001 "Contemporary Latin American Perspectives on Masculinity." *Men and Masculinities* 3(3): 237–60.

Warren, Kay B.
    2001 "Telling Truths: Taking David Stoll and the Rigoberta Menchú Exposé Seriously." In *The Property of Words: Rigoberta Menchú, David Stoll, and Identity Politics in Latin America,* edited by Arturo Arias, 198–218. Minneapolis: University of Minnesota Press.

Weber, Max
    [1919] 1946 "Science as a Vocation." In *From Max Weber: Essays in Sociology,* edited by H. H. Gerth and C. Wright Mills, 129–56. Reprint, New York: Oxford University Press.

Weiner, Tim, and Ginger Thompson
    2001 "U.S. Guns Smuggled into Mexico Feed Drug War." *New York Times,*
    19 May, p. A-3.

Williams, Heather L.
    1996 *Planting Trouble: The Barzón Debtors' Movement in Mexico.* La
    Jolla: Center for U.S.–Mexican Studies, University of California at San
    Diego.

Williams, Patrick, and Laura Chrisman
    1994 Introduction to *Colonial Discourse and Post-Colonial Theory: A
    Reader,* edited by Patrick Williams and Laura Chrisman, 1–20. New
    York: Columbia University Press.

Willis, Paul
    1979 *Learning to Labor: How Working-Class Kids Get Working-Class Jobs.*
    New York: Columbia University Press.

Wolf, Eric
    1999 *Envisioning Power: Ideologies of Dominance and Crisis.* Berkeley: Uni-
    versity of California Press.

Womack, John, Jr.
    1999 *Rebellion in Chiapas: An Historical Reader.* New York: W. W. Norton.

Zermeño Padilla, Guillermo
    1997 "Unión Nacional Sinarquista (UNS)." In *Encyclopedia of Mexico: His-
    tory, Society, Culture,* edited by Michael S. Werner, 1471–72. Chicago:
    Fitzroy Dearborn.

Zolov, Eric
    1999 *Refried Elvis: The Rise of the Mexican Counterculture.* Berkeley: Uni-
    versity of California Press.

Index

Index   287

Modernity: and elections, 91; and EZLN, 91, 150, 155; and NAFTA, 83; and 1968 Olympics, 65; and progress, 41, 164, 166, 175, 220
Molyneux, Maxine, 160–161
Momo, 18
Monsiváis, Carlos: on EZLN, 154; on Oscar Lewis, 27; on NAFTA, 82; on popular politics, 173, 187, 210, 216; on Tlatelolco, 62
Monte Albán, 222
Mothers. *See* Kinship; Women
Movements: accomplishments of social movements, xviii, xx, 76, 90–91; analysis of social movements, xxx, 19, 122–23; El Barzón debtors, 21, 131, 186, 187; campesino, 70–71, 130, 185, 199, 204, 205; ecology/green, 71, 82, 186; independence of social movements, 66, 70, 114; lesbian and gay, 71, 82; national liberation, 116; radical, 70, 113, 122, 145, 171, 193, 224; right-wing in Europe, 94; student, 7, 61–72, 130, 145, 172, 174, 185, 192–206, 210–12, 238 n. 4; women in social movements, 1–2, 43, 47, 158–61, 174, 180, 184, 190, 237 n. 18. *See also* EZLN; Feminism; Indigenous peoples of Mexico; Politics; Rights
Moynihan, Daniel Patrick, 39
Murder. *See* Crime

Nations: national integrity/sovereignty, 76–78, 90, 92, 94, 107; nationalism, xx, 18, 74–76, 82, 88–94, 187, 223, 239 n. 4. *See also* Movements; Politics
Nazism, xxii, 243 n. 22
Neoliberalism, 10–11, 50, 143 46, 193–94, 206, 211–12, 221, 235 n. 2
New Year's celebrations, 12, 15, 17, 95, 132, 147, 157, 162
Nicaragua, 34
Niños Héroes, 239 n. 9
Nivón, Eduardo, xxvi–xxvii
Noche de Tlatelolco, La (Poniatowska), 63
Norma, 17, 23, 124, 135, 195–96
North American Free Trade Agreement (NAFTA): passage and implementation of, 8–9, 132, 139, 146, 220–21; popular response to, 11, 24, 72–96, 212
North Carolina, 113

Oaxaca, 106, 222
Ocosingo, Chiapas, 219
O'Donnell, Guillermo, 233 n. 2
Olympics, 1968, 7, 65–66, 71, 202

Omar, 124
Ong, Aihwa, 113
Oppenheimer, Andres, 170
Orfila, Arnaldo, 27

Paredes, Américo, 36–38, 42, 81, 237 n. 15
Parenting. *See* Kinship
Partido Acción Nacional (PAN), xxix, 10, 20, 163, 171–72, 191, 207, 226
Partido de la Revolución Democrática (PRD): and elections, 20, 148, 162–63, 168, 173; and EZLN, 156; as leftist, 18; popular support for, xvi, 13–14, 88, 171; and UNAM strike, 204
Partido Revolucionario Institucional (PRI): and elections xv, xviii, xxix, 8–10, 22, 67, 148, 162–65, 191, 207, 219, 226; and EZLN, 151; legitimacy of, 19, 67, 70, 167–73, 182, 215; and machismo, 229
Patriarchy. *See* Kinship
Paz, Octavio, 59–60, 150, 234 n. 6
Pedro, 120–21, 140, 217
Pedro Martínez (Lewis), 30, 49
Peña, Guillermo de la, 86, 98, 188, 208–9
Peru, 155
Petroleum/PEMEX. *See* Economic conditions
Police. *See* Crime
Political economy, 28, 40, 116, 146, 212, 236 n. 4. *See also* Economic conditions
Political science, 5, 74, 158, 244 n. 5
Politics: *abstencionista*, xvi, 21, 168–69, 207; accountability, 40–41, 51, 54, 57, 183, 200, 230; alienation/marginalization, xxiii, 50, 58, 74, 154, 159, 170; autonomy/self-reliance, 2, 86, 90, 146, 156, 166, 176, 197, 209, 224, 245 n. 20; blame, 23, 24, 26, 29, 50–52, 150, 231, 235 nn. 12, 5; citizenship and democracy, 21–22, 70, 106, 164, 169, 182, 218, 220, 233 n. 2; complicity, 40, 42, 66, 102, 115, 133, 136, 212; cultural citizenship, xxiii–xxiv, 98, 175, 219; electoral, xv, xviii, 8, 21, 66, 115, 158, 159, 165, 168, 180, 209; expectations, 4, 14, 23, 73, 114–15, 142, 207; independence/sovereignty, 14, 47, 76, 86, 123, 192; integrity, 8, 90, 107; passion for, xvii, 1, 26, 95; power, 42, 46, 59, 78, 102, 106, 115, 117–18, 152, 176, 180, 218, 235 n. 5; rituals of, 21, 70, 100, 109, 130–31, 141, 164, 190. *See also* Armed conflict; Elections; Feminism; Gender;

Compositor:	G & S Typesetters
Text:	10/13 Sabon
Display:	Sabon
Printer and binder:	Thomson-Shore, Inc.